"There are major forces moving in iceberg fashion into the complex but symbiotic education environment. It is possible to see the tips of the icebergs moving with enormous power, but the key question is, where, how, and when will higher education institutions intersect with these forces?"

-From *Dateline 2000: The New Higher Education Agenda* by Dale Parnell

What the Experts are Saying About *Dateline 2000...*

"*Dateline 2000* contains an astonishing amount of information in a well organized and highly readable form. The forecasts accompanying each chapter provide a provocative agenda for discussion and action." Richard C. Richardson, Jr., Associate Director, National Center for Postsecondary Governance and Finance

"I find *Dateline 2000* to be Dale Parnell's usual standard of excellence. I especially like the way each chapter can stand alone and is a valuable contribution within itself without relying totally upon the previous chapter....Incidentally, I have already cited the book in a chapter I am doing for another volume." George B. Vaughan, Director, Center for Community College Education, George Mason University

"I have spent the last few evenings reading *Dateline 2000* and extracting ideas and quotes for speeches I am giving in the next few weeks. The book is excellent work with a great deal of good information. Congratulations to Dale Parnell for a job well done and done at a very appropriate time." Joe McDonald, President, Salish Kootenai College

"The work will stand as one of the most important for the future of U.S. education in this century....Many students forming the next generation of productive employees will have Dale Parnell to thank for giving them the chance to obtain the knowledge and vital skills required in the 21st century." Robert J. Pond, Professor of Engineering, Central Ohio Technical College

DATELINE

2000

The New Higher Education Agenda

DALE PARNELL

THE COMMUNITY COLLEGE PRESS
A division of the American Association
of Community and Junior Colleges

One of the central messages of this book is the advancing impact of technology on American enterprises. To show that we practice what we preach, this book has been produced entirely on Apple Macintosh desktop publishing equipment and programs instead of through traditional typesetting procedures. –D. P.

Published by the Community College Press, a division of American Association of Community and Junior Colleges
National Center for Higher Education
One Dupont Circle, N. W., Suite 410
Washington, D. C.   20036

Phone: (202) 728-0200

ISBN 0-87117-198-8

Library of Congress Catalog Card Number: 89-85388

A nation is never finished. You can't build it and then leave it standing as the pharaohs did the pyramids. It must be re-created for each generation by believing, caring men and women. If we don't care, nothing can save the nation. If we do believe and care, nothing can stop us.

John Gardner

Contents

Foreword

Drawing on his nearly forty years of experience in education, Dale Parnell has brought to the forefront the challenges facing our educational system as we move into the twenty-first century. He also has provided an array of workable solutions.

Parnell identifies the environmental, societal, and demographic changes that will confront us in the 1990s and the human development needs these changes will create. Higher education's contribution to America's future economic prosperity, he says, will be to educate, train, and retrain the emerging workforce at all levels.

Three paramount needs emerge from this discussion: to increase minority participation in higher education, to better educate the "neglected majority"—the 65 to 75 percent of high school students who will not likely pursue a baccalaureate degree, and for college and universities to give priority attention to the outcomes of the higher education experience. All of these needs have been recognized by the higher education community as top priorities and Parnell details how these goals can be served by partnerships between higher education and the communities it serves.

Parnell identifies economic development as a key community service for many colleges. In the future, communities will call on colleges more frequently to help solve economic problems, conduct economic surveys, train and retrain workers, and share facilities, equipment, and professional staff. Successful partnerships between colleges and their communities already exist, and Parnell provides useful descriptions of how several of them work.

He also reiterates the importance of establishing partnerships between two- and four-year institutions to enhance minority and low-income student participation in higher education through transfer. Coherent college transfer agreements, coordinated academic calendars, common course credit systems, and sequential curriculum planning for all institutions are some of the mechanisms that can be developed to improve the articulation process.

Dateline 2000: The New Higher Education Agenda helps us focus on the opportunity we have to help the disadvantaged and undereducated reach higher educational levels. Parnell predicts the passage of new federal initiatives designed to solve problems facing urban America—plans that would bring higher education into partnership with city governments, local communities, and the federal government.

Technological advances will require colleges, universities, and secondary and elementary schools to work more closely in what Parnell terms "the search for synergy." Liberal arts and technical education will become more integrated, he says, to help develop flexible, well-educated, and technologically competent individuals.

This book issues a challenge to colleges and universities of all kinds. The strength of their leadership, combined with their ability to define a clear and attainable mission and to develop partnerships with their students, faculty, alumni, governing boards, and communities, ultimately will determine whether higher education can meet the needs of a changing America in a changing global society and economy as we move into a new century.

The imperative has never been greater for those of us in higher education to move beyond the boundaries of our campuses and into the community to educate those populations that will comprise the majority of our society by the close of the 1990s. This important new volume provides us with a road map and guideposts to measure our progress.

Robert H. Atwell
President
American Council on Education

Preface

In the course of collecting information for this book I have talked with hundreds of people in education, government, business, labor, finance, and think tanks, including former presidents Jimmy Carter and Gerald Ford. I find a surprising amount of cautious optimism about the future. Certainly, the optimism is not even, and is tempered by many of the tough problems of poverty, terrorism, urban and inner-city challenges, drug problems, environmental problems, and educational problems. But despite these sobering challenges and the pain involved in solving, or even partially solving, these perplexing problems, a cautious optimism about the future, particularly for higher education, seems to be emerging.

In the chapters that follow I have attempted to analyze some major external forces that will fuel a new education boom and impact higher education institutions of all kinds in the 1990s. No attempt has been made to be inclusive. As an example, environmental challenges remain unexamined. Certainly, the rising cost of cleaning up the environment and maintaining water quality and supply will be large issues in the decade ahead. The terrible drug problem facing our country has not been examined in this analysis, but higher education institutions have a heavy responsibility to help stem the tide of substance abuse on and off campus. The rising tide of college faculty unionism and the challenges of making the collective bargaining process work within the academy have not been discussed here. These and many other issues have been left for others to explain and analyze.

An attempt has been made in this book to forecast for the future of higher education based upon an analysis of the overarching forces that are, by and large, external to colleges and universities of all types and sizes. As an example, the link between the economy, education, and human resource development is solid and becoming more important every day. It is an umbrella external force that will impact all education institutions regardless of mission.

Nothing written here will be a guarantee for the financial or educational health of all colleges and universities. Some institutions will do better than others in the new technological environment. But all U. S. institutions of higher education will be offered more opportunities in the 1990s than ever before. There are rich possibilities, as well as hazards, ahead for those colleges and universities that respond to these opportunities in dynamic rather than static ways.

The leaders of higher education institutions are urged to utilize this book to expand the dialogue about how the future will impact their college or university, and to initiate the dialogue where it has yet to begin. This book is intended to be a resource for helping guide these discussions.

Even though the opinions expressed in this book are my own, a large number of individuals deserve thanks and recognition for their suggestions, research, and critical comments.

Special words of appreciation go the American Association of Community and Junior Colleges Board of Directors and the executive staff for the inspiration and for allowing the author the time away from the office to complete the writing.

Dan Savage, private entrepreneur, and Jim Flanigan, information officer for the Peace Corps, made many early suggestions and helped with some of the early research. Jim Murray, director of publications for the American Council on Education and manager of the ACE/Macmillan Series on Higher Education, made many invaluable suggestions. Elaine El-Khawas, vice president of the American Council on Education, provided much background material and information. A special word of thanks must go to Robert Atwell, president of the American Council on Education, for his encouragement and for writing the foreword.

Several individuals reviewed manuscript drafts and made invaluable suggestions. This list includes Dan Angel, president of Austin Community College in Texas; Lloyd Chilton, executive editor of the Macmillan Publishing Company; Jim Palmer of George Mason University in Virginia; Larry McClure, former colleague in the Oregon State Department of Education and now with the Northwest Regional Educational Laboratory; and James Gollattscheck, Connie Odems, Frank Mensel, Jack McGill, Phillip English, and Lucy Cooper, all of the AACJC executive staff.

I am grateful to Lela Sallis, who translated the writing into manuscript form, and to Mark Winter, who helped edit the book with unflagging care and understanding. Special appreciation is expressed to Diane Eisenberg for coordinating the editorial and artistic services in the production of the book.

Dale Parnell
President
American Association of
Community and Junior Colleges

Chapter I

Opportunities and Challenges

The future cannot be feared ... it is the only future we have, so we had better figure out how to deal with it!

Gerald Baliles
Former Governor
Commonwealth of Virginia

Y ou are invited to step into what well could be the most important decade of human history—the 1990s. It is the end of a century, the end of a millennium, and the end of many aspects of our current way of life. The 1990s will introduce us to the new age of technology, the new learning age, and it will bring rich possibilities as well as challenges for colleges and universities.

What follows is a look ahead into a decade that portends to be the most promising, but fast-moving and unsettling, ten years in memory. As the old saying goes, "If you can keep your head while all about you are losing theirs, you simply do not understand the situation."

In one brief lifetime this writer has gone from cow chips to potato chips, to computer chips, to nanochips. Over the past fifty years the U. S. has experienced enormous upheaval and absorbed turbulent changes. We have had a major war, where we introduced the atomic bomb to the world, and two other wars of considerable magnitude and pathos. We have experienced turbulence on the college campus, a social revolution in mores, a civil rights struggle, antitax revolts, and a flood of new individuals, particularly females, into the labor force and into higher education. We can now travel faster than the speed of sound, including travel into space, and experience instantaneous visual communication around the world. We have become a global community in terms of trade, travel, and telecommunications. The computer is revolutionizing the publishing industry, the defense industry, the financial world, health sciences, and basic manufacturing.

Who would have forecast these developments fifty years ago, or even two or three decades ago? But the astonishing fact is that our country has experienced all of this in real-life living color and our system has not collapsed. Our political, economic, and educational institutions have a certain resiliency to be able to bounce back from trouble and adversity.

When one weighs the evidence on all sides, it appears that the U. S. is on the edge of a major period of economic growth and technological expansion, which will be fueled by education. Publisher Austin Kiplinger states the case this way in his book *The New American Boom:*

> In 1925 Calvin Coolidge said, "the business of America is business." Today, I say "the business of America is EDUCATION." Education constructs the foundation of technology, and technology in turn provides the track for industry and commerce to advance into the 21st century. . . . Evidence is mounting that the U. S. economy, in the 1990s and extending into the 21st century, will raise American living standards to new high records for U. S. consumers and will increase the American share of business in world markets.[1]

The decade of the 1990s will be a decade of challenges, but promises to be a boom period for higher education. The road to the year 2000 will not be free of potholes and regional problems, but scientists, engineers, and business leaders are predicting that an education-based technological boom is on the way that will take off in the 1990s in a steep upward curve.

This new higher education boom will happen in an environment of automation and increased productivity; slow population growth; higher wages for a more experienced, older and better-prepared workforce; better education-training and more opportunity for the unskilled workers; more and better research and new and improved procedures for technology transfer to the marketplace.

When one analyzes American higher education institutions, the startling discovery is the sheer diversity of the enterprise. For example, out of 2,785 colleges and universities admitting freshmen students, some 45 percent, or 1,258, have open admissions, and only about 16 percent are identified as being highly selective, admitting students who are in the upper academic quartile of their high school graduating class. It is necessary to gain some appreciation for that diversity in order to understand why and how the contemporary

4

higher education system works in the United States. And it does work, primarily because that diversity meets the needs of an increasingly diverse population.

Our democracy can and must work in the face of enormous population diversity. Americans meet that diversity by providing and supporting both open access and quality standards in American higher education. But these twin goals have presented higher education with unprecedented challenges, and indeed working them out has been one of the major challenges of the 1980s. Even though much remains to be done, great progress has been made. But what about the 1990s?

You can stimulate an animated discussion in higher education circles when you talk about faculty tenure, but a glaze moves over eyes when you try to discuss institutional mission, or intergroup human relations or even learning outcomes and value-added education. What Albert Einstein observed many years ago is true today, that this age can be characterized by a concentration upon means and a confusion about ends.

A church bishop was riding on a transcontinental flight. The scientist sitting next to him could not help but observe that the bishop was a religious man. In an effort to make conversation he said, "Bishop, do you know what my religion is? Do unto others as you would have them do unto you." The bishop said with a gleam in his eye, "Professor, do you know what my science is? Twinkle, twinkle, little star, how I wonder what you are?" This tongue-in-cheek story illustrates the tendency in our culture to oversimplify matters and major in minor issues.

What will be the major forces impacting our nation in the last decade of this century, and where does higher education intersect with these forces? That is the key focus of this book.

What can colleges and universities do to help develop a deeper sense of civic responsibility among our citizens? What is the practical link between the economy and education? How can higher education help the U. S. meet the international economic challenges? How can higher education help millions of at-risk Americans move into the economic mainstream of life, particularly those surviving in a large urban environment? How can colleges and universities adjust collegiate programs to meet the needs of the new, older college student, or the nontraditional, ethnic minority student?

Former president Theodore Roosevelt once said that a great democracy must be progressive or it will soon cease to be either great or a democracy. That progressive search for access and excellence in education presses on in this country. There is a relentless pressure to improve the quality of American life, and millions of individuals see higher education as the major road leading to a fuller and more satisfying life.

Led by the clarion call to the American people in *A Nation at Risk*, the 1983 report from the National Commission on Excellence in Education, at least twenty-five other major national reports were issued in the 1980s calling for substantive changes in American schools and colleges. Never in history has the public been so conditioned to think seriously about education.

Change in education, particularly higher education, comes slowly, and that may be a blessing. Perhaps slow change gives American education a type of stability that is much needed in a dynamic and changing society. But the flip side of that coin is that educational institutions do not exist in an isolated environment. Schools and colleges are part and parcel of a community, state, and nation. Some may be set apart for certain important purposes, such as church-related schools and colleges, but no educational institution can be immune from the major forces impacting our society. Students are being prepared for life in a technological society and learning age, a life that is becoming increasingly complex, and filled with change.

Edward Bellamy, the nineteenth-century futurist and author of *Looking Backward—2000–1887*, saw a twentieth-century America in transition with free public education, women working outside the home on an equal basis with men, occupational safety, credit cards, retirement provisions and early retirement, and a shorter work-week. Even as Bellamy envisioned twentieth-century changes, so we in the 1990s can glimpse some trends and a time of transition into the learning-technology age. For the leaders of higher education not to see their institutions as related to the gathering forces in this complex and symbiotic world is a grievous error.

6

It is relatively easy to look backward and enumerate the sweeping economic, political, and social changes that came about as a result of the industrial revolution. It is much more difficult to look forward and outline the coming changes with any degree of accuracy. Yet it is possible to see the tips of the icebergs on the move, barely visible, yet moving with enormous power into the American economic sea. Here is the key question for the decade ahead: Will there be serious attempts to steer these iceberglike forces and convert them to productive use, or just allow them to go where they will, altering or destroying all in the way? Here is a second and allied question: Where and how will higher education institutions intersect with these forces?

One of the problems facing the leaders of higher education is keeping up with the sheer speed of change. This problem can be symbolized by an observation from a General Motors executive when queried as to why GM did not enter into more partnership arrangements with colleges and universities. He replied, "Their speed is deceptive . . . they are slower than they look." To be sure, colleges and universities are developing new attitudes, new organizational structures, better response time, and a host of other modifications to address the speed of change. But some analysis of the forces now moving in our society and around the world should be of assistance in steering the collegiate enterprise toward Dateline 2000.

Since the end of World War II, American education has undergone tremendous change. As an example, contemporary colleges and universities have been transformed from the insulated (and sometimes isolated) halls of learning for young people into more complex and multifaceted institutions serving all ages and a variety of new constituencies. The agents of change—population demographics, economic policies, changing social mores, international economic competition, technological developments, and political decisions—will continue to reshape the form and substance of higher education in the decade ahead. But how will colleges and universities respond? Are there major restraints that will inhibit the ability to respond?

When college presidents and other leaders in higher education discuss the challenges and opportunities and how colleges and universities might respond to the forces of change in the decade ahead, seven basic institutional challenges emerge: (1) understanding and acting upon the relatedness of issues; (2) building a sense of community within and outside the college; (3) recruiting and retaining more ethnic minority students; (4) increasing institutional flexibility; (5) developing funding stability; (6) solving the faculty shortage problem; and (7) improving governance and leadership effectiveness.

Relatedness

Can the diverse American education system ever be viewed as a seamless garment? Our nation, as well as its colleges and universities, is caught in a web of relatedness. As an example, most of our nation's competitiveness problems are interrelated, sometimes making them seem insoluble. A world-class economy depends upon the development of a world-class workforce, but in too many ways the needs of the American workforce have been neglected. Superior manufacturing, in turn, relies on top-flight research and development, but there are signs that other nations are gaining ground on the once-commanding U. S. lead in technological innovation and technology transfer. Economic success in the learning-technological age depends upon well-educated citizens, but the multiple educational shortcomings of America's school systems have been amply documented.

Time after time, when discussing one issue we find ourselves zeroing in on others. A discussion of developing a world-class economy almost inevitably turns toward the problems of inadequate education, or America's lack of global awareness. Most national leaders now agree that most of the key issues must be addressed simultaneously; we simply cannot afford the luxury of solving problems one at a time. Systems must interact in support of each other in a synergistic way. Growth and improvements in whole industries such as financial services, computers, communications, biotech research, and higher education will have a multiplier impact across many other industries, improving their profitability and productivity. The impact on these industries will then spread out across the country in thousands of new and different ways.

These connections and relationships are already at work in our country, knitting something that looks like a fish net. There is a cell here and a cell there tied together by nodules of information, or cooperation, or just by individual contacts.

It is reality that many of the most pressing issues in our society have no home in the college curriculum and disciplines. Where is the curricular responsibility for discussing the improvement of intergroup race relations on or off the campus? Where is the curricular home for studying the environment: in biology, in chemistry, in physical science, in political science? What discipline has the responsibility to study the drug abuse problem: in health classes, in law enforcement classes, in political science classes? There is little congruence between the disciplines and organization of the college curriculum and the tough multidisciplinary issues of real life.

Even in the transfer of students' credits from one college to another one can find little consistency or relationship to real-life applications. What is the academic rationale for allowing the transfer of college credits in modern dance because it is in the liberal arts tradition, but denying the transfer of credits in self-defense for a law enforcement officer because it is a career course? One can almost conclude that the rationale for transfer of credits from one college to another has little relationship to the need for it in real life. Should a college be condemned because of efforts to connect the practical with the theoretical, or connect the employer community with the academic talent and resources of the college? This "relatedness" approach to higher education stands in stark contrast to traditional forms of higher education and creates a persistent tension, particularly in the transfer of credits.

The connectedness issue also runs vertically into the secondary schools as well as horizontally into the community. College and university leaders all across the land are discovering that their students had a life before college and that their institution's roots grow deep into the soil of the secondary and elementary schools. However, there has been precious little communication among college and high school faculty. Baird Whitlock writes for the College Board about this problem:

> The willingness on the part of many college faculty members to believe that secondary school teachers can teach at the college level has not changed much. Robert Frost once said that the basic difference in post-lecture parties he attended in Britain, along with the college faculty, local doctors, lawyers, clergy, and businessmen, there would always be secondary school teachers; in America this latter group was almost never present. For easier articulation to take place for students, the inner wall of separation within the academic community must be broken down. The distrust will never melt away until genuine conversation between the two groups of teachers begins.[2]

The day is clearly over when colleges and universities can exist in splendid monastic and scholarly isolation from real-world activity and problems. College leaders are busy endeavoring to improve their connections with the employer community, the financial community, the political community, the high school community. Networking has become a new lifestyle for many college and university faculty and administrators.

Building Community

Building and strengthening community life inside and outside the academy is an energizing challenge, but also a great opportunity. *Building Communities* is the title of the report of the American Association of Community and Junior Colleges' Commission on the Future of Community Colleges issued in 1988. This commission, chaired by U. S. Senator Nancy Kassebaum of Kansas and Ernest Boyer, president of the Carnegie Foundation for the Advancement of Teaching, stated in this widely acclaimed report:

> We propose, therefore, that the theme "Building Communities" become the new rallying point for the community colleges in America. We define the term community not only as a region to be served, but also as a climate to be created.[3]

10

Even though this report was prepared for community, technical, and junior colleges, the theme of building communities is applicable to all kinds of colleges and universities when the term "community" is defined as a climate to be created. Certainly, the concept implies more than colleges simply sponsoring public events. Given the broad definition of "community," what are the implications for all of higher education?

College and university students must feel a sense of belonging and involvement if a sense of community is to be achieved. This is particularly true for ethnic minority students. Not only must more minority students be encouraged to enroll in college, they must also experience success and a feeling of belonging in their college experience if they are to stick with it. This issue argues for all sorts of new collaborative efforts between colleges and junior and senior high schools. Students and parents must be counseled early with regard to what a college or university expects of them so that students can better prepare while in high school.

A good bit more attention must also be given to commuter students (young and old) if this majority number of college students is to feel a climate of community on a college campus. Ways must be found to help the commuter student interact more with campus life. Bruce Smith states the case for the commuter student this way:

> Virtually no research has addressed ways to foster the types of development among commuter students that are taken for granted among residential students. While the 18- to 21-year-old commuter student frequently enters the college experience with characteristics that differ from the residential student in the same age group, it does not necessarily follow that the commuter student does not need similar types of development. In fact, it is assumed that the commuter student needs and deserves comparable academic programs. Should it not also be assumed that 18- to 21-year-old commuter students need and deserve comparable development of self-concept, autonomy, social and academic integration?[4]

We have been conditioned in our Western culture to accept competition among students as the standard operating mode. Research on study habits among various groups of students at the

University of California (Berkeley) has discovered that the key difference between Asian American and African American students is that the Asian students tend to study together, seminar together, and generally help each other, while African American students tend to study alone, work alone, and generally approach collegiate studies on an independent basis. Colleges of Dateline 2000 must understand that most students learn better when they study together and support each other. Students and faculty alike are beginning to understand that creating a climate of community operates best on the premise that students and faculty derive mutual benefits from getting to know each other as people.

The college or university of Dateline 2000 must encourage cooperative learning experiences not only among students but also among faculty. Because community and state regional colleges work between high schools and universities, they might logically serve as conveners of regional educational consortia. The resulting partnerships among various levels of education could include cooperative efforts aimed at developing teaching-learning excellence, enhancing teacher enrichment, developing continuity in learning, improving student retention and the further education of disadvantaged students. Formalized discussion among faculty from various levels of education could also encourage feedback related to student performance.

Recruiting and Retaining Ethnic Minority Students

Between now and the year 2000, college classes will increasingly be made up of minorities and economically disadvantaged as a result of changing demographics and the growth of single-parent households struggling to survive against the predominantly double-income households. Marian Wright Edelman points out that:

> One feeder system creating those single-parent households is adolescent pregnancy, a paradigm of America's social neglect of children and youths, a symptom of pervasive lack of hope and too few positive life options.[5]

Of those who will be eighteen in the year 2000, one in four

will be poor, and if they are African Americans or Hispanic Americans, one in two will be poor. There will be significantly increased competition for the attention of eighteen-year-olds in all walks of life because of their decreased numbers, and this competition will have an impact upon college and university enrollments in the future.

One disturbing trend is the declining proportion of African American students who go on to college. Many reasons are given for this decline. However, Solomon Arbeiter has studied the variables for the College Board and has concluded that the primary reason for declining minority youth enrollment is competition and economics. Black high school graduates are increasingly selecting the workforce, the military, and proprietary schools for short-term training.[6]

Black participation in the armed services has increased during the 1980s, from 399,729 in 1980 to 410,901 in 1986. While figures are difficult to obtain on proprietary school enrollments, the Pennsylvania Higher Education Assistance Authority does collect this information. In 1976 there were 7,129 Black students in Pennsylvania postsecondary institutions, with 496 (or 7 percent) in proprietary schools. Ten years later, in 1986, there were about the same number of Black students in postsecondary institutions at 7,185, but 1,353, or nearly 19 percent, were enrolled in proprietary schools.

An increasing proportion of Black students have also been entering the workforce upon graduation from high school. In 1977,

Employment of High School Graduates
(in thousands)

	1977	1980	1983
Black number in labor force	126	149	183
White number in labor force	1,184	1,173	971

Source: Solomon Arbeiter, *Enrollment of Blacks in College*, Research and Development Update (New York: College Entrance Examination Board, 1987).

High School Graduates and College
Enrollments of 18- to 19-Year-Olds
(in thousands)

	1973	1978	1984
White			
No. high school grads	5,029	5,391	4,632
% of total age 18-19	76.7	76.3	75.5
Enrolled in college	2,281	2,553	2,541
% of White high school grads	45.4	48.3	54.95
Black			
No. high school grads	563	586	688
% of total age 18-19	56.5	55	63
Enrolled in college	194	270	265
% of Black high school grads	34.5	46.1	38.5

Source: U. S. Department of Commerce, Bureau of the Census, *Population Characteristics: Social and Economic Characteristics of Students,* Current Population Reports, 1973, 1978, 1984.

126,000 Black graduates entered the labor force. This increased to 183,000 six years later, up 32 percent. At the same time, the reverse was true for White graduates, with a decrease of 18 percent.

It is clear that colleges and universities have their work cut out for them in the challenge to increase the college enrollment of minority young people. The competition will be keen. However, it must be pointed out that with the GI Bill thousands of military service personnel will have served their active duty commitment and will be leaving the service during the 1990s with dollars in hand that can only be used for education.

One must be careful in analyzing college-going patterns by race. Ethnic minority individuals vary as much in composition and socioeconomic outlooks as the White population. Even though racism is much alive today, the issue of college enrollment hinges far more upon economics than upon race. It is clear that individuals of low-income backgrounds, of any race, are making their postsecondary choices upon the basis of what they think they can afford.

Increasing Institutional Flexibility

Demands will be made upon colleges and universities by Dateline 2000 that cannot be fully anticipated today. The technological society is motivating change at an ever accelerating speed. Higher education leaders are increasingly concerned about balancing the need for institutional flexibility and the need for institutional stability. The employer and political communities criticize colleges and universities for moving too slowly and for inflexibility, while the academic community criticizes the college president who moves too fast or makes too many changes. Peter Drucker writes in *Psychology Today*:

> More than ever, education will fuel our economy and shape our society. . . but it cannot be education as usual. . . . Education must recognize that learning is now a lifelong process of keeping abreast of change.[7]

Here is what several university presidents are saying about the need for institutional flexibility and the ability to change:[8]

- George Johnson, President, George Mason University, Virginia

> Given the changes and the challenges of the next century, universities have the opportunity to act as a leading and unifying force in society. To do this, universities themselves must accept the need to change. But our universities are still constructed on the factory model, with education pursued along the assembly line of the credit hour and the semester through a watertight segmentation of the disciplines by department.

- Stephen Trachtenberg, President, George Washington University, Washington, D. C.

> There is a need to establish a better balance between teaching and research and to blend the "hands on" experience of community colleges with the more theoretical work of the research-oriented universities. There must be greater synthesis of theory and practical needs of the

15

workplace and employers. Those who accomplish this will be able to honestly say: "We prepare our students for a lifetime of learning in a society where skills must be continually renewed and revised." We can assure the families who pay tuition that their sons and daughters will not be segregated from our most talented faculty members.

• Leroy Keith, President, Morehouse College, Georgia

Partnerships will become more prevalent in the education system of the future. The system, from kindergarten through graduate school, needs to be seen as a continuum. We also need to eliminate the disjointed relationship between the public school systems and the nation's colleges and universities. There will have to be more partnerships among our colleges and universities and the corporate sector, local and federal government, and among the schools themselves.

• King Jordan, President, Gallaudet University, Washington, D. C.

A revised understanding of educational principles is now emerging. Instructional quality must now be the preeminent mission of postsecondary institutions. The proportion of effort and resources dedicated to student learning and performance assessment must increase. We must accept responsibility for the failure of our students to learn. The values and methods of American higher education in the 21st century must alter markedly. The higher education community cannot spend the next 10 years refining its academic programs at its leisure. The time for pilot testing and isolated efforts is over. The time for application of exemplary practices has arrived.

The major finding from educational research in the last thirty years is that the most important difference among learners is speed. There are fast learners and there are slow learners, there are no dumb students and there are no smart students. Colleges and universities are challenged to match administrative practices with differing learning styles and modes. Yet most colleges cling steadfastly to the eighteen-week semester or the eleven-week quarter as though it were handed down by Moses from Mount Sinai. The 1990s will see much more experimentation among colleges, with flexible calendars and attempts to meet individual learning differences among students.

Who would have guessed, even ten years ago, that the American public would favor, on a two-to-one basis, the flexibility of parental choice for which public school a child could attend within a state regardless of where the family lived? Minnesota, Arkansas, and Iowa have already written parental choice into state law. Or who would have guessed that nearly three out of four Americans now say they would support a standard national curriculum and nationally established standards and goals for education?[9]

The Minnesota postsecondary enrollment options program, which allows high school juniors and seniors to take college courses at state expense, appears to be a success. While the four-year-old experiment has not received much national publicity, this flexible high school-college attendance program is generally accepted by Minnesota educators. The competition it poses for high schools and colleges appears to be stimulating more students to go on to college, and more advanced courses to be offered in high school.

If this flexible attendance program is working so well in Minnesota, one must ask why other states are not doing the same thing. By Dateline 2000 they probably will, but not without a good bit of motivation from college leaders and some educational statesmanship from high school colleagues.

For many students in many high schools the twelfth-grade experience does not amount to much. Students arrive at that point in their high school experience needing only two or three credits to graduate. As a consequence, the twelfth grade becomes a "goof off" year, a phenomenon that has seemed to increase since the late 1960s. Far too many high school seniors appear to be enrolled in unstructured and unfocused programs lacking in substance. Many educators are asking if excellence can be cultivated and a first-rate education achieved when half or more of high school seniors do not see this as a very important year of learning for them? With so much to be learned and so many new skills to be developed, why can't educational programs be more flexible between high schools and colleges?

Reducing barriers between and within educational institutions to form new networks of cooperation will be a large challenge in the 1990s. This will require college and university leaders to examine the flexibility index of their institution and generally improve their college connections.

Funding Stability

Money matters always seem to be near the top of the challenges facing college and university leaders, and in the decade ahead there will be no letup of the financial pressures. In many colleges the financial pressures have become so great that all other aspects of college life are affected, from tuition charges, to faculty pay, to building maintenance and renovations.

Carol Simpson Stern, president of the American Association of University Professors, sees a clear relationship between the financial pressures and the educational and social policies and practices in a college: "Faculty shortages mean that professors may command higher salaries, and if that problem is not solved, the educational program may suffer. It is also a social issue because a shortage of funds means less financial help for minority students who in turn could become the role model faculty of the future."[10]

Each year the College Board issues a report on college costs that generates much hand wringing and editorial ink about the high cost of higher education. It is charged that soaring tuition rates are outstripping students resources to pay for a college education. The College Board states that neither student aid nor family income has kept pace with rising college costs in the 1980s.[11]

Adjusted for inflation, student aid from all sources increased 10.5 percent between 1980 and 1989 and disposable family income increased some 16 percent. During this same ten-year period tuition and fees at private colleges increased 56 percent and at public colleges 30 percent.

These and other figures about college costs have generated some spirited and well-publicized debate. Led by the criticisms of former education secretary William Bennett, many other politicians have joined the chorus demanding investigation into the cost of higher education. Bennett charged in 1986 that colleges and universities were not underfunded but underaccountable, underproductive, and motivated by greed. While Bennett speaks of greed, college and university presidents are speaking of need. James Freedman, president of Dartmouth, countered the Bennett argument in a September 1987 appearance on the ABC News program *This Week with David Brinkley*:

> I think the most important thing that parents have to appreciate about the cost of college tuition is that they pay about 50 to 60 percent of the entire cost of educating a student in a private college. Throughout the 1970s, tuition rose at a rate lower than the price of inflation. During the 1980s, it's been rising at a slightly higher rate in order to catch up. It's rising for that reason. It's also rising because universities and colleges are competing with private industry for the most important talent in the country, especially in the sciences and in the professions. It's rising because the cost of carrying out high-quality world-class science in this country is expensive. And, indeed, the cost of putting computers on a campus, and . . . giving students access to computers is expensive. Education is an expensive business.

The argument is joined by Congressman William Goodling (R-Penn.), ranking member of the House Education and Labor Committee. Goodling, a consistent supporter of more funding for higher education, stated in a 1989 speech at York College in Pennsylvania:

> Skyrocketing costs are the number one problem facing students who want a college education. . . . The cost of attending college will rise faster than inflation for the eighth year in a row, putting student access to a college at risk.[12]

Robert Atwell, president of the American Council on Education, points out that in the decade of the 1970s college costs went up at an average annual rate of 6.6 percent, while the inflation rate was moving along at about a 7.8 percent annual increase. During the 1980s tuition increased an average annual rate of 9.8 percent, while the inflation rate hovered between a 4 and 5 percent annual increase. Atwell sees a slowing trend in the rise of college costs and predicts a leveling during the 1990s.

Also, fewer people talk about the true cost of inflation during the 1980s for frequently purchased items. The Manufacturers Hanover Trust indicates that during 1985-87 air fares went up 17 percent and gasoline went up 20 percent, and the inflation rate on frequently bought items commonly used in colleges and universities was 13 percent. These increases are coupled with huge increases in liability and health insurance, mandated fringe benefits, new state and federal regulations like asbestos removal, and renovation or replacement of worn-out buildings and equipment.

In the constant search and pressure for stable funding and ways to control college costs, it is important to have some knowledge of where the support dollars come from and how the dollars are spent. There is no mystery attached to the issue of college tuition and fee increases. In the public institutions between 50 to 70 percent of the support dollars are derived from state and local taxes. Tuition costs are tied to this factor. When state or local appropriations go down, tuition increases and cost-cutting measures are the only recourse for college decision makers. State and local governments are caught between the conflicting demands of tough social issues (the drug crisis, the homeless, building prisons) and the demands for supporting and expanding the investment in education.

Private colleges and universities rely upon tuition and fees for between 50 to 70 percent of the support dollars. Private giving and endowment fund returns account for about 20 percent. When private giving goes down, and when interest rates are down, tuition increases and cost-cutting measures are the only recourse.

However, it is important to point out in this discussion that 75 percent of all the higher education enrollment will be found in the lower-cost public colleges and universities. The media tend to concentrate attention upon the higher-cost private institutions largely situated in the northeast. As an example, 40 percent of the total higher education enrollment is now in the lower-cost community, technical, and junior colleges. There are 1.5 million community college students in the state of California alone, where the tuition charge remains at $100 per year. Tuition charges in community

20

colleges and many state colleges have remained near or below the rate of inflation in recent years.

Different segments of higher education face different funding challenges. But they all seek a more stable funding base that allows for better long-range planning and stability in tuition increases.

Faculty Shortages

The faculty shortage has arrived and will only get worse during the 1990s, particularly in certain fields and most importantly among ethnic minority faculty. Forty-six percent of all college and university faculty are fifty years of age or older.[13] Because of its size and ethnic diversity, the state of California provides us with a useful micromodel of the faculty shortage issue. William Pickens, former executive director of the California Postsecondary Education Commission, makes this projection:

> By the year 2000 . . . the University of California will need a total of 6,000 new faculty members at 400 hires per year. The California State University system currently has 11,000 ladder-ranked faculty and a projected turnover of 8,700 by the year 2000. They plan to recruit 8,000 replacements. Our third segment, the California Community Colleges . . . currently has 15,600 faculty, of these 6,900, or 44 percent, will reach age 65 by year 2000. So we do have a substantial number of faculty who will reach that point (retirement), and many who will probably take early retirement before then. . . . If this is not a crisis in numbers, it surely is a crisis in terms of the distribution of ethnicity and, perhaps, of gender of the faculty.[14]

The prospect of significantly improving upon the underrepresentation of Black, Hispanic, and Native American faculty is not promising. The competition throughout the professional labor force is keen today for well-educated ethnic minority personnel. As the technological-learning age demands an increasing volume of professionals, the competition will become fierce during the 1990s.

The reasons for the faculty shortages are many and varied.

Some colleges and universities in certain parts of the country are experiencing growth problems, which translates into the need for more faculty. In some cases faculty salaries have not kept pace with the competition. However, the predominate reason for the shortage is the advancing age of the current faculty. Many faculty in their early sixties are taking advantage of early retirement programs offered by some colleges. Other older faculty are teaching on a reduced-load basis. The Labor Department is projecting a large downturn in the workforce of those fifty-five and older due to "golden handshake" early retirement or partial retirement programs.

An important study of faculty attrition was done in 1986 by Howard Bowen and Jack Schuster. After considerable study of the new entry and replacement variables in four-year colleges and universities, they concluded that 70,000 to 130,000 new faculty will be required during each five-year period through the year 2010. If we use the midpoint of 100,000 of their prediction, this would mean that 20,000 new faculty must be hired each year over the next twenty years in four-year colleges and universities.[15] Where will they come from?

Many leaders in higher education are advocating a "grow your own" program. Promising students would be identified in the freshman or sophomore year of college and encouraged to enter teaching. Special financial support programs would be developed, including a loan forgiveness element added to the federal guaranteed student loan program, for those who enter and remain in teaching for a period of time.

At the same time, salaries will be improved, and this is already under way. Faculty salaries have increased at a rate higher than the rate of inflation for eight consecutive years. The average salary for all ranks of college professors has more than doubled, from $17,930 in 1976-77 to $37,000 in 1987-88. At the same time, the fringe benefits package, as a part of the compensation package, has increased threefold, from $2,740 to $8,140. It is problematic if this same progress will be made in the 1990s, but if it does the *average* annual professor salary will be $74,000 by Dateline 2000. Of course, averages are deceptive when combining all ranks of professors and all kinds of colleges. Many professors could be well above the average salary of $74,000, and many well below.[16]

Since there will be a slight trough in the faculty demand cycle during the early 1990s, colleges and universities still have time to develop plans to address the faculty shortage problem. It is not likely to be solved by chance, and specific efforts must be crafted to recruit and retain talented African American and Hispanic American individuals for teaching careers.

To underscore the importance of the faculty replacement problem, David Pierce, executive director of the Illinois Community College Board, recently completed a study of Illinois community college faculty based upon age. By 1992 approximately 40 percent of the current full-time faculty in Illinois community colleges will have retired, or will be eligible for retirement.

Large-scale faculty retirements will challenge colleges and universities of all kinds to strengthen the faculty recruitment and selection process, particularly if the number of ethnic minority faculty is to be increased. But this challenge also provides colleges with a great opportunity for renewal and reconfiguration of faculty patterns.

Vital people and vital organizations are interdependent. Perhaps the greatest internal challenge facing college and university leaders in the 1990s will be the recruitment, retention, and renewal of vital faculty members. How this challenge is handled will significantly impact how higher education institutions fare with the large external forces.

Improving Governance and Leadership Effectiveness

Every college or university chief executive officer has four basic constituencies: faculty, students, community (or perhaps alumni), and governing board. Of these four, the relationship with the governing board is the most personal, and sometimes tenuous. It has the power to hire and fire. It has the responsibility to establish policy for the college. It does not administer the institution, but it does need assurance that the college is administered effectively. The governing board is concerned about the whole college and not just pieces of it. Since the governing board is not involved in the day-to-day operation of the college, it is the job of the president to keep the board well informed. It must share in the bad news as well as the good news. In many way the college president is a teacher, continuously teaching the members of the governing board about the needs of the institution.

Probably the most difficult but most important constituency is the faculty. They are a highly diverse group with diverse interests and, by and large, they consider the college president their equal, not their superior. The college president is the leader of the faculty, but they know it is the governing board who hires him or her. There are no sure times in the faculty-president relationship. The president is always in the middle, among, and between the constituency groups. But it is the faculty who can breath life into the presidential vision of the institutional mission. The president must bring the diversity of the faculty into a unified effort aimed at fulfilling the overall mission of the college. It is the faculty that will make or break the institution. The president must inspire and challenge, but above all the president must persuade.

Father Theodore Hesburgh, longtime popular president of Notre Dame University, writes about the faculty-president relationship:

> The normal faculty criticisms of a president are many and varied, often contradictory. If he is always home, he is a nobody; if he is often away, he is neglecting his homework. If he spends little time with faculty, he is aloof; if he spends much time with them, he is interfering in their proper business. If he balances the budget, he is stingy; if he cannot balance the budget, he is irresponsible and incompetent. If he is big on fringe and retirement benefits, the younger faculty can't meet their expenses; if he stresses faculty raises, the older faculty are impoverished on retirement. If he spends much time on fund raising, he is a huckster; if he doesn't, the financial situation gets worse. In a word, it is Scylla and Charybdis every day. We might as well admit that willy-nilly, the president will always be between the rock and the hard place.[17]

However, despite the built-in tension between a strong faculty and a strong president, most colleges and universities have been able to make the collegiate form of governance work, and in most cases work with mutual understanding and cooperation. As a bottom line the faculty of the 1990s expect the college president to have accurate empathy with the teaching-learning process and be able to discuss educational issues with the faculty intelligently. If that element of presidential competency is missing, the president has sacrificed leadership.

A third constituency is the student body, the primary reason colleges exist. The students are a diverse group and becoming more diverse each year. The college president who does not demonstrate that he or she cares, and cares deeply about students, will not be serving the highest and best interest of the institution. Probably the greatest contribution a college president can make to students is the offering of example, of practicing what you preach. The president declares by daily living, by the causes supported, by the services rendered, a set of values. One of the most difficult but necessary jobs of the college president is to develop, on a continuing basis, some form of two-way communication with students. The pressure to improve communication with the students will only grow in the 1990s. Nothing can replace "the pressing of the flesh," as politicians like to say, in student-president relations. However, it must be honest two-way communication with genuine interest in student concerns.

The fourth constituency is loosely called the community of supporters. It may be alumni, or legislators, or the governor, or the mayor, or community groups. By and large it is the community of supporters who financially support the institution and make judgments, for better or worse, about the work of the college. The college president of the 1990s may be the best internal administrator in the world, but community groups expect the president to be a leader who can work with them and clearly communicate where the college is going and how to get there. They relate to clarity and not to fog.

This discussion of dealing with constituencies leads into the subject of leadership. What kind of leadership will be required to overcome the restraints and take advantage of the opportunities in the decade ahead?

Leadership cannot be described by the square boxes or dotted lines of an organizational chart. It is a concept that is both difficult to define and subject to popular distortions. Leadership is often confused with power, prerogatives, and prestige. Both a law enforcement officer and the red and green lights of an intersection have the power to direct traffic, but do not confuse this power with leadership. The wealthy enjoy an array of perks, but they are not necessarily leaders because of their good fortune. A Rolls Royce may symbolize prestige, but it is not a certain signal of leadership.

Leadership is also confused with time-honored management tasks of planning, organizing, staffing, directing, and evaluating; however, the mastery of these functions does not make one a leader. Most leaders can also manage, but leadership is much more. While leadership is evident when it is present, describing it is like trying to catch a cloud or a fog. It is difficult to put in a box.

It will be important for the college and university president of the 1990s to understand that management talent and leadership talent are not necessarily the same. It is a blessing when these two attributes are combined in one person. Management tasks have generally been well defined; leadership tasks have not. Nonetheless, clues to the attributes of leadership are provided by examining the tasks and responsibilities that an effective leader must face. These leadership tasks fall into three essential categories of mission clarification, climate development, and concept building.

Nothing is more important for the effective college leader of the future than to clarify the mission of the institution. The Good Book says, "Without a vision, the people will perish." Communicating vision is a fundamental task of leadership. Mission clarification and goal setting, therefore, are priority tasks for an effective college president. We live best by living on our hopes rather than on our fears; by looking to the future, not the past. The president sets the tone, the motivation, and the positive attitudes about the future of the college and articulates these clearly as part of the mission and goals of the institution. One wag has simplified the whole issue of defining a leader as a person who has followers. If so, it is vital for followers to have a vision and pride in their contributions to shared mission and goals.

Related to the clarification of mission is the task of affirming institutional values. When broad consensus about values is absent, is unclear, or loses its motivational force, college health and vitality decline. Most individuals are value-driven, and they can be motivated to live up to institutional values if these are clearly communicated by both the practice and the preaching of the college president.

A great college president is also usually a great teacher, and one of the key tasks of a leaders is to teach. Systematic explanation of the purposes of the college and the high standards expected of its members is a critical teaching function that falls to the president. An effective president does not forget that cows will not stay milked with just one milking; systematic and continual explanation of organizational purposes and values is required to create the climate of an organization, the environment within which its members operate. This teaching function includes not only instruction in how to fulfill organizational expectations, but also motivation and inspiration to convince individuals that they are capable of quality performance.

Another key to institutional climate development in the 1990s will be continuing attention to institutional and staff renewal. It is an important leadership task to encourage creativity, diversity, and even dissent—without tearing up the college. The college president must assure that the institution balances continuity and change in correct proportion. As the great American philosopher Mae West once said, "Too much of a good thing is simply wonderful." The college leaders of the 1990s must be sensitive to how much change an organization can stand. The effective college president is also sensitive to the need for staff development. He or she must assure that the college provides ample opportunity to its individual members for growth and renewal and must participate visibly in the institution's own staff development programs.

Taking symbolic action is a third element of climate development. This leadership task is ignored in much of literature, even though every leader is necessarily involved in symbolic action. However, symbolic action can be both positive and negative, and it is both planned and unplanned. The college president of the 1990s must understand the importance of symbolism and be sensitive to the meanings attached to a range of activities. The effective leader plans and shapes the symbolism of his or her actions.

Leaders live by metaphors. It has been proclaimed by Lakoff and Johnson that:

> Metaphor is pervasive in everyday life, not just in language
> but in thought and action. Our ordinary conceptual sys-
> tem, in terms of which we both think and act, is fundamen-
> tally metaphorical in nature. . . . Our concepts structure
> what we perceive, how we get around in the world and
> how we relate to other people.[18]

Many U. S. colleges and universities have risen to places of distinction because they have been able, at least in part, to develop and nurture certain metaphorical concepts, or common images, and communicate these to the public. Most of us operate on the basis of "pictures in our heads," or images. These images are developed based upon what we have seen, heard, or experienced. If the college or university of the 1990s cannot communicate a common image, how will the students or community deal with that? Of course, they will develop their own "pictures in the head."

The college president must continually focus the image of the college to maintain clarity of vision and expectation. Adjusting the focus knob of the college image projector is, in a nutshell, a fundamental task of leadership. The Avis car rental company says, "We try harder." A judge wears a robe in a courtroom. IBM founder Tom Watson insisted on dark suits and white shirts for company representatives. Yet not all leaders have consciously established a "picture in the head" for their organization. Certainly, not all college executives could articulate the distinct image of their respective institutions.

The college president of Dateline 2000 will articulate the image by consistently representing the college to constituents, by networking with other organizations, by paying unrelenting attention to the purposes of the institution and the quality of product. People develop images of organizations one way or another and effective leaders significantly influence the development of those pictures.

Leadership is not tidy. It is difficult to define, and even more elusive to quantify. At the same time, it can be observed in action, and clues to the attributes of effective leadership are provided by examination of the essential tasks required by an effective leader. The decade of the 1990s will require strong, insightful, and perceptive college leaders as well as managers. The colleges and universities that will thrive in this turbulent atmosphere will be led by leaders who know and implement exemplary leadership practices.

Dateline 2000 Forecast

1.   There will be many more opportunities than restraints for colleges and universities in the years ahead, if the leaders see and act upon the manifold possibilities.

2.   The 1990s will see all of education moving closer together, sponsoring more cooperative programs with fewer turf battles, and coming close to tailoring that seamless education garment for all students.

3.   Tuition increases will level out to about the inflation rate during the 1990s as state appropriations and private giving for colleges increase.

4.   The faculty shortage problems facing higher education will be solved as salaries increase, as early retirees from other careers move into education, and as more individuals see teaching in a college or university as a satisfying and rewarding lifestyle.

5.   Schools, colleges, and universities will pull together in new forms of partnerships to develop "grow your own" programs for recruiting, educating, and retaining more ethnic minority individuals in teaching careers. The current emphasis upon minority student education will begin paying off in the 1990s.

6.   An increasing number of women and minority individuals will be selected for chief executive officer positions in colleges and universities in the 1990s.

7.   New and more productive ways will be designed to develop a sense of community and improve college faculty and administration relationships. The problem-solving approach to collective bargaining will replace the confrontational approach.

8.   Increasing attention will be given to staff development on the college campus. These renewal efforts will apply to all staff and not just faculty. Even the time-honored sabbatical leave for faculty will

30

come under scrutiny as leaders look for more effective and efficient ways to help people grow and develop new competencies to match the fast-moving changes in society.

9. New and better ways will be developed to help the increasing volume of commuter students on college campuses interact more with campus life and feel a greater sense of involvement.

10. Much attention will be given by higher education leaders in the 1990s to the subjects of building community, assuring student success, and developing value-added outcome measures.

11. The new definition of scholarship in higher education will place great emphasis upon the application of existing knowledge along with the basic research to generate new knowledge.

12. Most colleges and universities will develop flexibility measures to determine the institutional ability to respond with wisdom to the forces of change.

13. The twelfth grade will be eliminated for many high school students as more and more states adopt the Minnesota postsecondary attendance options program.

14. Many regional state colleges and community colleges will break free of the traditional university model, developing a new model emphasizing their role as regional learning centers, technology transfer agencies, and as regional economic development organizations.

Executive Summary

The decade of the 1990s will present colleges and universities with rich new possibilities and opportunities as well as some challenges. Higher education leaders who can recognize and take advantage of the external windows of opportunity and solve some of the internal operating problems will be the leaders required for Dateline 2000.

How colleges and universities will respond to the forces of change in the decade ahead will depend in large part on how well they handle seven basic internal issues. How can the institution:

- Understand and act upon the relatedness of issues?
- Build a sense of community within and outside the college?
- Recruit and retain more ethnic minority students and faculty?
- Increase institutional flexibility?
- Develop funding stability?
- Solve the faculty shortage problem?
- Improve governance and leadership effectiveness?

The decade of the 1990s will be a decade of challenges, but promises to be a boom time for many colleges and universities. The road to the year 2000 will not be free of potholes and regional problems, but a learning age boom is on the way. There are major forces moving in iceberg fashion into the complex but symbiotic education environment. It is possible to see the tips of the icebergs moving with enormous power, but the key question is, where, how, and when will higher education institutions intersect with these forces?

Notes

1.   Kiplinger Washington Letter Staff, *The New American Boom: Exciting Changes in American Life and Business Between Now and the Year 2000* (Washington, D. C.: Kiplinger Washington Editors, 1986).
2.   Baird Whitlock, *Don't Hold Them Back: A Critique and Guide to New High School-College Articulation Models* (New York: College Entrance Examination Board, 1978).
3.   American Association of Community and Junior Colleges, Commission on the Future of Community Colleges, *Building Communities: A Vision for a New Century* (Washington, D. C.: American Association of Community and Junior Colleges, 1988).
4.   Bruce Smith, "The Personal Development of the Commuter Student," *Community College Review* (Summer 1989).
5.   Marian Wright Edelman, "The Future at Risk," *Liberal Education* (May/June 1987).
6.   Solomon Arbeiter, *Enrollment of Blacks in College: Is the Supply of Black High School Graduates Adequate? Is the Demand for College by Blacks Weakening?* Research and Development Update (New York: College Entrance Examination Board, 1987).
7.   Peter Drucker, "How Schools Must Change," *Psychology Today* (May 1989).
8.   *Trends and Learning Newsletter* (Summer 1989).
9.   Stanley M. Elam and Alec M. Gallup, "The 21st Annual Gallup Poll of the Public's Attitudes Toward the Public Schools," *Phi Delta Kappan* (September 1989).
10. *New York Times*, 6 September 1989.
11. College Entrance Examination Board, *Trends in Student Aid: 1980-1989* (Washington, D. C.: College Entrance Examination Board, 1989).
12. *New York Times*, 23 March 1989.
13. Figures are according to preliminary unpublished data collected in a national survey of faculty by the National Center for Education Statistics, U. S. Department of Education.
14. William Pickens, "California Response to Faculty Supply and Demand," paper presented at the Annual Meeting of the Western College Association, Los Angeles, California, 1988.

15. Howard Bowen and Jack Schuster, *American Professors: A National Resource Imperiled* (NewYork: Oxford University Press, 1986).
16. American Council on Education, *1989-90 Fact Book on Higher Education* (New York: American Council on Education and Macmillan Publishing Co., 1989).
17. Theodore M. Hesburgh, *The Hesburgh Papers: Higher Values in Higher Education* (Kansas City, Kan.: Universal Press, 1979).
18. George Lakoff and Mark Johnson, *Metaphors We Live By* (Chicago: University of Chicago Press, 1980).

Chapter II

The Missing Link

America's success in meeting the challenges of swift, far-reaching, uncertain change depends primarily on how we will develop and apply the knowledge, skills, wisdom, enthusiasm, and versatility of the nation's prime resources, the American people.

Pat Choate
Vice President
TRW Corporation

The missing link in current U. S. economic policy is systematic attention to human resource development. It is puzzling how any national economic policy can be successful for very long in the world today when the development of the most precious resource in a country, the human resource, is given short shrift. The United States has no coordinated national human resource development policy, or even a national strategy; there are only bits and pieces. Yet most of the contemporary economic development challenges focus significantly on the human resource development issue. It is true that economic policy is far more complicated than simply developing a national human resource development strategy, but human resource development is becoming an increasingly important factor, and the link between the economy and education must be strengthened.

There is little economic logic in encouraging capital investment in machines and equipment through tax incentives and other public efforts, if our country fails to make a similar level of investment in the people who will operate, maintain, repair, and build the machines. Much of the nation's economic well-being in the decade ahead will be tied to full development and utilization of human resources. When unemployment rises, governmental expenditures for unemployment insurance and welfare rise as well, while tax receipts fall. Some of the costs of social unrest and crime can also be tied to an idle, indeed, a wasting population.

Federal social policies of the past seem to have been designed primarily to foster social equity rather than to encourage the development of human potential, economic self-sufficiency, and individual empowerment. People must be educated and trained not just because they are poor, but because they represent a fundamental resource for maintaining the economic health of our nation. It does make a difference when governmental leaders at all levels recognize people as untapped resources instead of seeing people as merely causing more social problems to be alleviated.

A large majority of the jobs of the future in this country will require some form of postsecondary education or training for entry. The need for employees with higher levels of competence will greatly expand as U. S. employment expands from 106 million in 1985 to 123 million in 1995. As a result of these changes much attention will be given in the decade ahead to the linkage between the economy, education, and human resource development.

There are five interrelated components to consider when analyzing the linkages between higher education and the economy. They are human resource development, research, technology transfer, economic development, and curriculum reform. We will examine each of these in this chapter.

The Human Resource Development Component

First and foremost is the human resource development component. America's success in meeting the challenges of uncertain but far-reaching economic change will depend, in part, on how well the knowledge, skills, and resources of colleges and universities are utilized, and how flexibly these institutions respond to the human resource development challenge.

Significant changes are expected in the type of work to be done in the future, and the workers available to do the work. These changes hold some large implications for colleges and universities. The workforce of the future, at all levels, must develop higher levels of problem solving and reasoning abilities. The workers must also be computer literate. They must be broadly educated with the ability to apply knowledge.

In analyzing future workforce needs we find the greatest need for workers with significant levels of postsecondary education and training. According to the U. S. Bureau of Labor Statistics, in the decade of the 1990s the most significant growth in jobs will come in professional, managerial, and technician categories. It is estimated that by the year 2000, 70 to 75 percent of all job classifications will require some form of postsecondary education for entry.

John Naisbitt has indicated that he can recite the economic history of the U. S. with the three words of "farmer," "laborer," and "clerk." At one time the largest block of workers were employed in farm or farm-related occupations. Today less than 3 percent of the workforce are employed in the farm categories. With the advent of the industrial revolution came the laborer or blue-collar worker. In about the mid-1950s another transition occurred, with the largest block of workers becoming the clerical, or white-collar, worker.[1]

The United States is now experiencing another economic transition between the industrial and technological age. There is speculation that the next word to describe the largest block of the workforce will be "technician." Between now and the year 2000 most new jobs created will be in the technology-related and service parts of the economy. This does not mean that manufacturing jobs will disappear, it means that many manufacturing jobs will change. Even though manufacturing jobs dropped from 25 to 20 percent of the workforce, the actual number of manufacuring jobs increased by 343,000 over the past ten years. The goods-producing sector of the economy continues to grow at a slow pace, but the technology-service sector has become the major job creation machine, and will

Occupational Distribution of Labor Force Entrants in 1983 and Total Projected Growth, by Category, 1984-1995

Occupation	1983 Employment Ages 16-24 (%)	1984-1995 BLS Forecast Employment Change (%)
Technicians and related support workers	2.9	+28.7
Executive, administrative, and managerial workers	3.5	+22.1
Professional workers	5.3	+21.7
Service workers, except private household	19.2	+21.3
Sales workers	14.2	+19.9
Precision production, craft, and repair workers	8.9	+11.7
Admininstrative support workers, including clerical	17.6	+9.5
Private household workers	1.7	-18.3
Operators, fabricators, and laborers	18.3	+7.3
Farming, forestry, and fishing workers	3.2	-3.0
Active duty military	5.3	n.a.

Sources: The figures for 1983 employment are based on unpublished data from the BLS January 1983 Current Population Survey and unpublished (1987) information from the Defense Manpower Center, Arlington, Virginia. The 1984-1995 BLS forecast data are from the U. S. Bureau of Labor Statistics (1986).

continue to be for the decade of the 1990s.

Between now and the year 2000 the U. S. Department of Labor projects a significant increase in higher-skilled, better-paying occupations that will require some form of postsecondary education for entry. Occupations such as "professional workers" are projected to increase 22 percent over the 1990s; the number of executive, administrative, and managerial jobs will also likely increase 22 percent; jobs for technicians and related support workers will increase nearly 29 percent. The need for better-educated workers will be great.

Technology will be the driving force of the U. S. economy of the 1990s. It is creating millions of jobs, revitalizing older industries, and spawning entirely new fields. In the process many jobs will be eliminated, others will be radically altered, and new kinds of occupations will be born. The technology age will force decision makers to consider hard new policy choices. Do we import workers and export jobs? Or do we invest in the full development of our own human resources?

Human resource development threads run though economic development plans, with education and training as the central focus. In analyzing state-level economic development efforts, eight trends emerge and five relate to education. These trends are:

- Improve elementary and secondary education in order to improve the skills of the future workforce.
- Expand the work of community, technical, and junior colleges in technical education, adult worker training and retraining, and technology transfer.
- Fully utilize the research resources of colleges and universities and develop better technology transfer methods.
- Promote more partnerships between public and private employers and colleges and universities.
- Develop a more literate adult workforce.
- Develop and attract technology-based industries to the states.
- Accelerate job creation efforts.
- Help businesses participate more fully in the global economy.

The gap between high-wage skilled employment and low-wage unskilled jobs tends to widen as technology moves forward. New education and training programs will be required to train the unemployed and underemployed to perform in occupations in which shortages are growing. According to the Department of Labor, significant shortfalls are expected for a number of skilled workers, including craftspeople, machinists, mechanics, and technicians of all kinds.

At the same time, the high school dropout rate—according to some estimates as high as 30 percent—must be trimmed. The unemployment rate among twenty- to twenty-four-year-olds with less than a high school diploma hovers between 15 and 20 percent. The gap between the needs of a growing technological economy and the ability of schools and colleges to help a greatly increased percentage of their students develop higher-level competencies must be narrowed. The U. S. is facing a major skills shortage unless steps are taken soon to remedy the situation.

The Bureau of Labor Statistics indicates that legal immigrants were 22 percent of all new U. S. labor force entrants in 1989, compared to only 11 percent during the decade of the 1970s. Some 600,000 immigrants are admitted into this country each year, with an increasing number coming into the U. S. by employer requests to help alleviate skilled worker shortages. This is particularly true in severe shortage areas like nursing. In effect there seems to be an unwritten federal policy operating to import skilled workers and export jobs for unskilled workers.

Immigrants may be one answer to the pending skill shortage crisis, but other solutions must be found. One answer could be the development of a new national upward-mobility retraining program aimed at identifying talented individuals now in the workforce and working in dead-end jobs. These people will have demonstrated that they know how to work and have an aptitude for more technical employment. A targeted upward-mobility retraining program could be designed in which these individuals are prepared for jobs in skill shortage occupations, thereby alleviating the skill shortage problem and opening more entry-level jobs for new or unskilled workers.

In the decade ahead the nation will complete an economic

cycle that started with the introduction of new technology, to retraining the workforce, to worldwide marketing. Eventually, the retooled technology-age industries should be able to reduce prices and increase quality, given increased productivity from a better trained and higher-skilled workforce. This kind of progress will be fundamental in helping the U. S. to maintain a competitive edge in world markets. Such progress will not occur in a skill shortage, inflation-producing economic environment.

International competition, existing and looming skill short-

Educational Upgrading of the Labor Force
(Distribution of the Labor Force by Level of Education Completed)

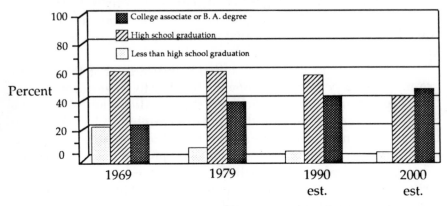

Source: U. S. Department of Labor, Bureau of Labor Statistics.

ages, deficiencies in training and education programs, and new, more technical national defense requirements are motivating a new national interest in human resource development efforts. Higher education will not be allowed to sit on the sidelines. The economic future and educational future of our country are inextricably linked together.

Early in this century the U. S. experienced a societal shift of similar magnitude as the contemporary agrarian mode of life gave way to a rising industrialized society. America's tradition of welcoming change and rejecting reactionary approaches is reassuring.

New challenges bring forth new solutions, such as the land-grant universities and extension programs, and the Smith-Hughes Vocational Education Act of 1918. The GI Bill of 1945 is, perhaps, the best known and most successful national human resource development program. In the 1960s the community college movement blossomed, in a grassroots movement, opening wide the doors of higher education to baby boomers and the adult population.

Unfortunately, there are some danger signs on the horizon. The number of jobless across the nation continues to hover between six and seven million. Another estimated one million have simply given up looking for work because of limited competencies. Add to these figures an estimated five million individuals who are working part time and/or are undereducated and underemployed, and you have some twelve million people looking for work even in good times. Unfortunately for many of the unemployed, they lack the necessary job skills to match the job needs.

The job match-mismatch dilemma was underscored by former secretary of labor William Brock when he said that America is simultaneously creating more high-skill jobs and turning out more low-skill workers. Unless our nation resolves that problem, we will create a de facto class segregation between the happy and productive citizen and the miserable and unemployed citizen.[2]

Unemployment and the wasting of human resources have become a staggering expense to our nation, even in good economic times. Unemployment and the related programs cost the federal government close to $21 billion in 1986 alone. Unfortunately, the traditional victims of unemployment continue to be the unskilled, the transient, and the poor. But a new group of unemployed are emerging; they are experienced workers displaced by rapidly changing technology and vigorous international competition. As a result, the nation is grappling with the most massive adult education and retraining challenge it has ever faced. Community, technical, and junior colleges report that up to 15 percent of their students already possess at least a bachelor's degree, with many returning to local colleges to upgrade skills or train for new careers. Indeed, an entirely new kind of graduate program has emerged.

Providing the education and training necessary to prepare the new generation of adult workers to perform at higher skill levels

Major Federal Programs for the Unemployed

Program	Fiscal 1986 Outlays
Unemployment Compensation Authorized by the Social Security Act of 1935, as amended, to compensate eligible workers who are temporarily out of work and looking for a job. Benefits are paid by state tax on employers; administration paid by federal tax; extended benefits shared by federal/state governments.	$ 16.4 billion
Block Grants to the States Authorized by the Job Training Partnership Act of 1982, title II-A, to make grants to the states for the operation of programs ... prepare disadvantaged youth and unskilled adults with job training and employment services.	$ 1.78 billion
Summer Youth Employment Authorized by the Job Training Partnership Act of 1982, title II-B, to make grants to the states to subsidize minimum wage public sector jobs and related training during the summer for youth between 14 and 21 years old.	$781 million
Dislocated Workers Authorized by the Job Training Partnership Act of 1982, title III, to assist dislocated workers with training and employment services.	$ 95 million
Employment Service Authorized by the Wagner Peyser Act of 1933, as amended, to place persons in employment by providing a variety of placement-related services—without charge—to job seekers and to employers seeking qualified individuals.	$754 million
Job Corps Authorized by the Job Training Partnership Act of 1982, title IV-B, to provide remedial education and job skills to disadvantaged youth, now in more than 100 residential centers that provide meals, room, recreation, medical care, and living and readjustment status.	$612 million
Work Incentive Authorized by the Social Security Amendments of 1967, to provide job services, training, and public service employment for the recipients of Aid to Families with Dependent Children.	$152 million

Source: U. S. Department of Labor Employment and Training Administration, 1986 Budget.

than in the past is a major challenge facing postsecondary education. Flexible higher education programs must be developed to enable adults to move in and out of programs easily while acquiring new knowledge and new skills. Jobs in the 1990s will be more interesting and rewarding for those who are qualified, but helping individuals acquire the qualifications for these jobs will be a major challenge for schools, colleges, and universities in the coming decade.

The Bureau of Labor Statistics predicts that sixteen million new jobs will be created by the end of the 1990s. During the same period, the workforce is expected to increase by about fifteen million. The question is not whether there will be sufficient numbers of jobs, but whether the entrants to the labor force will have the competencies to fill the available jobs.

National economic policies in the decade ahead must include development of human resources as an integral part of overall federal economic strategy. Historically, our country's strength reflects an unflagging faith in the investment in human potential. Any new vision for a revitalized economy in the 1990s will fall short of its goals unless it addresses human resource development needs. In many ways colleges and universities hold the key—through the provision of education, training, retraining, and research—to America's future economic prosperity. The technological age is reshaping how we live and work, and it is certainly reshaping educational programs.

The Research Component

Another opportunity and challenge facing America will be to maintain worldwide leadership in research and the transfer of new technology to the marketplace. According to Bruce Merrifield, former assistant secretary of commerce for production, technology, and innovation, 90 percent of all scientific and technical knowledge has been generated in the last thirty years, a major proportion of which was gained in the United States. By the end of the 1990s the field of knowledge will have doubled again. The "half-life" of this new knowledge is now estimated to be as little as five to ten years.

For well over a hundred years there has been an understanding of the vital connection between university research and the application of knowledge. But it was not until the end of World War II that university-based research became a national interest. Led by Vannevar Bush and other prominent scientists, a national plan of action was developed, leading to the establishment of several science and research agencies, including the National Science Foundation, the Atomic Energy Commission, and the Office of Naval Research.

Today approximately forty federal agencies provide $4 billion in support of research activities at more than 350 universities. As a result of this huge investment, the United States has achieved undisputed leadership in nearly every research field. Americans have dominated the Nobel Prize competition in science and technology. From 1953 to 1973 U. S. researchers produced two-thirds of the major technological innovations.

Technology and technology-related research have created a dazzling array of new goods, services, and jobs. As an example, in 1965 a single space satellite carried 240 telephone circuits at a cost of $22,000 per circuit; today's satellite carries fifty times more circuits at a cost of less than $800 per circuit. Improvements in optical fibers, robotics, automated production, graphics, and computers have rendered many products and processes obsolete over the past few years and transformed millions of jobs. Millions of workers are requiring new and improved skills to cope with the technology of the present and future.

However, high-technology research and high-technology industries will account for only a small percentage of the new jobs of the future. Each high-tech job creates between five and fifteen support jobs. It is the small and medium-size low-technology industries that will provide the economic stability in terms of sales, jobs, and other measures of economic performance. Indeed, the future of our nation as a global economic force will be linked in the future to thousands of smaller companies scattered all across the country, most of which do not have a training or retraining capacity. From 1978 to 1984 companies with fewer than 1,000 employees *added* more than 8.4 million jobs to the U. S. economy, while companies with over 1,000 employees *lost* nearly 280,000 jobs.

William Rentschler, chief executive officer of the Medart Company, states the case for low-tech industries this way:

46

> We should not forget—despite our preoccupation with megatrends and robots, rocketry and genetics—that there's profit in the prosaic, the basic, the unglamorous, the tried-and-true. And there are jobs—many, many jobs. There are profits and jobs in toasters and toys, glassware and greeting cards, lockers and fasteners, cornflakes and cookies, dress shirts and machine tools, lift trucks and linens.[3]

Smaller companies that do not have the education and training capacity of the larger corporations will increasingly be turning to schools, colleges, and universities for assistance, even as the small farmer turned to the land-grant university and county extension agent over this past century.

This will require colleges and universities to develop new programs and new services for the small business sector of the economy. As an example, Gonzaga University in Spokane, Washington, has joined with Spokane Community Colleges and local businesses, too small to afford state-of-the-art CAD/CAM systems, to provide this service. Each partner buys into the program on a "use" base and it is running night and day. Often college students join with local engineers, college professors, and technicians to solve problems.

But what about the future of research? While scientists around the world generally agree that American research efforts continue to lead those of other countries by a wide margin in all but a few fields, there is concern that the U. S. edge may be eroding, because of insufficient funding as well as a drop in the number of young scientists entering the research community. Moreover, American manufacturers have not been able to capitalize on the research edge and have lost important battles—perhaps even the war—in the consumer marketplace, especially in consumer electronics.

One of the perplexing problems facing research communities is the matter of who should police basic research. How can the research community get a handle on questionable research practices, including fraud, fudging on findings, ordinary error, and financial conflict of interest? The National Science Foundation and the National Institutes of Health, as well as many universities, have introduced investigative policies and procedures.

Scientists and researchers argue that the process of peer review, publication, and retesting of results makes the current research system a self-correcting enterprise. Governmental leaders, on the other hand, point out that in an era of tight money, many researchers and university-based scientists have commercial ties, like holding stock in companies that directly benefit from their research work. As a consequence, the collegial information-sharing process, so necessary in research, is hampered by competing commercial interests.

Fortune magazine has documented the growing trend in which colleges and universities establish active research partnerships with employers. While the government continues to be the primary source of research funds, industry added $600 million in 1986 to support campus-based research, three times the amount provided in 1980. *Fortune* reported that the college-corporate partnerships often "go beyond mere affiliation, to merge forces in joint ventures." In one example, the Monsanto Company signed a multimillion-dollar joint research agreement with Washington University of St. Louis. As part of a strategic corporate decision to diversify its main business as a chemical manufacturer into the growing field of biotechnology, Monsanto looked to the university to acquire research and development expertise at reasonable costs.[4]

The entrepreneurial stories are almost legend growing out of the Stanford University-motivated "Silicon Valley" research and development efforts. Duke University and the research triangle in North Carolina, Massachusetts Institute of Technology and Harvard University in Massachusetts, have all contributed significantly not only to research, but to the economic health of these regions of the country.

Regardless of the problems that surround researchers and scientists, it is safe to say that a vibrant and unhampered research community will be required to lead the U. S. into a healthy and competitive 1990 economy.

The Technology Transfer Component

Another major influence contributing to high state-level emphasis upon economic development has been the changing structure of the overall economy. About half of the governors report that declining industries are the most important economic issue facing their state.[5] The constriction of several industrial economic sectors, particularly heavy manufacturing, has forced many states to rethink and reanalyze their entire approach to competitiveness and economic development. The most significant result of the shifting economy has been a growing state-level emphasis upon existing businesses, strengthening the existing economy, and improving the competencies of the existing workforce.

But of all the trade and competitiveness problems to be solved, the most important problem is technology transfer. How can employers of all kinds keep up with the rapid developments and translate the findings of research into a product or service? Universities have a long history of technology transfer efforts in agriculture through the county extension program and in medicine, where clinical faculty link the classroom and the practice. However, in fields like computer-aided manufacturing, advanced materials, and biotechnology, successful technology transfer to American manufacturers is less certain. It appears that many foreign firms are adapting new technologies at a rate faster than U. S. firms and, consequently, increasing their share of U. S. and world markets.

Some experts believe that America is losing its competitive economic edge in the world economy. The Panel on Technology and Employment of the National Academy of Sciences, led by Richard Cyert, paints a disturbing picture:

> With the significant exceptions of portions of the National Aeronautics and Space Administration's aeronautics research program and the research programs of the U. S. Department of Agriculture and the National Institutes of Health, federally funded non-defense research (outside of energy in the 1970s) has focused largely on basic research; there have been few funding activities supporting the adaption of new technologies. This focus of U. S. public research support contrasts with publicly funded research

programs in Sweden, West Germany, and to some extent, Japan; in those programs, greater emphasis is placed on support for both applied and adaption-related research. Such differences in national science and technology policies may contribute to the more rapid diffusion of advanced manufacturing technologies in other nations. In addition to supporting long-term research relevant to the generation of new technologies, then, public financial resources may also be important for the support of technology transfer. The U. S. public research budget currently provides little, if any, support for the adaption of new technologies. U. S. industry must operate closer to the technological frontier if this nation is to maintain high employment levels and high living standards.[6]

Relatively few American inventions or industrial improvement ideas make it from the research organizations to the marketplace, or they are developed so slowly that aggressive international companies are allowed to capture that particular market niche. On top of that, few American companies have been able to penetrate on a continuous basis into foreign markets. It is becoming increasingly clear that higher education institutions of all kinds are being urged to help solve the technology transfer problem.

Here are some examples of how two states are utilizing colleges and universities to help solve research and technology transfer problems.

The state of Ohio has focused its attention over the past several years on the problem of technology transfer and has produced innovative solutions. Facing a severe statewide economic crisis in the early 1980s, Governor Richard Celeste formulated a multi-agency strategy that combined the resources of the Ohio Department of Development and the higher education Board of Regents. Called the Thomas Edison Program, with initial funding of $67 million, it was designed to stimulate working partnerships between business and academia that would stimulate new technological ideas, products, and companies. As part of the Edison program, a network of agents was established at each community or technical college. The Ohio Technology Transfer Organization's (OTTO) agents served as college and employer liaisons, similar to the role of county extension agents in the agricultural program.

According to state officials, the Edison program, along with other initiatives, played a key role in helping Ohio move from a dismal forty-ninth place nationwide in job creation in 1982 to third place in 1986. During the same time period Ohio's unemployment rate dropped from 14 percent to 7.9 percent.

Under the leadership of Governor Gerald Baliles, the Virginia Higher Education Economic and Technology Development Program (ETD) was developed under a partnership arrangement between the Virginia Community College System and the Center for Innovative Technology (CIT). (The CIT is a private nonprofit corporation chartered by the Virginia General Assembly in 1984 to fund high-quality applied research at state universities, assist in commercializing that research, and aid technology development in a variety of ways.) A technology transfer program was also developed utilizing the community colleges.

The state-funded technology transfer program is a unique three-year pilot program. Technology transfer efforts attempt to match technology solutions with business needs. Specially selected and trained ETD directors, located at nine community colleges, work with local businesses to help improve economic performance through the application of technology. The program is available at no cost to small and medium-sized businesses that typically do not have much research and development capability. Drawing from their knowledge, skills, and experiences, the directors help firms:

- Solve existing problems and expand their operation through technology applications;
- Arrange for services with their host community colleges, including education and training courses, business development resources, and technical skills of faculty and staff members;
- Access the latest scientific and technical information through national and international computer searches;
- Identify available specialists for clients from federal laboratories and state universities;
- Locate private sector consulting resources;
- Find appropriate technology-based equipment for clients

51

to buy or lease; and
- Utilize college faculty expertise to assist employers and provide technical information.

These represent two state-level technology transfer examples. There are many, many other efforts. As an example, the General Motors Corporation contracts with local community colleges to train local auto dealers and auto technicians, particularly as new General Motors products are developed. The Ford Motor Company has developed a similar program. This kind of employer-college cooperation, along with state technology transfer programs, is likely to expand significantly in the decade ahead.

The Economic Development Component

In *Workforce 2000: Work and Workers for the Twenty-first Century*, the landmark study prepared by the Hudson Institute for the U. S. Department of Labor, two divergent paths are outlined for the country's economic future. The first, the "deflation" scenario, sees a world in which America turns inward and toward the past in an effort to protect old, faltering industries and traditional jobs. In the other, the "technology boom" scenario, favorable technological and institutional changes are advantageously incorporated into the underlying economy. It pictures lightning-speed strides in service industry productivity, potent stimulants to encourage global demand for goods and services, rapid economic expansion in developing countries in a free and open trading atmosphere, and a rebirth of interest in educating and training the nation's workforce.

The study concludes:

> The central lesson of these two alternative scenarios is that leadership policies—wise and unwise—can make a difference. But strategies for holding back the pace of change and clinging to the industrial structure of a previous era have little chance of success and great likelihood of doing severe damage to the economy. On the other hand, the policies that appear to take risks by pushing the limits of growth, accelerating investment in human and

52

> physical capital, and removing the institutional barriers
> to productivity enhancements in services, can pay huge
> dividends.[7]

In a similar vein, America's colleges and universities face divergent paths in responding to the economic challenges of the future. When examining the role of a college or university in economic development activities, some view increased attention to economic issues as a threat to the purely academic mission of the institution. Others recognize that the college has a vital stake in the long-term economic health of its community or region, and that its role in economic development and the application of learning to real-life issues are as relevant to the institution's mission as is the traditional community service role. Indeed, economic development activities are a key new community service for many colleges.

A 1986 report from the American Association of State Colleges and Universities entitled *Issues in Higher Education and Economic Development* concludes that higher education institutions, of all kinds, today constitute the single most significant resource that can influence economic development. Federal officials, business, labor leaders, and state policymakers are increasingly looking to colleges and universities for assistance in solving economic problems.

An increasing number of colleges have resolved the internal conflicts and are vigorously moving ahead to provide cooperative economic development program services. Many colleges recognize that they can make a significant contribution to the economy of a region or state, and are actually providing economic development community services. While this increased attentiveness to economic issues may be new for some colleges and universities, there is a long history of economic development activity in the collegiate community. Established by the Morrill Land-Grant College Act of 1862, the land-grant university was designed to educate and train technical personnel for industry and agriculture. The large, sophisticated university extension service—complete with vigorous research and agricultural experiment stations and community-based extension agents—has become the worldwide model for technology transfer. In realizing its goal to make two blades of grass grow where only one grew before, the agricultural extension service has helped make American farmland the most productive in the world.

The work of the county extension agents has become synonymous with public-private partnerships at their best. In many ways some of the newer college-employer partnerships parallel the county extension agent experience. When the Ford Motor Company began to face reduced long-term demand for manufacturing during the 1980-82 recession, it initiated a program with neighboring schools, colleges, and universities to retrain its labor force. The comprehensive program included career counseling, tuition assistance, and targeted vocational retraining. By 1989 in excess of 18,000 displaced Ford employees had benefited from this unique partnership.

Many state and local economic development authorities are already tapping the resources of colleges to provide an array of services, including economic surveys, foreign trade assistance, and sharing of facilities, equipment, and professional staff. Community, technical, and junior colleges are beginning to serve as "convenience stores" for small business assistance. Each Oregon community college operates a small business development center. Programs include long-term development assistance, short-term courses, workshops, consulting, and support services. The colleges report that hundreds of small businesses in Oregon have increased sales, employment, and their ability to attract financing as a result of local college efforts.

Located in the nation's bread basket, Northwest Missouri State University serves the four-state region of Iowa, Nebraska, Kansas, and Missouri. Some three million people live within a 150-mile radius of the university campus. Northwest Missouri State University has developed three partnership programs: Center for Applied Research, Small Business Development Center, and a Dietary Manager Program.

The Center for Applied Research was established to bring together management, teaching, and research talent to muster new ideas, processes, and products. As an example, officials of Frito-Lay, Inc., met with university personnel and area farmers to discuss potato chip production opportunities. University horticulturalists, graduate students, farmers, the director of the center, and Frito-Lay leaders met together and developed a Contract Potato Project with

54

Frito-Lay. The company furnished the seed potatoes and offered farmers a solid contract price to grow the potatoes. The Center for Applied Research brought producers and the market together, and provided a project manager from the faculty along with graduate student assistance.

The project proved economically beneficial to the farmers, the Frito-Lay company, and to the university. Faculty members and graduate students had the opportunity to work on a real-world agribusiness problem and be agents of change.

Alcorn State University in Mississippi has operated a cooperative education University/Industry Cluster Program for sixteen years. This program facilitates collaborative efforts among businesses, industries, government agencies, and the university to bring people together in workshops, task forces, and conferences to work on real-world problems identified by the employer community. Currently there are fifty businesses and government agencies involved in the cluster program. This program provides a medium for employers to work with faculty and students. It is particularly advantageous for employers to observe potential new employees (students) in problem-solving situations.

The first order of economic priority in any community is providing enough infrastructure support to retain existing employers successfully. Equally commendable is that unique employer, who, responding to considerable external forces of change, makes an exceptional effort to maintain its community loyalty while adapting to those forces of change. It was this confluence of wills that led to an extraordinary public-private partnership between Front Range Community College and IBM in Boulder, Colorado.

In April of 1986 the IBM Corporation directed its Boulder site to change its mission from manufacturing to software development and systems support. Two thousand employees, or two-fifths of the workforce, were directly involved with this mission change that represented one of the largest workforce transitions ever attempted by IBM.

Two unique courses, "Retraining Preparedness" and "Career Transition Training," were developed as a response to the indicators that employee needs for adaptation must be addressed in order for them to succeed at retraining. The preparedness course

55

was quickly developed to enhance self-management skills and self-confidence, to improve attitudes toward change, and finally, to raise learning skill levels. A follow-up transition training course was developed and implemented for several hundred employees who were still working toward a complete job transition.

This partnership has been successful for IBM and for the college. However, the big winner has been the Boulder community in its quest to maintain economic stability. Congressman David Skaggs (D-Colo.) captures the importance of this project for all concerned: "This project is a good example of what industry and education together can accomplish. In addition to assisting IBM employees who had to change jobs and careers, the project addressed the community's need—to create a more flexible workforce."[8]

Johnson County Community College in Overland Park, Kansas, has developed an innovative program in cooperation with Burlington Northern Railroad and the city of Overland Park. An industrial training center was built on the college campus for the primary lease-back use of Burlington Northern.

The key discussions in planning this facility centered on a complicated set of terms for placing a private sector facility on public property in conjunction with critical industrial revenue bond (IRB) support. Most of this effort represented a pioneering effort for all concerned. The city agreed to issue $2,920,000 worth of tax-free industrial revenue bonds—a first, as Overland Park had never issued IRBs to promote development within city limits. The college, on the other hand, agreed to deed the development site to the city, which erected the building and leased the space to Burlington Northern. Alternately, Burlington Northern subleased one-third of the space back to the college for the same rate.

The fruits of this partnership prompted Overland Park mayor Ed Eilert to comment: "The impact of this innovative business, industry, and education compact has already been felt in our community."[9] Alternately, Burlington Northern's pleasure is captured in the words of Donald Henderson, vice president for technology, engineering, and maintenance: "The environment of this new technical training complex is important to the kind of view we want our employees to have about their work and themselves. . . . To be the best, you have to expect the best from yourself, and having the best training is the foundation of that expectation."[10]

Somerset Community College in Kentucky is the only public institution of higher education in its service area, an area that has been labeled the least educated population in the U. S. This distinction had lead to a sluggish economy and a dim future for that region of Kentucky. It is within this grim background that the role of Somerset Community College, working with a Cornell University professor, can be fully appreciated.

The college developed something it called "worksite strategy." The program was initiated with the Kingsford Charcoal Company. Kingsford had a workforce of 140 employees, of which only 40 percent were high school graduates. The college entered Kingsford with a modest basic skills program. The effort was so fruitful that it stimulated the creation of a comprehensive literacy program at Kingsford. The immediate result was the completion of twenty-eight GED certificates and increased college enrollment from this same group of employees.

Concurrently, the county government began to seek strategies in which it could enhance economic development prospects through an improved local labor market. With this in mind, the county imposed a 1 percent employee occupational tax with the intent that 30 percent of the revenues be targeted toward industrial education and training. Taking advantage of this new tool, Somerset Community College leveraged a $107,000 county grant to play a critical role in the elevation of productivity levels for the county's largest employer, Tecumseh Products Company, Inc. A year-long management program was developed that addressed employee feedback, team building, employee attitudes, and skill preparation in a workplace structure. The immediate result was a significant reduction in the product-quality defect rate. Secondly, there was a workforce increase from 800 to 1,250 employees. And finally, Tecumseh donated $20,000 to the college's labor-management resource center to assist other local industries in improving labor relations. The capstone of this kind of college-labor-employer partnership has been an economic resurgence for this region of Kentucky, with new companies moving to the area and older companies expanding.

Each of the fifty states has some form of economic development activity either in the planning or operational stage. This widespread interest in economic development on the part of state government leaders has been motivated primarily by the size and extent of the 1981-85 recession. What had become an economic crisis of major proportions in many states forced political leaders into economic development action. The high level and duration of unemployment alone was a major factor in stimulating economic development efforts. Seven states—Alaska, Alabama, Louisiana, Michigan, Mississippi, Ohio, and West Virginia—experienced the highest levels of joblessness since the Great Depression of the 1930s. Eleven states posted unemployment rates above 8 percent as late as 1987. The most disturbing aspect of the 1980-85 economic recession was that, unlike previous postwar recessions, a high proportion of the unemployed would never return to their same jobs again.

By 1987 about half the nation's governors reported that a decline in their manufacturing industries and related jobs was the most important economic obstacle facing their states.[11] The erosion of several industrial sectors, particularly heavy manufacturing, has forced many states to rethink and reanalyze their entire approach to economic development. A significant result of this review has been a reorientation in the thinking of business and labor leaders geared to strengthening the economy by improving the competencies of the workforce at all levels.

The good news from higher education's point of view is that the needs of the technological economy have refocused attention on education as a vital component of economic development. During the 1970s and early 1980s economic development meant passing revenue bonds, building industrial parks, and wooing large industries from other states. The emphasis for the 1990s will be on human resource development, embracing the wisdom of eighteenth-century economist Adam Smith, who recognized that people are the prime economic resource and first responsibility of a nation.

One of the key emerging roles for colleges and universities to play in the decade ahead can be pictured in a new kind of economic development paradigm. Economic development has traditionally been defined as the process by which individuals or organizations are motivated to invest capital in a community, generating or expanding industrial, commercial, or service activities and, thereby, increasing or retaining jobs. Increasingly, this process has required the cooperation of three diverse groups: public-private employers and labor; public and private community, technical, and junior colleges; and research universities. Working together they form a new kind of economic development triangle. The success of this new paradigm hinges upon the commitment and cooperative efforts of the partners. Where it has been tried in states like North and South Carolina the benefits returned have been significant.

New Economic Development Triangle

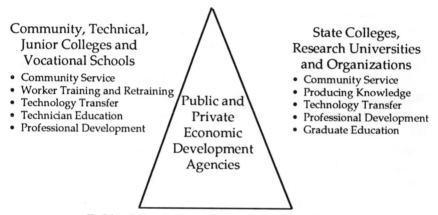

Community, Technical, Junior Colleges and Vocational Schools

- Community Service
- Worker Training and Retraining
- Technology Transfer
- Technician Education
- Professional Development

Public and Private Economic Development Agencies

State Colleges, Research Universities and Organizations

- Community Service
- Producing Knowledge
- Technology Transfer
- Professional Development
- Graduate Education

Public-Private Employers and Labor Groups

The America of the 1990s will again invent new solutions to meet new problems. And a strengthened relationship between the employer community and the college community will be at the center of new initiatives to meet the challenges of the coming decade. Yet, adapting to change is never easy, especially in academia. Higher education institutions must develop new attitudes, new organizational structures, improved response time, and a host of modifications to match the pace of change.

The Curriculum Reform Component

The need for collegiate curriculum reform to match the economic and workforce needs of our technological age was underscored in 1988 at a meeting of more than 500 delegates from 121 countries in Geneva, Switzerland. The subject of the UNESCO-sponsored conference was "The Diversification of Postsecondary Education in Relation to Employment." Conference participants concluded that postsecondary education in most countries lacked a sufficiently employment-related practical focus.

These UNESCO officials voiced great concern that higher education, in too many instances, did not help students understand the real-life applications of their learning. In many parts of the world it is simply a fact of life that a wide chasm exists between higher education and the need for it in meeting real-world conditions. Can this observation also be applied to U. S. colleges and universities?

In their book *New Priorities for the University*, Ernest Lynton and Sandra Elman argue that universities are out of step with the society they serve by failure to emphasize the application of learning. They push for the university faculty to reach beyond the traditional search for new knowledge and stress the application of existing knowledge. This will require a new definition of scholarship to include the synthesis, interpretation, and application of existing knowledge as well as sponsoring basic research generating new knowledge.[12]

One exciting new technical education program developing across the nation is a liberal-technical education called the tech-prep/associate degree program. Some colleges and universities are also developing a bachelor of technology four-year college degree program. This four-year 2+2 program is intended to run parallel with, and not to replace, the time-honored college-prep/baccalaureate degree program. It combines a common core of learning with technical education courses that rest upon a basic proficiency in science, math, and communications, all taught in an applied setting.

Beginning with the junior year of high school, students select the tech-prep program (even as they now select the college-prep program) and continue for four years or six years in a structured and closely coordinated high school-college curriculum. They are taught by high school teachers in the first two years, but also have access to college personnel and facilities when appropriate. Starting from a solid base of applied science, applied math, literacy courses, and technical programs, the high school portion of the career program is intentionally preparatory in nature. Built around career clusters and the study of technical systems, such a tech-prep approach helps students develop broad-based competence in a career field and avoid the pitfalls of more short-term and narrowly delineated job training.

The history of cooperative and coordinated program articulation between high schools and colleges would not even fill a slim book. But there are signs that progress is being made. High school and college faculty are talking together as never before, and they are talking about the real "beef" of education called the curriculum.

America's economic system has been extraordinarily successful. It has provided material abundance that far outstrips anything experienced before. But that very success dare not lull the U. S. into thinking that the models and solutions applicable to an industrial age will be sufficient to meet the challenges of the future. The path to the Great Society of the 1960s and 1970s was more of everything. In the 1980s the United States learned—the hard way—that quantity is no substitute for quality. And no matter how many advances are made in technology, there will never be a true substitute for well-educated, superbly trained, energetic individuals to keep the technology working and the economy healthy.

Dateline 2000 Forecast

1.   A congressionally mandated national human resource development policy will emerge in the decade of the 1990s with well-established priorities that fully utilize public and private higher education institutions.

2.   This compelling national interest in human resource development will fuel a new boom in higher education to be supported by new sources of state and federal funding.

3.   Many colleges and universities will reexamine their mission statements as related to community service, updating that mission to match the economic development needs of their service region or constituency.

4.   More cooperative efforts will be developed among research universities, state and private colleges, community colleges, and the employer community in each state with an eye toward developing a more effective system to support technology transfer efforts.

5.   New and strengthened partnerships will be developed between the employer community, schools, and colleges. It will be a rare community college or state college that will not have established some kind of special employer-college liaison office.

6.   Colleges and universities will increasingly examine internal institutional policies and procedures as to flexibility and responsiveness. If community service is a part of the institutional mission, then flexibility and response time become important operational issues.

7.   The associate degree will become an increasingly important credential in helping meet the emerging technical workforce needs of the employer community.

8.   Special efforts will be made by colleges and universities to bring ethnic minority individuals, persons with handicaps, and women into careers where they are greatly underrepresented. These efforts

will be successful, but with much remaining to be accomplished by the year 2000.

9.   State and federal government leaders will support, and fully utilize, the research capabilities of colleges and universities to stimulate continued economic development activities.

10.   An increasing number of colleges and universities will reach out to help the eleven million or so small business owners of the country. Such help will take many forms (small business incubators, consultants, and worker training or retraining).

11.   A new and integrated 2+2+2 tech-prep/associate degree/bachelor of technology degree program will become commonplace in schools and colleges. This will be an applied academic program combining the liberal arts with technical education, requiring interdisciplinary and multidisciplinary teaching approaches.

Executive Summary

The missing link in current U. S. economic policy is the limited attention given to coordinating local, state, and federal human resource development programs.

The U.S. Labor Department is now predicting that by the end of the 1990s an estimated 70 to 75 percent of all job classifications in this country will require some form of postsecondary education or training for entry. The need for employees with higher levels of competencies will greatly expand as employment increases from 106 million in 1984 to 123 million in 1995. As a result of these changes, much national and state attention will be given in the decade ahead to the subject of human resource development.

Five interrelated components must be analyzed when studying the economy and higher education: human resource development, research, technology transfer, economic development, and curriculum reform. There is an increasing strong link between a healthy economy and how well institutions of higher education relate to these components and the economic needs of our nation.

Pioneering partnerships among America's schools and colleges and employer-labor groups have shown how links between education and the employer community can produce more skilled workers and significant economic payoffs. Corporations, colleges, and labor unions are also working together on such issues as illiteracy, unemployment, underemployment, foreign trade competition, fast-changing technology, and community service programs. Educators and employers are beginning to discover that it is in their own enlightened self-interest to work together. But new and expanded education and adult retraining programs will be needed to reverse economic currents that have forced thousands of job displacements. The new wealth of America will come from people who excel in mathematics, science, and applied technology, and from skilled entrepreneurs. This will require a much closer linkage between education and economic interests.

The new linkages between the economy and education will fuel, at least in part, a new boom in higher education. The new economic development triangle partnerships will certainly forge some new relationships.

Notes

1. John Naisbitt, *Megatrends* (New York: Warner Books, 1984).
2. "Altering the Face of Work," *Washington Post*, November 1986.
3. William H. Rentschler, "The Logics of Low Tech," *American Way* (May 1987).
4. Jeremy Main, "Business Goes to College for a Brain Gain," *Fortune* (16 March 1987).
5. Marianne K. Clarke, *Revitalizing State Economies* (Washington, D. C.: National Governors' Association, 1986).
6. Richard M. Cyert and David M. Mowery, *Technology and Employment: Innovation and Growth in the U. S. Economy* (Washington, D. C.: National Academy Press, 1987).
7. Hudson Institute, *Workforce 2000: Work and Workers for the Twenty-first Century* (Indianapolis: Hudson Institute, 1987).
8. American Association of Community and Junior Colleges, Keeping America Working Project Report (Washington, D. C.: American Association of Community and Junior Colleges, 1988).
9. Keeping America Working Project Report.
10. Keeping America Working Project Report.
11. Clarke, *Revitalizing State Economies*.
12. Ernest A. Lynton and Sandra E. Elman, *New Priorities for the University* (San Francisco: Jossey-Bass, 1986).
13. Dale Parnell, *The Neglected Majority* (Washington, D. C.: Community College Press, 1985).

Chapter III

The Global Community

Our world has undergone immense transformations. It has become a more crowded, more interconnected, more unstable place. A new generation of Americans must be educated for life in this increasingly complex world. If the undergraduate college cannot help students see beyond themselves and better understand the interdependent nature of our world, each new generation will remain ignorant, and its capacity to live confidently and responsibly will be dangerously diminished.

Ernest Boyer
President
Carnegie Foundation for the Advancement of Teaching

W hile the technology revolution is reshaping the American economy, an even more profound change is occurring in the international economy. Man has been on the moon. Planets millions of miles away have been photographed at close range, and their images have been beamed back to earth at the speed of light. Communication satellites allow us to see news as it happens around the world, weather stations in the sky track storms as they are developing in midocean, and fiber-optic cable speeds communications under the sea.

Stock market traders and farmers speculate in global financial markets that never sleep. Rumors circulating in Tokyo affect prices in New York. Asian speculators drive up the price of pork bellies and corn futures in Chicago when weather forecasters predict a sustained dry spell in the U. S. midwest.

The opening of the Berlin Wall between the East and the West is a fitting symbol of what is happening around the world. Communism's weakened grip on Eastern European countries is opening the doors of freedom to another 110 million people, and there will be no turning back.

With some 160 independent nations of all sizes, shapes, and socioeconomic situations scattered around the globe, the world looks considerably different to them than it does to the citizens of the U. S. It is a world of reciprocity, bilateral and trilateral agreements, trading blocks, and economic alliances. No one automatically stands to salute when the United States speaks. People in other countries today simply do not usually act or think in unison with the U. S. In 1992 twelve Western European nations will officially launch the European Economic Community, eliminating virtually all barriers to trade, capital, labor, and education for 320 million people.

Even in the U. S. the steady flow of immigrants from other countries brings a new vigor and vitality with them, but they also bring new ways of thinking and working. It is interesting to note that thirteen of the seventeen high school valedictorians in the Boston public high schools in the 1989 graduating class were foreign born. They came from around the globe, including Czechoslovakia, Jamaica, Italy, France, Portugal, El Salvador, Vietnam, and China.

The period of America's single-country supremacy in the global economy is clearly over. Twenty years ago only 25 percent of U. S. manufactured goods faced competition from imports; now that number has risen to 70 percent. For the first time in a century there is widespread and vigorous worldwide economic competition. And in a paradoxical fashion this competition has engendered a much higher level of cooperation and interdependence among the nations. The whims of the U. S. consumer dictate economic conditions in Japan, and a rise in the value of the yen means that Americans will spend higher percentages of their income on consumer electronic products and automobiles.

The huge appetite of American consumers for imported products, as well as the increased tendency of U. S. manufacturers to produce goods in foreign locations, has caused a most vexing economic challenge to America's future prosperity, particularly getting the rising U. S. trade imbalance under control. America continues to pile up deficits in the world merchandise trade account, though it appears that a lower dollar value in the U. S. may begin to restore some economic advantages to domestic production in the decade ahead. The dollar trade figures in 1988 and early 1989 certainly point toward some modest improvement in the trade balance.

The U. S. Department of Commerce is now estimating that for every billion dollars worth of increased imports into the U. S., 25,000 jobs for Americans are eliminated. An estimated 60 percent of the exports to the industrialized nations of the world come from Japan, Taiwan, Korea, Singapore, and Hong Kong. Some 36 percent of all Japanese exports go to the United States, while 33 percent of all Latin American exports go to the U. S. Japan has virtually captured the consumer electronic business (VCRs, etc.), 95 percent of the motorcycle business, 90 percent of the computer memory chip business, and is making major inroads into other businesses, not the least of which is auto manufacturing. The European Airbus Industry has now captured 20 percent of the wide-body aircraft jet market. Ariane, the French space energy company, has captured 50 percent of the space-shot business. Many of the developing nations are now entering the global competition with cheap labor and natural resources to capture markets sensitive to these factors. It is becoming the norm to see "Made in Taiwan," or Korea, or Singapore, or China, on goods sold in U. S. stores.

U. S. Trade Balance
(Billions of Dollars)

Period	Exports	Imports	Trade Balance
1982	216.4	244.0	- 27.6
1983	205.6	258.0	- 52.4
1984	224.0	325.7	-101.7
1985	218.8	345.3	-126.5
1986	227.2	365.4	-138.2
1987	254.1	406.2	-152.1
1988	321.8	441.0	-119.8

Source: U. S. Department of Commerce, Bureau of the Census, *Statistical Abstract of the United States, 1989.*

But to keep the international competition in perspective, here are a few statistics: If the entire world consisted of a hundred people, sixty-seven would be poor; fifty-five would have an annual income of less than $600; fifty would be in substandard housing; fifty would be without safe drinking water; forty-seven would be illiterate; thirty-five would be hungry and malnourished; six would be Americans and would earn 33 percent of the entire annual world income; and only one would have a baccalaureate degree education.

The world of the 1990s will largely be demographically divided between those countries with slow and those with fast population growth. In one set of countries, which represent nearly half of the world population, the number of people is decreasing or growing slowly and incomes are increasing. In the second group of

71

countries, representing the other half of the world, the populations are growing rapidly and incomes are falling. The perplexing aspect of a demographically divided world is that the situation will likely become even more divided along economic lines unless population growth can be stabilized. Southeast Asia, representing some 414 million people, very well could join the slow-growth countries by the year 2000. Thailand and Indonesia already have decreasing fertility rates and an increasing per capita income rate.

1986 World Population Growth

Region	Population	Population Growth Rate
	(million)	(percent)
Slow Growth Region		
Within Europe	381	0.2
North America	267	0.7
E. Europe and Soviet Union	392	0.8
Australia and New Zealand	19	0.8
East Asia	1,263	1.0
(primarily China and Japan)		
Totals	2,322	0.8
Rapid Growth Region		
Southeast Asia (primarily Burma, Indonesia, Philippines, Thailand, and Vietnam)	414	2.2
Latin America	419	2.3
Indian Subcontinent	1,027	2.4
Middle East	178	2.8
Africa	583	2.8
Totals	2,621	2.5

Source: Population Reference Bureau, 1986 world population data.

Already the slow-growth countries are experiencing a shortage of workers to match their economic growth needs. Japan is now estimating it will be short 2.7 million workers by the year 2000. Some Japanese leaders are recommending that Japan allow foreign workers into Japan as guest workers with a minimum wage that would allow them to maintain a living standard comparable to Japanese workers.

Can the United States move smoothly from a national to an international economy in the next decade? How will the United States deal with the economically competitive and the not-so-competitive nations of the world? Probably not without some strains, struggles, and stretching. First, it will be necessary for U. S. leaders and citizens to widen the viewing lens for a fresh look at a more competitive, but more open and interdependent, world. The globalization of the marketplace alone will require many changes in our way of thinking and working.

Spurred on by machines and other communication breakthroughs, the decade ahead will see a significant movement toward the development of trading blocks, international joint ventures, and licensing deals across national borders. Investments will be made in many different currencies.

Many more "free trade" agreements will be developed among countries, like the recently developed U. S -Canada agreement. It is now predicted that by 1995 the U. S. trade with Pacific Rim countries will be twice that with Europe. But Europe will not be standing still, either. The 1992 economic integration of an energized European Community will provide stiff market competition for the rest of the world. Even the newly opened Soviet bloc countries are beginning to participate at a higher rate in the wider European economy.

The United States is in the midst of some powerful changes. First, we are shifting from an isolated national economy to being part of an interdependent global economy. Second, we are becoming a working partner with other economically strong countries, where reciprocity will be the key ingredient.

Bruce Stokes, writing in the *National Journal*, calls for some new ways of thinking, impacting the way we work, save, and allocate our time:

> The United States today lacks the values of a competitive economy. American culture is oriented to the present rather than the future. It places a higher premium on pleasure than it does on work. And, it touts quantity rather than quality of production. As a result, in comparisons of productivity growth, savings, and educational achievement—the fundamental building blocks of an internationally competitive economy—the United States has clearly fallen behind many other industrialized nations.[1]

According to a 1987 Harris poll conducted for the Carnegie Forum on Education and the Economy, nine out of ten Americans believe that the challenge from foreign competition is serious. Some 97 percent of business leaders conclude that the U. S. must have a well-educated workforce to do more skilled jobs and to produce new products and services that will be competitive in the international market. It is becoming increasingly clear that the quality of the workforce will be the major factor in whether the U. S. maintains a leading economic position in the world.

In spite of the pressing need to prepare students to enter a world of global competition, support for collegiate international and intercultural education programs has been on the decline for the past twenty years. As of 1986 only about 15 percent of all colleges required any study of foreign language for admission, compared to 34 percent in 1966. The share of high school students with at least some skills in a second language has declined from about 33 percent in the 1930s to 17 percent half a century later in the 1980s.

Federal government and national foundation commitment to international education has also declined. Between 1965 and 1985 federal funding for programs administered by the U. S. Information Agency, including the Fulbright teacher exchange program, has been reduced by about 40 percent. The Ford Foundation provided $27 million annually for international education in the 1960s; twenty years later the annual support had been reduced to about $4 million. In 1981 the Reagan administration proposed cutting the Fulbright program by one-half and seriously reducing other international-intercultural programs. Under pressure from the worldwide economic competition, however, the administration's attitude was reversed in the later years of President Reagan's term and the administration showed new enthusiasm for international programs that might help to ease the trade deficit.

Commenting on the critical importance of training skilled internationalists for government service, Cassandra Pyle, executive director of the Council for International Exchange of Scholars, asked, "Can you cite a single country in which the U. S. has 'lost' only because of insufficient U. S. military strength? There are numerous examples where America has lost because of failure to understand the cultural and economic dynamics of a region or country."[2]

If the new international economy were the only major force shaping higher education in the 1990s, that influence alone would cause some significant changes in the operation of colleges and universities. Leaders at all levels in higher education are increasingly recognizing that the global community concept places new demands upon higher education institutions. More cooperative efforts at home and abroad will be required.

However, there has been a kind of ambivalence among higher education leaders about international education programs. Robert Kaplan, professor of applied linguistics at the University of Southern California, states: "A great many institutions that admit international students don't fully understand why they do so, and don't yet have any clear notion of what they are doing in international education."[3]

A National Commission on the Role and Future of State Colleges and Universities, under the leadership of former secretary of education Terrel Bell, in 1988 recommended three major areas of international education focus. First, college students must be provided with an international perspective that reflects the world in realistic social, political, cultural, and economic terms. Second, college students must develop international communication skills that will enable them to think, behave, and work effectively in a world of rapid change. Third, colleges must assist—through research, technical assistance, study, and international service programs—in the resolution of international problems with the same commitment that education institutions now address domestic issues.[4]

Many of the critical issues arising during the decade ahead

75

will require international rather than domestic solutions. What can the U. S. alone do about the problems of narcotics distribution, nuclear war, terrorism, pollution of the global environment? All these vexing challenges will require international solutions. The college and university students of the 1990s must develop the understandings and values required to meet these and other challenges in an increasingly interconnected world environment.

Language studies alone will not be enough. Tomorrow's college graduate must possess a real understanding of a multicultural and interrelated world. Community, technical, and junior colleges face special challenges in the field of international-intercultural education. Two years is not usually sufficient time for most students to develop the competencies required in most technical education fields. The decade ahead will see community colleges reaching out to feeder high schools to develop new programs offered over the four years of grades eleven through fourteen. This would allow time for students to develop some proficiency in a foreign language and some amount of cultural understanding.

The development of new knowledge and human resource development will be the basis of the world's economic order in the decade ahead. This will require a new kind of flexibility in educational institutions and in individuals. The pace of technological change and the challenges of international economic competition will require individuals to change occupations and retrain several times during their working lives. The diversity, flexibility, and quality of the U. S. schools, colleges, and universities will be the key pegs upon which the individuals in our society will hang their collective hats of hope.

It will be necessary in the future for colleges and universities of all kinds to help students to understand the culture of other countries, be able to communicate in at least one or two other languages, be knowledgeable about the political and economic climates of other countries, and also be competent in a specific career field. This challenge calls for internationalizing the college curriculum in new and more flexible ways.

International Student Enrollment

The enrollment of foreign students in U. S. colleges has, traditionally, been the single most important contribution to internationalizing our institutions. Beginning after the end of World War II, foreign student enrollment in U. S. colleges and universities began to grow dramatically, helping to establish their preeminent reputation throughout the world. During the thirty-year period from 1955 to 1984, foreign enrollment in U. S. colleges increased tenfold, from 34,200 to 342,110 students.

Foreign Student and Total College Enrollment, Selected Years, 1954-55 to 1985-86

Year	Foreign Enrollment	Total Enrollments	% of Total Enrollment
1954-55	34,200	2,499,800	1.4
1959-60	48,500	3,402,300	1.4
1964-65	82,000	5,320,000	1.5
1969-70	135,000	7,978,400	1.7
1974-75	154,000	10,321,500	1.5
1975-76	179,600	11,290,700	1.6
1976-77	203,100	11,121,400	1.8
1977-78	235,500	11,415,000	2.1
1978-79	263,900	11,392,000	2.3
1979-80	286,300	11,707,000	2.4
1980-81	311,880	12,087,200	2.6
1981-82	326,300	12,371,700	2.6
1982-83	336,990	12,425,800	2.7
1983-84	338,890	12,393,700	2.7
1984-85	342,110	12,467,740	2.7
1985-86	343,780	12,387,726	2.8

Source: Institute of International Education, *Open Doors: 1985-86 Report on International Educational Exchange* (New York: Institute of International Education, 1985).

Today the situation is beginning to change. Some foreign governments have become disillusioned with the "brain drain" that has resulted from students deciding to stay on in the United States after completing their studies. Other countries, dependent upon petroleum-based export revenues, have considerably less revenue to spend on student exchanges as a result of lower crude oil prices. Consequently, during the decade of the 1980s there has been little increase in the number of foreign students enrolled in U. S. collegiate institutions.

Competition from other countries has also cut the flow of international students to the U. S. The Soviet Union has funded nearly as many students from Latin America alone as the U. S. does from all parts of the world. During the 1984-85 academic year, an estimated 7,000 Latin American students were studying in the U.S.S.R., another 3,000 studied in Eastern bloc countries, and some 6,000 studied in Cuba. The Soviet Union annually funds the college education of an estimated 90,000 Third World students, and Soviet bloc countries sponsor another 40,000. It is believed that 37,000 students from African nations were enrolled in Soviet colleges during 1982. During a similar period the U. S. government sponsored a total of only 20,000 students from the entire world to study in the U. S.[5]

Today, faced with declining enrollments, an increasing number of U. S. colleges and universities are developing active foreign student recruitment programs. In April 1989 the American Association of Community and Junior Colleges sponsored a student fair in Tokyo, Japan, to familiarize Japanese students with U. S. community, technical, and junior colleges. Over the two days of the fair more than 1,000 Japanese students were counseled about attending a U. S. college. Edmonds Community College in Seattle, Washington, has, in cooperation with Japanese interests, opened a branch campus in Japan. Numerous colleges and universities are operating colleges and branch campuses in countries all around the world. In the 1985-86 college year seventy-eight American colleges reported enrolling 1,000 or more foreign students. By contrast, only one institution enrolled that number of foreign students thirty years earlier.

Engineering, business, and management studies attract the most foreign students to U. S. institutions. Substantial shifts in recent years have occurred in the choice of study. Business management, mathematics, and computer science are steadily increasing in popularity, while engineering, education, and fine and applied arts have leveled off. Enrollment of foreign students in the humanities and social sciences has also declined, as has enrollment of American students in these programs.

The enrollment decline of foreign students is also felt by some community, technical, and junior colleges. At a time when interest in international-intercultural education is increasing, the number of foreign students attending some of these institutions is decreasing. Ironically, political leaders' interest in the U. S. community college idea is rising dramatically in other countries, particularly in Third World countries.

The decline in foreign student enrollment in community colleges appears to be the result of three factors. First, the drop in oil prices and the depressing effect on economies dependent on petroleum exports is keeping many students at home. Less than 1 percent of the foreign students in community colleges receive financial aid, while nearly 15 percent of foreign students in four-year institutions receive some sort of financial aid. Second, an increasing number of countries are developing their indigenous version of the American community college. Australia, for example, has developed a network of Technical and Further Education Colleges (TAFEs), serving one million students on 200 major campuses. Consequently, foreign students are staying home for their first two years of college and then transferring to upper-division colleges, some of them in the United States. Third, many colleges have not been aggressive in recruiting foreign students. Few colleges employ specialized recruiters in foreign countries, and only a handful have developed foreign language "viewbooks" or other descriptive college materials aimed at the foreign student market.

Unfortunately for both two-year and four-year colleges, the present trend in foreign student enrollment is not likely to change during the decade ahead unless some new national initiatives are mounted. There are a number of organizations working to turn things around. Groups like the National Association for Foreign Student Affairs, the Institute of International Education, and the American Association of Collegiate Registrars and Admissions Officers have been promoting new programs aimed at attracting for-

Two-Year Institutions With the Most Foreign Students and Percentage Change, 1984-85 to 1985-86

Rank			Foreign Students		
1984 -85	1985 -86	Institution	1984 -85	1985 -86	Percent Change
1	1	Miami-Dade Community College, FL	4,316	4,730	9.6
3	2	Northern Virginia Community College, VA	795	1,774	123.1
-	3	Bunker Hill Community College, MA	483	721	66.9
4	4	Prince George's Community College, MD	751	694	(7.6)
2	5	Montgomery College, MD	812	694	(14.5)
8	6	Central Piedmont Community College, NC	545	602	9.0
5	7	City Colleges of Chicago, Loop College, IL	681	581	(14.7)
6	8	Los Angeles City College, CA	650	487	(25.1)
7	9	Santa Monica College, CA	616	483	(21.6)
-	10	Broward Community College, FL	460	481	4.6
Total, 10 Leading Two-Year Institutions			10,109*	11,247	8.9
Percent of All Two-Year Institutions			24.2*	26.9	
TOTAL, ALL TWO-YEAR INSTITUTIONS			42,083	41,773	(0.7)

* Totals are for the ten leading two-year institutions of 1984-85, which included Oklahoma City Community College (ranked ninth) and San Jacinto College (ranked tenth).

Source: Institute of International Education, *Open Doors: 1985-86 Report on International Educational Exchange* (New York: Institute of International Education, 1985).

eign students. But if it is desirable for foreign student enrollment in the U. S. is to increase in the years ahead, several policy changes will be necessary.

One obstacle to increasing foreign student enrollment is the disagreement among college faculty and administrators concerning the value of enrolling students from other countries. Some see international students as a drain on limited institutional resources.

Four-Year Institutions With the Most Foreign Students and Percentage Change, 1984-85 to 1985-86

Rank		Institution	Foreign Students		Percent Change
1984 -85	1985 -86		1984 -85	1985 -86	
1	1	University of Southern California, CA	3,761	3,741	(0.5)
2	2	University of Texas, Austin, TX	3,286	3,132	(4.7)
3	3	University of Wisconsin, Madison, WI	2,901	2,873	(1.0)
5	4	Ohio State University, Main Campus, OH	2,606	2,690	3.2
4	5	Columbia University, Barnard and Teachers College, NY	2,773	2,679	(3.4)
8	6	Boston University, MA	2,462	2,493	1.3
-	7	University of California, Los Angeles, CA	2,012	2,488	23.7
-	8	University of Minnesota, Twin Cities, MN	2,344	2,473	5.5
9	9	University of Houston, University Park, TX	2,424	2,434	0.4
10	10	University of Michigan, Ann Arbor, MI	2,366	2,413	2.0
Total, 10 Leading Four-Year Institutions			26,935*	27,416	(1.1)
Percent of All Four-Year Institutions			9.2*	9.1	
TOTAL, ALL FOUR-YEAR INSTITUTIONS			300,030	302,004	0.7

* Totals are for the ten leading four-year institutions of 1984-85, which included North Texas University (ranked sixth) and Southern Illinois University, Carbondale (ranked seventh).

Source: Institute of International Education, *Open Doors: 1985-86 Report on International Educational Exchange* (New York: Institute of International Education, 1985).

Others, more closely connected to foreign student programs, are concerned that the college provides adequate support so that international students feel a part of campus life and are not "ghetto-ized" into special foreign student programs and housing. Others on the college campus see foreign students as a way to enhance the financial resources of the colleges and stabilize the enrollment. The college rhetoric is often couched in terms like internationalizing the curriculum. But in too many situations the international students do not feel much of a part of college life. There is little evidence that internationalization of a college occurs simply by enrolling students from other countries, without the appropriate support programs.

On most campuses, however, education of foreign students suffers from benign neglect rather than from a conscious effort to downplay these programs. College personnel who work with students from other countries are relatively invisible and perform their duties with little recognition from senior administrators. Most foreign student advisors view their work as a kind of missionary effort. In some colleges there are few special services to help students from other countries find suitable housing, or find their way through the maze of admission and registration procedures. Relatively few colleges assign a special intermediary between the international student and the state or federal agencies in charge of alien and immigration services. Many students suffer in their studies as a result of inadequate English proficiency. Foreign students are often allowed to stumble along the academic path with little advice or guidance. Foreign student advisors, where they exist, are often excluded from management consultations or instructional administration.

A few years ago an informal survey was made involving some forty California public and private colleges, all enrolling a substantial number of students from other countries. Not one of these colleges had a written policy statement dealing with international education or international student exchange. The most disturbing finding of this survey was that three out of four colleges had no written policies or procedures for dealing with enrolled students from other countries. The attitude toward international students by most colleges and universities seems to have been "Here we are, come and get what you can, but we cannot give you any special help or support."

The Oregon State System of Higher Education has developed a new and important way to utilize the talents and services of international students. Students are given a partial scholarship in return for eighty hours a year of community cultural service in the public schools, nursing homes, businesses, or in cross-campus classes.

Even at the federal level, while other countries like the U.S.S.R. are enrolling foreign students in large numbers, the United States has yet to develop a coherent international student policy or include such statements in federal foreign policy statements.

American Students Abroad

Less than 1 percent of America's twelve million students currently study abroad, though we are likely to see that number expand greatly during the 1990s. While study-abroad programs have been among the most glamorous of college programs, they have enjoyed relatively small participation. The traditional junior year abroad has been the most popular model, although the program has been limited to the relatively small group of students who can afford to participate. In the years ahead there will likely be an expanded number of programs that provide opportunities for shorter stays abroad, thereby broadening the potential appeal of the program for students with limited financial resources.

Many colleges have developed semester- or quarter-long programs for foreign study. These shorter programs typically concentrate on one academic discipline or a specific aspect of technical education, allowing students to experience an international dimension in fields as diverse as law enforcement, literature, electronics, and language. Usually the academic program includes three courses taught in English and two courses taught in the language of the host country, and is frequently offered during the summer or January mini-term.

To increase the quality and diversity of programs offered abroad in a cost-effective manner, colleges often work together in consortia. The College Consortium for International Studies is one such cooperative effort devoted exclusively to the operation of semester-length and full-year academic programs in sixteen countries. Students are usually required to learn about the culture, history, and language of the host country before leaving the United States. While in the foreign country students learn about themselves and their own country by contrast and comparison. Well over 200 U. S. colleges and universities now send students abroad in special

Students Who Have Studied or Who Intend to Study Abroad, by Institutional Classification

All Institutions	Percent
Liberal Arts Colleges	17
Research universities	11
Doctorate-granting universities	8
Comprehensive four-year colleges	8
Community colleges	4

Source: Carnegie Foundation for the Advancement of Teaching, undergraduate survey, 1984.

international programs. Lewis and Clark College in Oregon, Kalamazoo College in Michigan, Goshen College in Indiana, the Fashion Institute of Technology and Kingsborough Community College in New York, and Lansing Community College in Michigan are among the rapidly increasing number of colleges leading in the study-abroad program.

College-to-College Ties

In addition to working through stateside consortia to share and develop expertise, an increasing number of colleges are establishing college-to-college relationships across international boundaries. While there are many sister college programs today, the relationships are often perfunctory and casual. New structural institution-to-institution study-abroad programs are now being developed that provide the U. S. college with a much greater degree of control over the student experience and the quality of the programs offered. Cornell University has developed such a relationship with the University of the Philippines. Lansing Community College has developed similar programs with colleges in Japan.

In another kind of consortial arrangement, El Paso Community College has joined forces with Arizona Western College, Imperial Valley College, Laredo Junior College, Southwestern College, and Texas Southmost College to form the Border College Consortium. This consortium has established a cooperative program between its members and fifteen technical institutes located close to the Mexican border.

Central and South American countries present U. S. colleges with many opportunities to develop a host of cooperative programs. While these countries need highly trained professionals, they have an even greater need for well-educated midlevel managers and teachers trained in technical areas.

The trend toward international institutional relationships will undoubtedly increase as more U. S. firms move portions of their operations to offshore locations or expand their ties with foreign companies. James Madison University in Virginia will be placing forty students in jobs around Europe in 1990 with the aim of greatly expanding the program around the world over a five-year period. The worldwide revolution of movement and communication is making the world a much, much smaller place, requiring college emphasis upon language, geography, technical education, and experience with employees in other countries.

The decade ahead will likely see an increasing volume of U. S. colleges and universities establishing consortia or other working relationships with colleges in other countries. Indeed, many colleges will be establishing branch campuses in other countries even as businesses have established branch plants or offices.

Study and Serve

One aspect of studying abroad that may be a growth area in the 1990s is the "study and serve" program. Goshen College has had an international study-and-serve requirement since 1968. While church-related independent colleges will likely find it easier to implement such programs, the decade ahead will see more colleges of all kinds establishing new relationships with the Peace Corps and other study-and-serve international programs. With the recent reawakening of interest in civic responsibility and calls for some form of community or national service for all youths, the 1990s will see many colleges and universities adding a study-and-serve dimension to international-intercultural programs.

Frank Newman, president of the Education Commission of

the States, has been one of the leading advocates of the study-and-serve concept. He states the case this way: "To succeed in the fullest sense, the graduates of American colleges and universities must see themselves as able to help shape the world in which they live and not simply as living in a world to which they must adapt."[6] Stanford University began a program in 1984 of competitive grants to students involved in service-oriented work around the world. Brown University has developed a program whereby a small number of students receive awards of $1,000 to $3,000 for contributing their time and effort to voluntary public service. Georgetown University operates a public service liaison center that puts students in contact with Washington, D. C., community service groups.

The handwriting is on the wall. Some form of federally funded community or national service legislation will be enacted in the decade ahead. It is likely that international study-and-serve programs will become a national service component alternative.

Faculty Exchange Plays a Vital Role

International faculty exchange is another important element of the international education program for colleges and universities. While there are a number of small faculty exchange programs, the mainstay of U. S. international faculty exchange remains the Fulbright Scholar Program, funded by the federal government and administered by the U. S. Information Agency and the Council for International Exchange of Scholars.

In the 1986-87 college year—the fortieth year of the Fulbright program—a record number 1,103 American educators received lecture or research awards for research, work, or teaching. Since 1947, the Fulbright program has aided in the exchange of more than 22,000 American and 23,000 foreign scholars.

Named after Senator J. William Fulbright, recognized as the father of international faculty exchange, the program has three major goals. The first, and probably most often cited, purpose of the program is to promote a better understanding in the United States of foreign nations and to help the leaders of other nations to better understand the United States.

A second goal is to create the understanding and motivation

American Scholars Abroad

Academic Year	1982-83	1983-84	1984-85	1985-86	1986-87
Applications	2,980	3,028	3,055	3,260	3,475
Grants	728	809	805	1,001	1,008
Lecturer	503	553	529	632	669
Research	225	256	276	369	339
Less than six months	290	362	342	414	497
Six months	438	447	463	587	511
Full benefits	654	712	725	916	925
Partial or travel only	74	97	80	85	83
Renewals	31	56	50	52	58
Distinguished Fellows- Fulbright 40th Anniversary					37
Total Awards	759	865	855	1,053	1,103

Source: Council for International Exchange of Scholars, Fulbright Scholar Program, 1986 Annual Report.

in different countries that will serve as the basis for nonviolent solutions to international conflicts and tensions. Senator Fulbright noted on the fortieth anniversary celebration of the program:

> To continue to build more weapons, especially more exotic and unpredictable machines of war, will not build trust and confidence. The most sensible way to do that is to engage the parties in joint ventures for mutually constructive and beneficial purposes, such as trade, medical research, and development of cheaper energy sources. To

formulate and negotiate agreements of this kind requires well-educated people leading or advising our govern- ment. To this purpose the Fulbright program is dedicated.[7]

The third and most all-embracing goal is to contribute to worldwide social and economic development and to enhance the spirit of international community through scholarship, teaching, and learning. While some might emphasize one goal over another, the three as a whole form the mosaic of purposes of a program that fosters faculty exchange reaching 120 countries. Those purposes are likely to be under continuing review in the decade ahead. Funding for the program, until recently, has been the sole responsibility of the United States, though some countries are now beginning to pick up a share of the costs. That trend will likely continue into the 1990s.

Some political leaders will want to see the Fulbright program

1986-87 Visiting Scholar Awards: Sources of Dollar Support

	U. S. Govern- ment	U. S. Private Sector	Foreign Sources	Total Dollars
Africa	807,475	96,050		903,525
East Asia and the Pacific	1,551,355	372,293	1,166,530	3,090,178
East/Southeast Europe and U.S.S.R.	1,834,450	298,551	11,000	2,144,001
Latin America and the Caribbean	1,101,022	103,681	156,350	1,361,053
Middle East and North Africa	473,085	337,692	661,385	1,472,162
South Asia	952,008	357,861	34,750	1,344,619
Western Europe	451,408	2,165,299	4,255,779	6,872,486
Distinguished Fellows—Fulbright 40th Anniversary	140,150			140,150
Worldwide	7,310,953	3,731,427	6,285,794	17,328,174
Percentage	42	22		

U. S. Government: U. S. Information Agency and other U. S. government agency funds. U. S. Private Sector: U. S. host institutions and private U. S. organizations. Foreign Sources: Foreign home institutions and governments, personal funds, binational commissions, and foundations.
Note: All funding totals are for the academic rather than fiscal year.

Source: Council for International Exchange of Scholars, Fulbright Scholar Pro- gram, 1986 Annual Report.

of the 1990s more carefully targeted to certain countries, especially if there is to be any expansion in the number of participants served. In the past the program has had a European orientation, in part because much of the non-U. S. funding derived from Europe. For example, in the 1986-87 college year, 345 of the 1,103 American scholars traveled to Western Europe. On the other hand, only 4 percent of foreign scholars came from Africa and 10 percent from Latin America.

In the decade ahead there will likely be expanded involvement in the Fulbright program of scholars from community, technical, and junior colleges. In 1986-87 community college faculty were noticeably absent from the program. Only sixteen, or just 4 percent, of the Fulbright recipients were from two-year colleges. Community colleges are still relatively newcomers to American higher education, and they have not, for the most part, aggressively promoted participation in the program. The 1990s will see much more active involvement in programs of scholarly exchange from this segment of higher education. The opportunity is simply too great for these community-based institutions not to bring a higher level of international and intercultural understanding to local communities at the very heart of Main Street America.

Foreign Language Study

Senator Paul Simon (D-Ill.) paints a dismal picture of foreign language study in the United States:

- In 1915, 36 percent of American students in high schools were studying foreign language. Today, the most reliable figure is 18 percent.
- America is the only nation in the world in which students can complete 16 years of education without having to complete at least one year of foreign language. It is even possible to earn a doctorate without studying a foreign language.
- Twenty percent of the nation's community, technical, and junior colleges offer no foreign language courses. By contrast, most of the developed nations—and many

of the developing countries—offer every elementary
student the chance to learn at least one foreign language.

- There are many more teachers of English in the Soviet
Union than there are Russian in the United States.
- There are more Soviet citizens studying English in the
city of Leningrad than there are students of Russian in
the United States.[8]

In Japan, a key economic competitor of the U. S., 80 percent
of the Japanese students take foreign languages beginning at age
twelve, and competency in two foreign languages is required for
graduation from a university. However, one must be quick, when
comparing U. S. and Japanese education, to point out that the
Japanese culture lacks the social, ethnic, linguistic, and religious
diversity that enormously complicates, but so largely enriches,
American education.

The rest of the world continues to be amazed that the United
States is largely monolingual. Timothy S. Healy, S.J., former president of Georgetown University, observes: "[Our] isolation goes
deeper . . . than our ears and tongues. It is really an isolation of the
soul. Our ignorance of language keeps us nationally from making
the kind of salving contact which ties people together, which enables
people to talk person to person, and which can in the long run
prevent embroilment, misunderstanding, and violence."[9] Unfortunately, most collegiate foreign language instruction has been left to
the linguistic scholars. Greater attention will be given by colleges in
the decade ahead to developing conversational competency in a
language. Indeed, learning to listen and speak in a foreign language
may become a vocational necessity in the decade ahead for many
college students.

Miami-Dade Community College, serving a large bicultural
region of southern Florida, has instituted several intensive foreign
language training programs. To serve the English-speaking business and professional communities of Dade County, the college
offers sixteen weeks of conversational Spanish, fifteen hours per
week, three hours per evening. The classes are taught by bilingual,
native Spanish speakers. A short-term, multimedia-based course,

"Survival Spanish," is offered as well for students seeking rudimentary conversational skills.

El Paso Community College serves a large bicultural region of western Texas. Spanish-speaking students begin their coursework in their native language, while concurrently learning English. At the same time, many of these students are used as teaching assistants to help other students become proficient in Spanish. Increasingly, colleges are taking advantage of the language skills of their non-English-speaking students by employing them as teaching assistants and tutors to teach the monolingual American student.

The education ministers of the European Community nations announced in June of 1989 a cooperative program of foreign language instruction. The program, called Lingua, has been developed as a way of promoting language learning throughout elementary, secondary, and higher education involving Danish, Dutch, English, French, Gaelic, German, Greek, Italian, Luxemburgian, Portuguese, and Spanish. Jauvier Solana, minister of education in Spain, describes the Lingua agreement as "the most transcendent ever in the area of European education."[10] Lingua has an initial five-year budget of $220 million. Incentives have also been built into the program to encourage private companies to include foreign language instruction as part of employee training. Translation services are becoming a boom industry in some U. S. businesses. More and more U. S. employers are requiring specialists to translate technical documents and sales contracts.

There can be no question that primary and refresher foreign language courses will again move up in popularity in U. S. colleges and universities during the 1990s, particularly as institutions move to strengthen foreign language requirements for associate of arts, bachelor's, master's, and doctoral degrees. New teaching technologies, like computers and the interactive compact disc, hold the potential to aid greatly in the process of foreign language acquisition and instruction.

The International Baccalaureate

As the international perspective has taken on new importance, a quiet but related curriculum development is growing in some high schools across the U. S. It is called the international baccalaureate (IB) program. Developed in Geneva, Switzerland, in the 1960s, the IB program is based on a common set of exams given in many languages in literature, science, language, and social science. High schools design courses around these four areas of study, and offer the IB program as a cohesive and comprehensive high school honors curriculum.

Most U. S. colleges and universities will allow students who have completed the IB program up to one year of college credit. About 1,200 students worldwide now receive the IB diploma, and nearly 2,000 earn credit for individual courses and exams. Four international schools in the U. S. now offer the complete IB program: the Anglo-American School and the United Nations School in New York, the Washington International School in Washington, D. C., and the French-American Bilingual School in San Francisco.

Gilbert Nichol, executive director of the New York-based IB program, indicates that the popularity of this high school honors program parallels a growing feeling of internationalization in the schools. Students enjoy knowing that at the same time they are taking an exam, students all over the world are taking the same exam. The international dimension of the program can be seen in the typical IB history exam question: "Compare slavery between 1800 and 1850 in the United States and Brazil."

One unique aspect of the IB curriculum includes a course called "Theory of Knowledge," which combines philosophy with critical thinking. Students in this program must also do a research project, plus engage in a creative or community service effort.

One reason for the slow growth of the IB program in the U. S. is the requirement that the program must be adopted as a unit and high schools must offer the full program in order to participate. But despite that restriction, more and more schools are adopting the IB program. Approximately 120 schools in the U. S. and Canada now offer the program. As the IB high school program continues to grow in popularity in this country, colleges and universities will begin to see an increasing flow of IB students into their institutions. Students from all around the world could be knocking on college doors in the 1990s with the IB diploma in hand.

If the IB program begins to catch fire in the U. S. and around the world, will U. S. colleges and universities be ready? What changes will be required in the college and university curricula in order to avoid duplication and sustain continuity in learning?

Immigration Impact

One aspect of the global community discussion that has received small attention in higher education circles is the impact of

U. S. Immigration: 1970-1987

1970	373,000
1975	386,000
1980	531,000
1985	570,000
1987	602,700

Source: U. S. Department of Commerce, Bureau of the Census, *Statistical Abstract of the United States, 1989.*

1987 U. S. Immigrants by Country of Birth

Europe	61,200
Asia	257,700
Central and South America	249,100
Africa	17,700
Other	17,000

Source: U. S. Department of Commerce, Bureau of the Census, *Statistical Abstract of the United States, 1989.*

immigration upon colleges. About all that is heard from the U. S. Immigration and Naturalization Service is the negative aspects of immigration, such as illegal aliens coming across the border, and requiring employers to screen individuals carefully to be sure aliens are not employed.

The Immigration Control and Reform Act of 1986 set up new immigration controls and procedures. However, the new act also established new programs and funding for immigrant education, training, and employment. Colleges and universities are viewed by many immigrants as the primary resource to help them move into the American life. Under the new federal legislation, higher education for immigrants becomes even more important. Many community colleges help immigrants by providing classes in preparation for citizenship. As an example, Austin Community College in Texas received a grant of $1.7 million for the 1988-89 college year and provided English as second language, American history, and government to more than 7,000 immigrants.

The U. S. Bureau of Labor Statistics and the Census Bureau think there will be a significant increase in jobs during the 1990s and a shrinking population to fill these jobs. Fewer births, more retirements, and more deaths mean a decreasing population, and a smaller workforce. In terms of the economy, a decreasing population means fewer dollars spent on housing, clothing, food, cars, and other consumer goods. In addition, fewer younger workers mean fewer individuals to help support a growing senior citizen and retiree population.

The truth is that not only must the U. S. develop all its human resources to higher levels to meet the global competition, but it will also need an increasing number of immigrants. Skill shortages are increasing all over the country. While most other countries are giving the cold shoulder to immigrants (and the U. S. Immigration and Naturalization Service has not been exactly lavish with its help to immigrants), the 1990s will see a reexamination of this issue.

Would the combination of fully developing our home-grown talent and wise immigration practices give the U. S. a competitive edge in the global economic competition? The West German population is already declining and aging, and Italy, Japan, and others will soon be in the same fix. The long history and past experience of U. S. colleges helping immigrants move into the economic mainstream of American life has made for a stronger nation. In fact, there is a dramatic, yet-to-be-told story in what colleges have done, and are doing, to empower the recent Vietnamese, Cambodian, and Laotian immigrant citizens. It will be increasingly incumbent upon colleges and universities to help enfranchise the flow of immigrants looking for new opportunities in their adopted land.

Dateline 2000 Forecast

1.   Colleges and universities will develop clear policy statements about the purposes of collegiate international and intercultural education programs.

2.   The 1990s will see colleges and universities strengthening the structure, quality, coverage, and utilization of their undergraduate offerings in the field of international-intercultural studies, and relate these offerings more directly to career as well as cultural and intellectual goals.

3.   A new interest will develop in ethnic and intercultural studies, but for quite different reasons than those espoused in the 1960s. Ethnic studies will be combined with language studies and closely related to various career programs.

4.   Conversational foreign language studies will be added to the curriculum as a legitimate part of the collegiate program. The time-honored, traditional, formal study of a foreign language will not meet the time commitments and needs of some students.

5.   Colleges will be reaching out to work with high schools to develop new kinds of four-year education programs (grades eleven through fourteen) to allow the time for students to develop some proficiency in one or more foreign languages.

6.   Colleges and universities will encourage and help faculty members to acquire, improve, and maintain international-intercultural knowledge, skills, and experiences that will enable them to incorporate international studies into various aspects of the curriculum.

7.   Students from other countries attending U. S. colleges will be utilized to teach and tutor U. S. students in foreign language instruction.

8.   The federal government will establish and fund an International Education Foundation, similar to the National Science Foundation, aimed at coordinating all federal international education programs under one federal agency, and encouraging the development of quality international-intercultural studies programs.

9.   An increasing number of U. S. colleges and universities will operate branch campuses in countries around the world and an increasing number of colleges from other countries will establish campuses (or partnership programs) in the U. S.

10. The high school international baccalaureate program, with its worldwide standardized tests, could become the new honors program in secondary schools, with important implications for higher education.

11. Faculty coordinators or directors of international education programs will be moved up in the collegiate hierarchy of importance.

Executive Summary

Internationalizing America's colleges and universities will become a dominant force for higher education in the 1990s, as the American people have awakened, belatedly, to a new global environment and have begun to realize the interrelatedness of the world economy. Wall Street nearly collapsed during 1987 in a wave of selling that started in Tokyo while Americans slept. Page-one newspaper articles around the world charted the financial drama of the Crash of 1987, bringing home the message to millions of small and large investors that the U. S. economy—forever linked through worldwide advanced telecommunication—does not live and work in isolation from the rest of the world.

For the first time in half a century trade policies have become the stuff of presidential campaigns, as voters ponder the impact of domestic and foreign trade policies upon their own communities. Regional manufacturers in Ohio have realized that their principal competitors are small Asian nations rather than factories in Pittsburgh and Detroit.

College and university graduates of the 1990s will be expected to participate in a worldwide economy, and that will mean major changes in the college curriculum and programs. Foreign language and ethnic studies will be combined in a resurgence of collegiate interest in these subjects.

More partnerships will be formed between U. S. and foreign colleges and universities than ever before. Foreign student enrollment in U. S. colleges and universities will not likely increase, but branch campuses and programs will be developed to operate in other countries. Other countries, such as Japan, will establish schools, colleges, and universities in the U. S.

Faculty exchange programs will increase slowly during the decade ahead, with increased emphasis upon Eastern Europe, Africa, and Central and South America. At the same time faculty exchanges are showing small growth, the study-and-serve-abroad programs for U. S. students are likely to expand rapidly.

The high school international baccalaureate could well become the preferred honors program in many high schools around the country. This development could have significant impact upon some colleges and universities.

Continued expansion of the immigration program will have an impact upon college and university enrollments.

Notes

1.   Bruce Stokes, "Moral Leadership," *National Journal* (24 January 1987).

2.   Cassandra Pyle, "Our Shortfall in International Competence," *AGB Reports* (March/April 1984).

3.   Robert B. Kaplan, "Foreign Students: Developing Institutional Policy," *College Board Review* (Spring 1987).

4.   American Association of Colleges and Universities, *To Secure the Blessings of Liberty: Report of the National Commission on the Role and Future of State Colleges and Universities* (Washington, D. C.: American Association of State Colleges and Universities, 1986).

5.   14 June 1984, *Congressional Record*, 98th Cong., 2d sess.

6.   Frank Newman, *Higher Education and the American Resurgence* (Princeton: Carnegie Foundation for the Advancement of Teaching, 1985).

7.   Council for International Exchange of Scholars, Fulbright Scholar Program, 1986 Annual Report.

8.   Paul Simon, *Tongue Tied American: Confronting the Foreign Language Crisis* (New York: Continuum, 1980).

9.   Newman, *Higher Education and the American Resurgence.*

10.   *Chronicle of Higher Education* (3 July 1989).

Chapter IV

The At-Risk Population

We share the conviction that there is no such thing as an expendable student. We will never accept the notion that vast numbers of illiterate and undereducated Americans can be offset by a well-educated elite. That's not the American way.

President George Bush
1989 AACJC Convention

Two converging forces, a skilled worker shortage and the development of a permanent underclass, are bearing down upon the United States. Demographers tell us that by the year 2000 there will be a significant shortage of qualified people to fill the available jobs, and many of the individuals who should fill these jobs will be unmotivated, undereducated, underhoused—a permanent underclass. A major challenge for the decade of the 1990s will be solving, at least to some degree, the twin problems of a surplus of disadvantaged individuals and a shortage of skilled workers. Many people refer to the disadvantaged as the "at-risk population." They are not only at risk in terms of their own lives, but they create a risk for our society. The future economic strength of our country is in danger if the at-risk population is not empowered to be a contributing force. The statistics are well known, and charts do not tell the story in terms of loss of human potential and loss of individual hope that things can get better. Will colleges and universities sit on the sidelines? If not, how can higher education institutions better serve that segment of the population considered undereducated and disadvantaged?

It is true that many of the at-risk group live in rural and suburban areas of the country, but in terms of sheer numbers and volume of people it is the urban population that is doubly afflicted by an inadequate education and the ills peculiar to urban life. In 1890 more than half the American people lived in small cities or rural areas and worked on the farm or in farm-related occupations. In 1990 only about 2 percent of the working population works on the farm or in farm-related occupations. Many, many individuals, for whom urban schools have barely made a difference, live in urban communities that offer, in too many cases, a drug culture, unemployment lifestyle, welfare checks, and jail cells.

It is a paradox of our times to see, within the same eye span, gleaming inner-city high-rise hotels, office buildings, convention centers—and deteriorating schools and neighborhoods. Within a two-mile radius of the capital of the United States one can see all too clearly the hard truth of this paradoxical situation. Is this the social dynamite of which James B. Conant spoke over forty years ago? Can America continue to waste precious human resources and be strong? Can America continue to build sparkling new inner-city office buildings and freeways and let urban schools and neighborhoods deteriorate?

According to a Carnegie Foundation for the Advancement of Teaching survey conducted in 1987, urban school teachers are four times as likely to face problems of violence, vandalism, and racial discord as suburban and rural teachers. Urban schools appear to be one of our most troubled institutions caught in between many conflicting and opposing forces.[1]

During the past fifty years one of the greatest migrations in human history has taken place in the United States, as an estimated fifty to sixty million people abandoned rural communities to move to the cities. The massive movement of people from agrarian to urban life has brought with it a host of vexing social problems, including poverty, unemployment, overflowing waste disposal systems, polluted air, water shortages, drug cultures, and overtaxed educational and social institutions. Feelings of fear and insecurity resulting from overcrowded living conditions have spawned polarized racial and ethnic divisions, alienation, and hostility toward governmental agencies, including those dealing with education.

Yet, urban America continues to grow. Between 1950 and 1985 the urban U. S. population increased from 84.4 million to 182.5 million. One out of every two Americans now lives in one of thirty-seven urban centers with a population of at least one million; three out of four live in urban areas with more than 250,000 people. Even the short-lived back-to-the-country trend of the 1970s has been reversed in the current decade, as the urban population increased 3.5 percent between 1980 and 1985. In the South the urban population grew at an even faster rate, 6.4 percent, during the same period.

Urban centers are expected to continue to grow slowly over the decade of the 1990s. By the year 2000 the greater Los Angeles metropolitan area is expected to surpass New York City as the nation's largest metropolitan area as it becomes home to more than ten million people, fusing with the Long Beach area in one giant megapolis. The Washington, D. C., metropolitan area is expected to more than double in size to 6.5 million people. Houston and Dallas/Fort Worth will likely become the fourth and fifth largest metropolitan areas, bypassing Chicago. By the year 2000 it now looks like two-thirds of the U. S. population will live in twelve major metropolitan and urban centers.

According to the U. S. Census Bureau, America now has eight cities with populations exceeding one million. Both California and Texas have two cities on the list. Urban growth is projected to continue in both the South and the West, while the urban centers of the Midwest and Northeast are expected to experience little or no overall growth.[2]

Population of Eight U. S. Cities
With More Than One Million Inhabitants

New York	7.2 million
Los Angeles	3.3 million
Chicago	3.0 million
Houston	1.7 million
Philadelphia	1.6 million
Detroit	1.1 million
San Diego	1.0 million
Dallas	1.0 million

Source: U. S. Department of Commerce, Bureau of the Census, *Statistical Abstract of the United States, 1989.*

Contrary to the generally held view that African Americans and Hispanic Americans are the majority population in most cities, only nine of the fifty largest cities have a Black majority and only three have a Hispanic majority. While both of these ethnic minority groups are overrepresented in urban populations, the problems of America are not confined to any single ethnic group. This observation does not diminish the urgent need to help more ethnic minority individuals move into the economic mainstream. However, the

Fifty Cities Above 300,000 in Population

City	1986 Population in Thousands	1980-86 Growth in Percent	Predominate Ethnic Minority by Group	by Percent
Albuquerque, New Mexico	376	10.4	Hispanic	34
Atlanta, Georgia	422	-.7	Black	67
Austin, Texas	467	34.9	Hispanic	19
Baltimore, Maryland	764	4.3	Black	55
Boston, Massachusetts	574	1.9	Black	22
Buffalo, New York	325	-9.2	Black	27
Charlotte, North Carolina	352	11.6	Black	31
Chicago, Illinois	3,010	0.1	Black	40
Cincinnati, Ohio	370	-4.1	Black	34
Cleveland, Ohio	536	-6.6	Black	44
Columbus, Ohio	566	0.2	Black	22
Dallas, Texas	1,004	10.9	Black	29
Denver, Colorado	505	2.5	Hispanic	19
Detroit, Michigan	1,086	-9.7	Black	63
El Paso, Texas	492	15.6	Hispanic	63
Fort Worth, Texas	430	11.5	Black	23
Honolulu, Hawaii	372	2.0	Asian	40
Houston, Texas	1,729	8.4	Black	28
Indianapolis, Indiana	720	2.7	Black	22
Jacksonville, Florida	610	12.7	Black	25
Kansas City, Missouri	441	-1.5	Black	27
Long Beach, California	396	9.6	Hispanic	14
Los Angeles, California	3,259	9.8	Black	17
			Hispanic	28
Memphis, Tennessee	653	1.0	Black	48
Miami, Florida	374	7.9	Hispanic	56
Milwaukee, Wisconsin	605	-4.9	Black	23
Minneapolis, Minnesota	357	-3.8	Black	8
Nashville/Davidson, Tennessee	474	4.0	Black	23
New Orleans, Louisiana	554	-0.6	Black	55
New York, New York	7,263	2.7	Hispanic	20
			Black	25
Newark, New Jersey	316	-3.9	Hispanic	19
			Black	58
Oakland, California	357	5.2	Black	47
Oklahoma City, Oklahoma	446	1.04	Black	15
Omaha, Nebraska	349	11.3	Black	12
Philadelphia, Pennsylvania	1,643	-2.7	Black	38
Phoenix, Arizona	894	13.1	Hispanic	15
Pittsburgh, Pennsylvania	387	-8.6	Black	24
Portland, Oregon	388	5.4	Black	8
Sacramento, California	324	17.3	Hispanic	14
			Black	13
St. Louis, Missouri	426	-5.9	Black	46
San Antonio, Texas	914	16.3	Hispanic	54
San Diego, California	1,015	16.0	Black	9
			Hispanic	15
San Francisco, California	749	10.3	Black	13
			Hispanic	12
San Jose, California	712	13.1	Hispanic	22
Seattle, Washington	486	-1.5	Black	10
Toledo, Ohio	341	-3.9	Black	17
Tucson, Arizona	359	8.6	Hispanic	25
Tulsa, Oklahoma	374	3.6	Black	12
Virginia Beach, Virginia	333	27.2	Black	10
Washington, D.C.	626	-1.9	Black	70

Source: U. S. Department of Commerce, Bureau of the Census, *Statistical Abstract of the United States, 1989.*

scourges of poverty, crime, drugs, unemployment, illiteracy, and undereducation do not discriminate on the basis of race or ethnicity.

In the following pages we will examine in more detail the persistent problems facing the at-risk populations of all ethnic minority groups and the resultant challenges for higher education in the decade ahead, but first here are a few projections and facts to ponder:

- By 2000 nearly three out of four jobs will require education or technical training beyond high school.
- The private sector demand for employees is expected to increase significantly during the 1990s.
- The number of young people sixteen to twenty-four years of age will comprise only 16 percent of the population during the 1990s.
- The average Black seventeen-year-old reads at the same level of the average White thirteen-year-old.
- Mean earnings of twenty- to twenty-four-year-old male high school dropouts declined 41.6 percent (from $11,210 to $6,552) between 1973 and 1984.

The Children

The largest proportion of poor families reside in urban centers. The child poverty rate is 45 percent in central cities and 28 percent in rural communities. According to the report *Schools That Work: Educating Disadvantaged Children,* published by the U. S. Department of Education, "poor children come from all racial and ethnic groups. Almost half are white, a third are black, and the rest are Hispanic or from other minority groups."[3]

Throughout American history the poorest segment of the American population has been the aged. Children were usually about as well off as their parents. Today 23 percent of children under the age of three are living in homes below the poverty line, compared to 14 percent of the population as a whole. The majority of inner-city children, two out of three, live in a household headed by a single parent, usually a female. The feeder system creating many of the single-parent households is teenage pregnancy, which springs from a pervasive lack of hope and few positive life options. Teen pregnancy and parenthood are the major reasons girls give for dropping out of school. It is important to point out that a teen parent earns about half the lifetime earnings of a woman who waited until age twenty to have a first child.

The U. S. Public Health Service reports that 828,174 babies were born to unmarried mothers in 1985. Illegitimate births were up 24 percent during the 1980-85 period. One out of every four babies is now born outside of marriage. Of every hundred children born today, twenty-one are born to unwed mothers, forty will grow up in a single-parent, female-head-of-household family, and twenty-five will be on welfare at some point prior to adulthood.[4]

Furthermore, the problem of illegitimate births is not confined to teenage mothers: 30 percent of illegitimate births are now from mothers twenty-five years of age or older. Moreover, illegitimate births among older women increased 11 percent during the period 1975-85, while the illegitimate birth rate among teenagers showed little change.

The Poor and Poorly Educated

Nearly one of two Black families earns $15,000 per year or less. Two out of five Hispanic families and one out of five White families have incomes of $15,000 or below. Educational attainment levels, like poverty, are disproportionately related to ethnicity and race. Forty percent of Black and 52 percent of Hispanic adults have not earned the high school diploma.

In terms of sheer numbers, twelve million White families dominate the nearly seventeen million families earning $15,000 or less. Some 6.5 million White families earn less than $10,000 per year, comprising 70 percent of all families at that level of income or below.

Child-bearing rates, as well, are linked to educational attainment and income. The birth rate for women with family incomes of at least $35,000 was 46 per 1,000. Of women with family incomes of $10,000 or less, the birth rate was more than twice as high, 94 per 1,000. College-educated women had a birth rate of 61 per 1,000, while women with less than a high school diploma had a birth rate of 98 per 1,000.[5]

During the period 1983 to 2000 the number of poor households is expected to rise 45 percent, based on current trends, from 11.9 million to 17.0 million. Over the same seventeen-year period the number of low-cost housing units (renting for $325 per month or less) will decline, from 12.9 million to 9.4 million. It is estimated that by the year 2000 some 7.5 million additional low-cost residential housing units will be needed to house the 17 million Americans living in poverty.

Education and Economic Characteristics of the 1985 Population

Family Income	Population	White	Black	Hispanic
Families	62,706,000	54,400,000	6,778,000	3,939,000
Less than $5,000	3,144,000	3.8%	14.7%	9.7%
$5,000 to $9,999	5,894,000	8.1%	19.2%	15.7%
$10,000 to $14,999	6,780,000	10.3%	15.0%	15.0%
$15,000 to $24,999	13,520,000	21.6%	21.7%	23.7%
$25,000 to $49,999	23,481,000	39.2%	23.6%	29.0%
	9,889,000	16.9%	5.8%	6.6%
Years of Schooling, Persons Age 25 or Over	143,524,000	124,905,000	14,820,000	8,455,000
Elementary, 0-8 years	19,893,000	13.0%	21.0%	37.7%
High School, 1-3 years	17,553,000	11.5%	19.2%	14.3%
High School, 4 years	54,866,000	39.0%	33.9%	24.8%
College, 1-3 years	23,405,000	16.5%	14.8%	11.0%
College, 4 years or more	27,808,000	20.0%	11.1%	8.5%

Note: Families and unrelated individuals are classified as being above or below the poverty level based upon an income index developed by the Social Security Administration in 1964, which is revised each year to reflect changes in the consumer price index. The poverty level for a family of two in 1985 was $7,231.

Source: U. S. Department of Commerce, Bureau of the Census, Current Population Reports, and U. S. Department of Labor, Bureau of Labor Statistics, Employment and Earnings, January 1986.

It is clear that much work remains to be accomplished in helping more ethnic minority individuals (who in terms of percentages have greater poverty problems) enter and complete collegiate programs. The issue of college enrollment hinges primarily upon

The Educational Flow of Students Into Higher Education

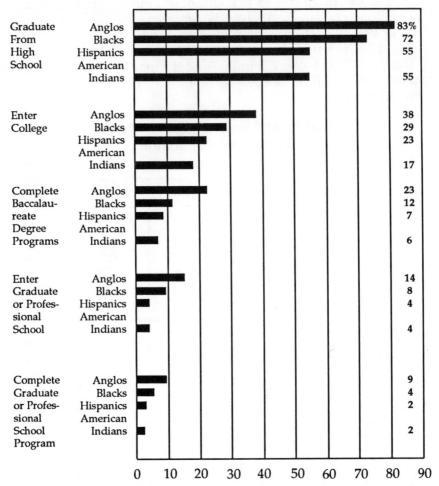

Source: Alexander W. Astin, *Minorities in American Higher Education* (San Francisco: Jossey-Bass, 1982).

economics. Individuals of low-income backgrounds are making their postsecondary education choices upon the basis of dollars. It is for this reason that the student financial aid programs of all kinds must be expanded and strengthened.

The 1990s represent a window of opportunity for colleges and universities to help the disadvantaged and undereducated gain an economic foothold in a society that most of this population have never seen. The impending labor shortage, and technological changes, will drive wages up for skilled workers and motivate a higher percentage of the population to seek some form of postsecondary education and training.

Urban Crime

The Bernard Goetz case has come to symbolize the fear of violent crime that is gripping urban inhabitants. Goetz told the New York City jury that his memory of an earlier mugging drove him to use his unregistered handgun on the four youths threatening him in a subway car. Posttrial news reports noted that the jury, which found Goetz innocent of all counts save a minor illegal weapons charge, included six persons who had, themselves, been victims of urban crime. Strong reactions to the trial came from all sides:[6]

To say this was a racism thing or that this was a vigilante thing is just garbage.

Michael Axelrod
Juror

I couldn't believe the good people of this city would convict that man for doing what was natural and was necessary and what anybody would have done. I think the verdict was fantastic; justice prevailed.

Roy Innis
Executive Director
Congress on Racial Equality

This case poses serious questions that go to the heart of living in an urban environment.

Gregory Waples
Prosecutor

Will the rising urban crime rates, and the personal fear they engender, infect urban citizens with a vigilante spirit? Already the Florida legislature has repealed laws that control citizens' rights to carry concealed weapons. Similar proposals are now under consideration in other states. Unfortunately, the crime rate has encouraged the rise of latent, and not so latent, racism actions that exacerbate the urban situation.

The connection between urban life and crime is abundantly clear. According to statistics compiled by the Federal Bureau of Investigation, the crime rate varies directly with the size of a city's population. In 1985 residents of cities with more than 250,000 people were nearly twice as likely to be crime victims than residents of cities with 10,000 or fewer inhabitants. The relationship between city size and crime was even more pronounced in the case of violent crime. Large cities had nearly four times the rate of violent crime than small cities. The murder rate was nearly six times as high in cities with more than 250,000 residents than in cities with 10,000 or fewer.

Urban Education

With some rare exceptions, urban educators are in a quandary. They daily face many of the most intractable social problems in America, operating in a survival mode because of inadequate political and financial support and a generally apathetic public. Impoverished students in America's large-city schools are public education's least well served group. The quality gap between urban and suburban schools widens each year. Many urban residents, regardless of race or ethnicity, send their children to private schools if they can afford it.

How long can higher education sustain vitality and forward movement when the homes, the feeder secondary schools, and a burdened system of human services produce young people with little hope of breaking the cycle of poverty? How can urban colleges perform their mission when one out of two urban high school students is not likely to graduate from high school?

It is estimated that one out of three students in urban schools comes from a family dependent on public assistance. School authorities in Boston estimate that 15 percent of the public high school

112

students report regularly to a probation officer as a result of previous convictions.

Judith Eaton, former president of the Community College of Philadelphia and now vice president of the American Council on Education, provides this bleak picture of an inner-city high school:

> Paint is dirty and blistered. Clocks don't work. Posters and signs don't stay up. One classroom is hot; another is cold. Broken, forgotten equipment takes up instructional space. . . .
>
> The students are young Blacks, Hispanics, Asians, and poor Whites. The faculty and administration are mostly White and mid-life. They are all victims of the barred windows, the police and hall monitors, the dirt, the disorder, the smell, the peeling paint, the clutter. They respond in various ways: with hostility, with indifference, with anger, with bravado, with moral indignation. . . .
>
> Teachers are defeated by the life circumstances of their students. Teachers are unable to distinguish competence from incompetence. Students are corrupted to conspire, not to learn. Administrators celebrate empty examples of success. The bureaucracy that drives the enterprise seeks only to preserve itself. The community that pays the bureaucracy does not wish to know it has failed.
>
> The message is despair. It comes from the dirt, the anger, the helplessness, the indifference, the misunderstanding. They all clearly signal: "don't hope, don't care, don't try." It cannot be any better for you. You are powerless. You are not entitled to proudly share in this rich nation. Opportunity is not yours.[7]

On any given day in most big-city high schools at least four of every ten students are absent. In Chicago over half the high school students fail to graduate. In all the Cleveland public high schools there was no semifinalist in the National Merit Scholarship competition in 1986; Boston and Detroit each had only one semifinalist. Ernest Boyer, president of the Carnegie Foundation for the Advancement of Teaching and former U. S. secretary of education, in a 1987 speech to the American Association of Community and Junior Colleges called the urban schools a kind of educational Third World serving the poorest children in one of the richest nations on earth.

In New York City six of every ten high school students fail to graduate after four years of high school. Some classrooms have not been painted in sixty years; many schools have toilets that do not work or inadequate drinking water. Middle-class families have largely deserted the urban school systems. The student population is 70 percent African American and Hispanic American. The school system must hire 40,000 new teachers by 1994, but teachers must first pass a New York Board of Examiners test, which can take as long as three years to process. Janitors have an agreement that allows them to decide whether to admit students or teachers to school buildings. Teachers, on the other hand, have little control over what goes on in their classroom and principals have little real authority over personnel and buildings.

While one can only applaud a new emphasis upon higher standards for teaching and learning, better discipline, more structure and substance in the school curriculum, these efforts can only help those students who choose to stay in school, not those who drop by the wayside. A number of national studies have shown that as standards rise, more students drop out. Between 1960 and 1983 the percentage of young people graduating from high school actually dropped slightly, from 72.4 to 71.8 percent. Moreover, the high school dropout rate has hovered at a stubborn 25 to 30 percent on a nationwide basis, in spite of dramatic increases in the percentage of young people completing one or more years of college.

In raw numbers, at current high school dropout rates, some eleven to twelve million students now enrolled in K-12 schools are not likely to earn a high school diploma during the decade of the 1990s. The dropout statistics for urban students present an even more perplexing prospect for urban colleges and urban society. As many as one out of every two urban students fails to earn the high school diploma.

The high school graduates of the year 2000 entered the first grade in 1988. Three out of four students attend a school in a metropolitan school district. Of these students, half of them attend an inner-city school. Unless there is a dramatic change, by the time of high school graduation the large majority of these students will not be prepared to enter college or secure a good job. If the projection is accurate that three out of four of the future job classifications will require some form of postsecondary education and training for entry, and the dozen fastest-growing occupations will all require some college-level education and training, where will this place the at-risk population in the economic milieu of American life? Perhaps the U. S. should develop some type of Social Guarantee Program, such as in Ireland, to pledge that all young people who complete high school will be offered some college, technical education, work experience, or all three.

High School Graduates and College Enrollment
1965 - 1985

Year	High School Graduation Rate	Percent of H.S. Graduates Enrolling in One or More Years of College	
		White	Black*
1965	72.1	-	-
1970	76.9	33.9	26.7
1975	73.6	-	-
1980	71.4	32.5	28.3
1985	73.2	35.0	26.5
1986	73.0	34.6	28.8

*Black category includes other minority groups.

Source: U. S. Department of Commerce, Bureau of the Census, *Statistical Abstract of the United States, 1989.*

The Literacy Challenge

Led by the good work of Barbara Bush, wife of President George Bush, Jim Duffy, president of ABC News, writer Jonathan Kozol, Public Broadcasting Service personnel, and many others, the subject of literacy has moved into a national priority position. The 1987 National Assessment of Educational Progress (NAEP) report *Learning to Be Literate in America* indicates that we are making

115

progress in the literacy business, but we have a long way to go. The NAEP reports provide the best base yet developed to examine the overall state of literacy in the country.

NAEP tests reveal that 97 percent of the young adults tested have attained a minimum level of literacy competency. Eighty-four percent of the young adults have moved above the minimum to what has been termed an intermediate literacy level. Consistent but slow progress has been made in improving literacy levels over the past fifteen years. All but a small percentage of young adults have developed basic literacy levels.

Percentage of Students and Young Adults at or Above Five Reading Proficiency Levels

Reading Skills and Strategies	Grade 4	Grade 8	Grade 11	Young Adults
Advanced (350): Synthesize and learn from specialized reading materials.	0%	0%	5%	21%
Adept (300): Find, understand, summarize, and explain relatively complicated information.	1	13	40	54
Intermediate (250): Search for specific information, interrelate ideas, and make generalizations.	20	63	85	84
Basic (200): Understand specific or sequentially related materials.	68	96	99	97
Rudimentary (150): Carry out simple, discrete reading tasks.	96	100	100	100

Source: Arthur N. Applebee et al., *Learning to Be Literate in America: Reading, Writing, and Reasoning. The Nation's Report Card* (Princeton: National Assessment of Educational Progress, Educational Testing Service, 1987).

However, in the world of the 1990s a minimum literacy level is not good enough. Only a small percentage of young adults have developed the competencies required to reason effectively about what they are reading or writing. Workplace literacy, in particular, requires the ability to understand, summarize, and explain what one reads and writes. This has been termed the "adept" level of literacy. Only about half of the young adults assessed can be classifed as "adept" readers.

Ethnic minority individuals are making greater progress, on a percentage basis, than their White counterparts. In 1971 only 7 percent of the Black seventeen-year-olds read at the adept level. This figure had risen to 16 percent in 1984. Between 1975 and 1984 the percentage of Hispanic seventeen-year-olds reading at the adept level increased from 13 percent to 20 percent. During this same time period White seventeen-year-olds had increased from 41 to 45 percent.

As a group, Black and Hispanic young adults are well behind their White counterparts in literacy skills development, but the gap is beginning to close slowly. It must be pointed out that some Black and Hispanic young adults are among the best readers and writers, while some White young adults are among the poorest. However, there can be no escaping the fact that obvious literacy inequities exist among various ethnic and socioeconomic groups. Special targeted help must be provided to the at-risk populations to help these individuals develop the literacy skills required to be a full participant in the new technological learning age.

Who Attends Urban Colleges?

A recent study of Hunter College, a low-cost New York City-supported urban university, found that its students are now typically minority female, older, and often juggling family responsibilities with college studies and work.[8] The traditional residential, full-time, younger student has become the minority group on most urban college and university campuses. A new generation of students are now attending urban colleges: working adults, single mothers often supporting families, Blacks, Hispanics, Asians, and recent immigrants.

While many urban colleges and universities like Hunter have taken steps to adjust their programs and services to the changing urban student population, overall the enrollment share of Blacks and Hispanics has declined during the past decade. U. S. Census Bureau statistics paint a disturbing portrait of Black male college enrollment, which has declined significantly since 1975.

While ethnic minorities now account for about 17 percent of total college enrollment, they comprise an estimated 22 percent of the population as a whole. Black student college enrollment peaked around 1976 and has declined overall, on a percentage basis, since that time. Among Black males in the eighteen- to twenty-year-old age group, the number of high school graduates who enrolled in college or completed one or more years of college has declined steadily, from 50.3 percent in 1975 to 43.7 percent in 1986, while Hispanic college enrollment has grown slightly over that same time

College Participation by High School Graduates*
14 to 24 Years Old
(by percent)

Year	Males		Females		All Persons	
	Blacks	Whites	Blacks	Whites	Blacks	Whites
1960	33.5	47.1	31.8	35.6	32.5	41.0
1970	41.2	60.8	39.0	47.1	40.0	53.4
1975	50.3	56.6	46.4	49.1	49.0	52.7
1980	44.4	51.8	47.5	51.0	46.2	51.4
1984	45.2	54.2	45.0	53.4	45.2	58.8
1985	43.5	55.5	43.9	55.2	43.8	53.3
1986	43.7	55.0	50.2	55.6	47.4	55.3

* Enrolled in college or completed one or more years of college.
Source: U. S. Department of Commerce, Bureau of the Census, *Statistical Abstract of the United States, 1989.*

period. Overall, however, Hispanics represented 8 percent of the population in 1986 and only 4.3 percent of the total college enrollment.

Faith Paul, staff member of the Metropolitan Opportunity Project at the University of Chicago, found a similar pattern of declining minority student enrollment at four-year colleges and universities in Chicago and Philadelphia. The study indicates that

118

Higher Education in Chicago

Percent of Enrollment in Bachelor's Degree Granting Institutions by Racial/Ethnic Group in Metropolitan Chicago in 1980 and 1985			
	1980	**1985**	**Difference**
Black	41.7	34.3	-7.4
Hispanic	52.2	42.3	-10.2
Majorities	42.5	37.0	-5.4
Percent of Enrollment in Community Colleges in Metropolitan Chicago by Racial/Ethnic Group, 1980 and 1985			
	1980	**1985**	**Difference**
Black	58.3	65.7	+7.4
Hispanic	47.5	57.3	+10.2
Majorities	57.6	63.0	+5.4

Source: Faith Paul, *Declining Minority Access to College in Metropolitan Chicago*, Working Paper No. 2, Metropolitan Opportunity Project (Chicago: University of Chicago, 1987).

the decline has been centered in baccalaureate-degree-granting institutions, while minority enrollment in community, technical, and junior colleges has increased.

While the data on minority enrollment are not as precise as needed, and the year-to-year changes can be dramatic, we can safely observe that urban colleges carry a heavy responsibility to actively recruit and educate larger numbers of ethnic minority students and to serve as a positive force for the social mobility of disadvantaged youth. The collegiate challenge of educating increasing numbers of the at-risk population is especially frustrating in the context of recent strides in employment opportunities. Employment of Black managers and professionals is now at an all-time high. In one year alone, between 1985 and 1986, employment of Black managers and professionals rose by 100,000, to 1.6 million. The number of Blacks employed in technical, sales, and administrative support jobs increased from 2.78 million in 1985 to 2.92 million in 1986.

Even if urban colleges are successful in vigorous efforts to recruit more of the at-risk population, an equally vexing problem will be student retention and persistence to the associate or baccalaureate degree level. According to a 1985 study by the Association of American Colleges, 59 percent of White students persist to the baccalaureate degree, compared to 42 percent of Blacks, 39 percent of Native Americans, and 31 percent of Hispanics.

The performance gap between White and minority students can be observed at every level of schooling. The National Assessment of Educational Progress (NAEP) reported in March 1987 that Black and Hispanic students are particularly at risk of school failure unless schools and colleges focus considerable attention on developmental programs.

Percent of Black, Hispanic, and White Children and Young Adults at or Above 4th-, 8th-, and 11th-Grade Reading Levels

Grade	Black	Hispanic	White
Grade 11	31%	52%	68%
Grade 8	53%	71%	85%
Grade 4	82%	92%	96%

Source: Arthur N. Applebee et al., *Learning to Be Literate in America: Reading, Writing, and Reasoning. The Nation's Report Card* (Princeton: National Assessment of Educational Progress, Educational Testing Service, 1987).

The good news is that the performance of ethnic minority students is slowly improving. The number of Black seventeen-year-olds reading at the "adept" level on the NAEP scale rose nine percentage points between 1971 and 1984, from 7 to 16 percent. Scores for Hispanic students increased seven percentage points to 20 percent, while scores for Whites rose four points to 45 percent. Black students across the country continue to make substantial gains on the Scholastic Aptitude Test (SAT). Between 1976 and 1986 the SAT scores of Black students rose forty-one points, while the scores for Whites remained relatively unchanged.

It is clear that the need to intensify efforts to improve the education of African American, Hispanic American, American Indian, and Asian American students will be a major challenge for all of higher education in the decade ahead, but particularly for urban institutions. Increasingly, educators at the postsecondary level realize that they must establish working partnerships with educators on the secondary school—even the elementary school— level in order to address this problem. It is in the enlightened self-interest of colleges to reach out to the schools, helping, supporting, and encouraging minority students to press on through higher education.

The State Higher Education Executive Officers Association addressed the need for improved performance by colleges in the education of minorities in a 1987 report recommending that higher education officials at all levels establish the issue of minority student access and achievement as a top priority in the years ahead:

> The decline in the pool of entry-level workers and the corresponding increases in both the median age and the minority constitution of the general population have import for the nation's economy as well as its educational system. Of particular concern to both sectors is the relative balance between the supply of jobs at various skill levels and the availability of appropriately trained individuals to fill them. The shrinking entry-level labor pool offers marked opportunities for advancement to minorities, if the economy can generate sufficient demand for highly-skilled individuals and if higher educators can provide sufficient numbers of minorities with the proper preparation to meet that demand. At the moment, prospects are relatively bright for the former, but clouded for the latter.[9]

Is Anything Working?

Many urban colleges have already successfully reached out to their communities. The University of Tennessee at Chattanooga has developed a Career Beginnings program designed to help at-risk high school students to overcome difficulties and to enter and succeed in college.

Northern Arizona University has established a literacy program, Principles of Alphabet Literacy System, aimed at improving the literacy levels of court-identified juveniles. Northern Arizona University president Eugene Hughes puts the university squarely in the process of dealing with at-risk youth by stating: "I believe it is time to introduce a 'new professor' who is in touch with the realities of the public schools and who is skilled in helping student progress through an experiential, developmental, competency-based training program. . . . Teacher preparation will never become relevant until it addresses the problems of at-risk learners."[10]

St. Louis Community College, which serves a sprawling urban area on the banks of the Mississippi River in Missouri, has operated the Metropolitan Re-employment Project (MRP) at its Forest Park campus since May 1981. MRP is a counseling and career-guidance referral service for displaced workers in the St. Louis metropolitan area. Initially established with a $150,000 grant from the U. S. Department of Labor, the project is currently funded by the Regional Commerce and Growth Association, the St. Louis Labor Council, St. Louis Community Colleges, Missouri Job Service, and the Missouri Department of Vocational Education. More than 3,000 unemployed men and women have been helped through personal and family counseling, financial planning, assessment testing, and one-day "job shops," which focus on such skills as resume writing, job interviewing, and skills assessment.

As another example, the Dallas County Community College District in Texas operates a metropolitan job training center (ECJTC) at its downtown El Centro College. Individuals are encouraged to move from dependency to independency and into the economic mainstream of American life. The ECJTC program is a partnership involving city, county, and federal government and the college. Oma Ruth Judah, a student in the program, captures the spirit of its success when she describes class hallways filled with serious individuals carrying books:

One thing stands out over all others. There are people here who are very young, as well as people who are not so young, but all are here to learn, to develop self-confidence, self-respect, and marketable skills to compete in today's work force. . . .

You see their outlook on life change drastically. We have been down a long road where it seemed impossible to reach the end. The crossroad stop at the ECJTC gives us the chance to replenish ourselves and the drive to push on to become more than we thought possible.[11]

Wayne County Community College in Detroit sponsors a number of partnership projects, including an extensive program for inner-city senior citizens. Classes are operated in senior service centers and at many community locations serving 4,000 to 5,000 senior citizens each college term.

Another example of a pioneering urban undertaking is the Neighborhood Home Repair Instruction and Consultation Partnership program in Detroit. Backed by financial support from the National Bank of Detroit, the project is sponsored by the Detroit Public Library and Wayne County Community College. At Mark Twain Public Library in Detroit, citizens may check out do-it-yourself manuals as well as about 170 hand tools appropriate for dozens of simple home repairs. Sam Brown, a Wayne County Community College instructor who runs the home repair workshop tied to the program, said the response has been enthusiastic:

Class members go home knowing how to make minor repairs . . . fixing a sagging step, repairing plaster, wallpapering or caulking around windows and drains. One person who had a problem with a bathtub drain saved $2100 by doing the job himself. All he needed was a 75-cent gasket and a little know-how.[12]

San Diego, projected to become the seventh-largest metropolitan area in the country within the next several years, provides still another excellent example of urban leadership. The San Diego Community College District, working with the city and county government, developed an exemplary urban project. In the heart of an economically depressed section of San Diego, an Educational Cultural Complex was established by the San Diego Community College District, providing technical education, basic and academic education, career counseling, child development programs, a community theater, a food service facility, and other community-oriented functions.

The city of San Diego has built a branch of its public library system on the grounds of the complex. Needs of the largely ethnic minority southeast San Diego community are met in creative, innovative ways at the complex, which serves as a one-stop facility for many urban services. The San Diego Educational Cultural Complex is an example of cooperation between city government and a local urban college system. This venture provides an illustration of the kind of coordinated effort that can breathe life back into urban areas in America. Urban institutions and urban people are brought together through a combination of resources to meet vocational, cultural, civic, educational, and personal needs.

Many urban colleges and universities are reaching out to their communities on a even larger scale by fully using advanced telecommunication instructional methods. The growing senior citizen population, many on low incomes, may not be able to visit a campus across town. Welfare mothers may also be potential students but lack mobility. The motivation for such groups to broaden their knowledge and fulfill their social needs is being accomplished by providing learning programs in neighborhood branch libraries, churches, and elementary schools at times when they sit idle or are unused. Holding noon-hour classes for workers in office lunchrooms is another example of college and urban communities working together.

The City University of New York has developed a middle college program in cooperation with the New York City Schools. The middle college has operated most successfully at LaGuardia Community College for many years. It is aimed at identifying those promising high school students who will likely drop out of high school unless intervention is undertaken. These students enroll in a middle college program (grades eleven through fourteen) at LaGuardia. The high school completion rate of students in this program approaches 90 percent on an annual basis.

An Urban Extension Act?

If urban colleges and universities are to provide the foundation for meeting an expanding list of urban needs brought about by explosive change, new community-based programs must be undertaken. City government and urban colleges are ready-made partners to undertake this task. By pooling resources wisely, America should be able to produce a new generation of urban citizens better able to handle the demands of urban living. However, the federal government must play a leading role in this effort, much as it has done in the Rural Extension Act.

A new generation of city leaders and urban college leaders are seeing and accepting the potential of cooperation and partnership development. Urban colleges, working in cooperation with city governments and the federal government, could lead the way in developing an Urban Extension Act patterned after the time-honored rural extension program.

Urban community, technical, and junior colleges in particular have led the way in responding to the demands of nontraditional education in the last two decades. They have grown in energy and strength because of the mass enrollment of individuals making their claim upon equal educational opportunity; the arrival of older students and women developing new careers; the growth of part-time students; and the development of the tremendous educational market of evening and weekend classes, plus short extension courses in how-to-do-it fields such as consumerism, home and auto maintenance, nutrition, and job training.

In Portland, Oregon, a group of small business owners has been meeting over coffee for the last several years at morning sessions with a college instructor and university consultant who also visit businesses to reinforce information learned in the classes. Recognizing the need for retraining, Passaic County College in Paterson, New Jersey, is waiving tuition for jobless residents who will be allowed to take six credit hours of classes a semester. The college is able to provide this innovative program by opening up courses to the unemployed when at least a dozen paid-up students are also enrolled. Some urban colleges and universities also serve as a clearinghouse for small business owners to come together to share

125

mutual problems and to learn from the experiences of others.

Whether it takes the form of an Urban Extension Act or not, the 1990s will likely see some new form of vigorous Marshall Plan-type federal action aimed at solving the problems facing urban America. The problems of living and working in an urban environment will not go away, and urban colleges and universities will not be allowed to sit on the sidelines remaining aloof from the action.

It has now been forty years since the Marshall Plan was inaugurated to help rebuild Western Europe after World War II. Five billion dollars was given out of the U. S. Treasury in direct aid, plus the best U. S. know-how. In ten years Western Europe was back on its feet, and has since become a major competitor in world markets. The same spirit is alive in America today to help develop a "Marshall Plan" Urban Extension Act for urban America. It could be a force shaping much of American urban higher education in the decades ahead.

Dateline 2000 Forecast

1.   Some type of federal Urban Extension Act will be developed in the 1990s forming a new kind of working partnership between the federal government, city governments, and urban colleges and universities. Even as the Rural Extension Act formed a time-honored partnership uniting the resources of the federal government, county government, and the land-grant university, so will a new parallel partnership be formed to meet the challenges of urban life.

2.   New partnerships will be developed between urban schools and colleges to help more ethnic minority students enter and succeed in college programs. The middle college model will become widely adopted whereby colleges and high schools join together to develop a new and more flexible program for grades eleven through fourteen. As a result, the high school dropout volume will decrease, particularly for minority youth.

3.   Much greater attention will be given to applied academic programs in urban schools and colleges whereby urban students will begin to see more clearly the connection between the classroom and the application of learning.

4.   Urban colleges will develop different and unique programs to serve two distinct populations: students aged twenty-five and younger and students twenty-six and older. Required courses will be rotated over a three- or four-year period so that students may complete a major while attending college exclusively in the daytime, or in the evenings and on weekends. Student support services will be different, but of the same quality in the evenings and on weekends as in the daytime.

5.   Child-care centers will be in operation on all urban college and university campuses to accommodate both day and evening students.

6.   Urban colleges will bring together in one place a full range of social services to serve at-risk students. In most cases this will mean

an unusual degree of cooperation among all social service agencies, with offices on the college campus as a part of the student support service program.

7.   Urban colleges and universities will develop more effective systems to monitor, in a personal way, the progress of each college student and motivate student success in college.

8.   Employers (public and private) will increasingly turn to the urban college to help train and retrain the urban adult workforce.

9.   Colleges and universities will be providing, on a universal basis, various types of financial support programs, like the Eugene M. Lang "I Have A Dream" program for at-risk children and young people. These programs will begin with fifth- and sixth-grade students.

10. Colleges and universities will develop aggressive "grow your own" programs to help and encourage more ethnic minority young people to enter teaching as a career and to promote racial diversity among higher education professional staff.

11. Colleges and universities will develop aggressive recruitment and support programs to help ethnic minority individuals attend and succeed in college programs.

12. Governors and state legislators will develop new funding programs to help urban colleges and universities more effectively serve the needs of the urban population.

Executive Summary

Many people refer to the disadvantaged, or the "at-risk population," and point out that the vast majority (although certainly not all) of these individuals are living in the great urban centers of America. Unfortunately the largest group of the at-risk population are children. Today 23 percent of the children under the age of three are living in homes with incomes below the poverty level, compared to 14 percent of the total population.

The at-risk population includes a large number of ethnic minority individuals. Nearly one of two Black families earns less than $15,000 a year. Educational attainment levels, and poverty level lifestyles, are disproportionately related to ethnicity and race. Colleges and universities are mounting new minority education initiatives to help more ethnic minority individuals enter and succeed in college programs.

Urban America continues to grow. The number of urban residents jumped from 84.8 million in 1950 to 182.5 million in 1985. Two out of three Americans now live in metropolitan areas of one million or more, and more than four out of five individuals live in population areas of 250,000 or more. The crises of urban America—isolation, illiteracy, crime, and other problems such as teen pregnancy and drug abuse—pose a tremendous challenge to our colleges. What can colleges and universities do to help meet the complex societal needs of the at-risk population?

Urban colleges and universities will increasingly be called upon to help the at-risk population move into the economic mainstream of American life. The federal government could mount a new type of Marshall Plan aimed at developing an Urban Extension Act to bring together the resources of the federal government, city governments, and colleges and universities to better serve the citizens of urban America.

Notes

1. *Washington Times*, 8 September 1987.
2. U. S. Department of Commerce, Bureau of the Census, *Statistical Abstract of the United States, 1989* (Washington, D. C.: GPO, 1989).
3. U. S. Department of Education, *Schools That Work: Educating Disadvantaged Children* (Washington, D. C.: GPO, 1987).
4. U. S. Departmernt of Health and Human Services, National Center for Health Statistics, Vital Statistics of the United States, 1986.
5. U. S. Department of Commerce, Bureau of the Census, Current Population Reports, January 1986.
6. *USA Today*, 18 June 1987.
7. Judith Eaton, "A Message Sent to Students," *The Philadelphia Inquirer*, 29 May 1987.
8. College Entrance Examination Board, *Today's Urban University Students: Part 2. A Case Study of Hunter College* (New York: College Entrance Examination Board, 1985).
9. State Higher Education Executive Officers Association, *A Difference of Degrees: State Initiatives to Improve Minority Student Achievement* (Denver: State Higher Education Executive Officers Association, 1987).
10. Mary Gordon and Meredith Ludwig, "Addressing the Problems of Youth: Public Four-Year Colleges Respond," *Memo to the President*, American Association of State Colleges and Universities (4 August 1989).
11. American Association of Community and Junior Colleges, Keeping America Working Project, unpublished reports, 1985.
12. Keeping America Working Project, unpublished reports.

Chapter V

Push-Button Accountability

We do not believe that a public commitment to excellence and educational reform must be made at the expense of a strong public commitment to the equitable treatment of our diverse population. The twin goals of equity and high-quality schooling have profound and practical meaning for our economy and society, and we cannot permit one to yield to the other either in principle or in practice.

National Commission on Excellence in Education
A Nation at Risk: The Imperative for Educational Reform

I n what has now become an annual national ritual, the U. S. Secretary of Education reveals the Education Department's yearly wall chart report comparing the quality of education among the states. This report makes a judgment about the quality of education, in part, on the basis of the Scholastic Aptitude Test (SAT) and American College Testing (ACT) scores. The Secretary of Education, chief state school officers, many higher education leaders, the media, students, and parents anxiously await this report to make a judgment about the quality of American education.

Statistics indicate that college entrance exam test scores have stagnated over the past ten years, even as per pupil expenditures have increased. On the surface, college entrance exam scores and expenditure levels sound like a reasonable basis for judging the quality of the national investment in education. The media and the public are demanding a simple and understandable basis for making judgments about educational quality, which motivates a "push-button accountability" response from many political leaders. But let's dig deeper. Consider the ten-year trend of SAT and ACT scores. Given the huge increase in the number of persons taking the SAT and ACT tests over the past decade, it is amazing that the average scores have not dropped. A significantly wider spectrum of the high school population is now taking the SAT or ACT exam than was the case ten years ago. The ranks of the test takers have expanded to include the middle 50 percent of high school students, as well as the top academic quartile.

Why haven't the college entrance exam scores gone down as increasing numbers of C-level students take the exams? We can only speculate, but one possible explanation is that American education may not be doing so badly after all. Considering the fact that many more students are now taking the college entrance exams, stable test scores over a decade may be a sign of progress and not of stagnation. Given the larger pool of test takers, educators have simply had to work harder just to maintain the same average test score year after year.

Of course, many of those convinced that all students should be above average will not be satisfied with this explanation. One could conclude that the trouble with American education is that half of the students are below average. For those who continue to see SAT and ACT scores as the primary tool for judging educational quality in this country, there is a simple tongue-in-cheek way to improve education. Just limit the student pool of college entrance exam takers to the top academic 25 percent of our high school student bodies, as is the case in many other countries. Test scores will rise dramatically, and educational leaders can be proud of the almost immediate improvements in the quality of the schools. Test scores will zoom upward, and the media can report that schools and colleges are "making great educational progress." Will the drive for push-button accountability really improve the education product?

Let there be no doubt that educators must continue to work hard at improving the quality of education at all levels of schools, colleges, and universities. But surely there must be a more accurate way to judge the quality of education than by college entrance exam scores. To the credit of the leaders of the College Board and American College Testing Program, they have consistently urged against using these test scores to make overall judgments about educational quality. In fact, there are some reputable researchers who state that college entrance exams, as popularly used, do not even help colleges make better decisions about student selection, nor do they help students make better college choices.[1]

Diversity is the major strength of American higher education. Through the combined offerings of the 3,406 degree-granting colleges and universities in the United States—including 2,070 four-year, 1,333 two-year, and 643 specialized institutions—programs can be found to meet any human need for postsecondary education and training. The individual missions of these colleges are as diverse as the programs offered. Approximately 16 percent of American colleges and universities employ some type of fairly rigorous "screen them out" admissions process. The remaining four out of five colleges utilize some type of "screen them in" procedures, testing students for the purpose of appropriate placement rather than for

134

College Entrance Exam Score Trends

SAT		
Year	No. Taking Exam (all students)	Average Score
1987-88	2,030,130	895
1986-87	1,979,061	897
1985-86	1,819,035	897
1984-85	1,704,187	900
1983-84	1,659,925	894
1982-83	1,600,511	890
1981-82	1,606,882	892
1980-81	1,600,159	893
1979-80	1,575,474	890
1978-79	1,519,345	892
1977-78	1,514,473	898
ACT		
1987-88	1,313,755	18.8
1986-87	1,193,722	18.7
1985-86	1,088,692	18.8
1984-85	1,036,058	18.6
1983-84	1,019,657	18.5
1982-83	1,025,075	18.3
1981-82	994,610	18.4
1980-81	1,023,283	18.5
1979-80	996,514	18.5
1978-79	962,647	18.6
1977-78	953,655	18.5

Source: The College Entrance Examination Board and the American College Testing Program.

admission. Despite all of the media rhetoric about getting into college, only about 2 or 3 percent of U. S. colleges and universities can be considered highly selective in their admissions standards. As an example of media attention given this subject, the June 4, 1989, issue of the national *Parade* magazine reports on the screen-them-out admissions standards of Stanford University this way:

> If you plan to apply for admission to one or more of the outstanding private universities or colleges in this country, or you know some student who does, here are a few facts and figures from Stanford University that afford an idea of the competition one faces.

- In the 1988-89 college year there were 14,912 freshmen applications for 2,547 slots.
- Of the 14,912 applications, 3,208 had a perfect 4.0 high school grade point average.
- Nearly half of the applicants had high school GPA's of 3.8 or higher.
- One thousand five hundred thirty-one had verbal SAT scores of 700 or higher on a scale of 800.
- Six thousand two hundred sixty scored 700 or higher on the math SAT.[2]

There can be little question that Americans, led by the media, judge the quality of higher education not upon the basis of who gets out of college, but who gets into the handful of so-called prestige schools. If that observation is accurate, then the majority of colleges and universities that screen them in must be considered second-rate by design. Surely, there must be a better way to judge quality in higher education than by who gets into the college.

Different College Types

The Carnegie Foundation for the Advancement of Teaching classifies institutions of higher education by mission, distributing colleges into ten broad categories based upon emphasis on research, graduate studies, diversity of programs, and degrees offered. Changes in the number of institutions classified in each of the ten categories provide clues to higher education trends into the 1990s, particularly toward developing different indicators of quality to match the diversity of institutional mission.

Between 1970 and 1987 the number of four-year colleges

Carnegie Classification of Colleges and Universities

Institution Classification	Number of Institutions and Enrollment Percentages by Year					
	1970		1976		1987	
	N	%	N	%	N	%
• Research Universities I (Give high priority to research and graduate programs)	52	1.8	51	1.7	70	2.0
• Research Universities II (Less federal support for R&D than Class I)	40	1.4	47	1.5	33	1.0
• Doctorate Granting Universities I (Emphasize research and graduate programs, but not as much as research universities)	53	1.9	56	1.8	51	1.5
• Doctorate Granting Universities II (Fewer Ph.D.'s awarded annually than Class I)	28	1.0	30	1.0	59	1.7
• Comprehensive Colleges I (Award more than half of B.A. and B.S. degrees in professional or occupational fields)	323	11.4	381	12.4	427	12.5
• Comprehensive Colleges II (Enroll less than 2,500 students)	133	4.5	213	6.9	174	5.1
• Liberal Arts Colleges I (Award more than half of degrees in arts and sciences)	146	5.1	123	4.0	125	3.6
• Liberal Arts Colleges II (Less selective than Class I)	575	20.2	460	14.9	439	12.9
• Community, Technical, and Junior Colleges	1,063	37.5	1,146	37.3	1,368	40.3
• Specialized Schools and Colleges	424	15.0	559	18.1	643	18.9
Totals	2,837	100	3,072	100	3,389	100

Source: Clifford Adelman, "A Basic Statistical Portrait of American Higher Education," unpublished paper, 1987.

classified as liberal arts colleges fell by 22 percent. At the same time, the number of colleges classified as comprehensive rose 32 percent, while the number of two-year colleges and specialized institutions rose 35 percent. Of this increase, 305 were community, technical, or junior colleges and 219 were specialized institutions. There were similar increases in the number of research and doctoral-granting universities. The number of research universities grew by 12 percent, and the number of doctoral-granting universities rose by 36 percent.

The trend toward higher-degree offerings, more comprehensiveness, and arguably, more emphasis upon prestige factors is clear. More universities are moving to greater emphasis on research and graduate studies, and more liberal arts colleges are adopting comprehensive missions. While this is going on in the four-year colleges, the open-door community colleges are increasing their share of undergraduate enrollment. In fact, community, technical, and junior colleges now enroll 51 percent of all first-time freshmen.[3]

While the overall number of colleges and institutions increased 20 percent from 1970 to 1985, the size of the colleges themselves expanded as well, particularly in the two-year college sector. Headcount enrollment grew 5.5 percent for four-year colleges and a whopping 46.5 percent for community, technical, and junior colleges. The large majority of college students are enrolled in a relatively small number of institutions, with 14 percent of the public colleges and universities enrolling 73 percent of all students. Three out of four students attend colleges with enrollments of 20,000 students or more, with the large community colleges showing the largest increases.

The U. S. participation rate in higher education is the highest in the world. In 1960 just under 8 percent of the population twenty-five years of age or older had completed four or more years of college. Today that figure stands at 20 percent, a 150 percent increase. Projections from the U. S. Census Bureau indicate that the 1990 census may document 24 to 25 percent. In the case of ethnic minority students, the college completion rate rose a significant 360 percent.[4] During the past twenty-five years enrollment in higher education rose 500 percent, the number of baccalaureate degrees awarded went up 165 percent, and the number of associate degrees conferred increased 200 percent.

Perhaps the single most important factor driving increased college enrollment and college program completions is the rising interest, on the part of high school seniors, in continuing one's education after graduation. A longitudinal study of 1972 high school seniors conducted by the U. S. Department of Education provides a rich source of information about this particular baby-boom-age cohort's postsecondary educational and work experience. The data from this study reveal that nearly half of all American

High School Graduating Class of 1972
1972 Educational Aspiration vs.
1986 Educational Attainment
(by percent)

	High School Diploma Only		Postsecondary Vocational		Associate Degree or Some College		Bachelor's Degree		Advanced Degree	
	Asp.	Att.	Asp.	Att.	Asp.	Att.	Asp.	Att.	Asp.	Att.
All	19.4	19.5	18.6	14.3	12.7	27.9	36.7	27.1	12.5	11.1
Male	NA	17.0	NA	14.8	NA	26.8	NA	28.1	NA	13.3
Black	14.7	23.4	19.2	19.7	10.1	27.5	43.4	21.0	12.6	8.4
White	15.7	15.5	17.9	14.3	11.7	26.0	38.3	29.8	16.5	14.4
Hispanic	14.1	29.6	16.1	15.1	22.9	35.0	34.7	13.8	12.2	6.4
Female	NA	21.8	NA	14.0	NA	28.8	NA	26.2	NA	9.2
Black	15.1	18.5	24.2	20.7	9.9	30.7	35.7	23.9	15.2	6.2
White	23.5	21.8	18.6	12.9	13.7	27.8	36.0	27.3	8.3	10.2
Hispanic	15.8	32.3	27.3	14.7	19.9	38.3	30.5	11.7	6.5	3.0

Note: This table is based upon self-reported information from a sample of 23,000 high school graduates in 1972 and a fifth follow-up sample of 12,500 in 1986.

Source: Clifford Adelman, Office of Educational Research and Improvement, U. S. Department of Education, unpublished paper, 1986

high school seniors in 1972 wanted to earn baccalaureate or advanced college degrees. Fourteen years later about three-fourths of the aspirants had earned bachelor's degrees.

The students' aspiration to attend college proved, over the fourteen-year period, to be a fairly accurate indicator of achievement. Nineteen percent of the high school seniors were content to stop at the high school level, and overall, 19 percent of the seniors had never enrolled in a college course. Another 19 percent planned to earn a vocational diploma or certificate, and 14 percent of them succeeded in doing so. With the community college emphasis upon the associate degree, of the 13 percent of the high school seniors who wanted to earn associate degrees, or wanted some higher education short of the baccalaureate, 28 percent did so, reflecting both the increasing popularity of the associate degree as a working credential in the economy and a desire for some form of higher education leading to a career.

It is clear from national studies, like the 1972 longitudinal study, that American higher education has been highly successful in opening the doors to higher education for students heretofore excluded from this opportunity. At the same time, some critics argue that the growth in access to higher education has compromised quality, that too many students are attending colleges, and too many are completing programs at lower-than-desired levels of performance.

Community colleges have, as open-door institutions, grappled with the persistent tension of access and quality from their inception. The challenge for two-year colleges has been to provide both access and quality, rather than holding the two as polar opposites. In 1987 the board of directors of the American Association of Community and Junior Colleges adopted a policy statement on access that states in part:

> The mission of community, technical, and junior colleges must go beyond the limited understanding and practice of open door admissions. Access must be seen as an effective process to ensure student success. A new definition of access must focus on the institution's responsibility to help its students succeed once they enter the "open door," with retention and program completion as key components. Effective student assessment, coupled with developmental support, can improve retention. Access and retention can then be measured by the number of students who enter and achieve their educational goals.[5]

The Historical Precedent for Access

The national commitment to providing increased access to higher education gained momentum at the end of World War II with the passage of the GI Bill. It was, beyond a doubt, the single most important piece of legislation ever adopted aimed at opening college doors to millions of previously excluded individuals. Among other benefits, the GI Bill demonstrated that a broad spectrum of the American population could benefit from higher education opportunity. It has been postulated that a vastly increased number of college graduates repaid, many times over, the government investment in their education through increased personal taxes and higher productivity.

In May 1954 Chief Justice Earl Warren delivered the momentous Supreme Court decision in the matter of *Brown v. Topeka Board of Education*, saying that in the field of public education the doctrine of separate but equal has no place. Thus began a new phase of the civil rights movement in the U. S., focusing attention on access to education at all levels. Subsequent acts of Congress in 1957, 1960, 1964, 1965, and 1968 put the force of law behind the access-and-equality movement. Perhaps the most powerful symbol of this new age was the picture of National Guard troops, under federal command, safeguarding the admission of James Meredith, a black, to the University of Mississippi in 1963.

During this same period the ranks of open-door community, technical, and junior colleges began to grow rapidly. From 1966 through 1968 more than 300 new community colleges were founded, an average of two per week.[6] Between 1960 and 1987 the number of two-year colleges increased 163 percent, from 521 to 1,368. Often called the "people's college," these institutions continue to provide accessible, low-cost higher educational opportunity on a scale unknown to the rest of the world. As a result of the growth of community colleges, the percent of high school graduates enrolling in college immediately following high school has jumped from 24 percent to 33 percent for Whites, and from 18 percent to 32 percent for Blacks.[7]

During the 1980s, however, interest in access to education has subsided in the face of concerns over quality. Some believe that the higher education enterprise experiences periodic, alternating cycles of interest in access and in quality, and that colleges and universities have now entered a quality phase. Some of the advocates of increased attention to quality have pointed to the stagnating scores on the Scholastic Aptitude Test as evidence that some institutions are falling short of quality goals, and that too many unqualified students are embarking on college careers without the proper academic preparation.

An advisory panel established by the College Board to examine the issue of stagnating test scores rejected the notion that increased access to higher education was the primary culprit in level test results. It was found that the early part of declining scores (1963-70) could be attributed to a greater number of individuals taking the tests and major changes in the composition of the test-taking population. The panel also suggested that stagnating test scores might be blamed on the lowering of high school standards, significant high school absenteeism, grade inflation, too much television, and too little family involvement in the elementary and secondary schools.[8]

Additional evidence that American higher education is entering into a new cycle of concern over quality, rather than access, is reflected in changed priorities at the federal level. In his first major address on higher education to the Congress in March 1970, President Nixon argued: "No qualified student who wants to go to college should be barred by lack of money. That has long been a great American goal; I propose that we achieve it now." With Nixon's leadership and the efforts of subsequent administrations, federal student financial aid programs expanded dramatically. During the ten-year period 1975 to 1985, Pell Grant recipients rose from 1.2 million to 3.5 million, and expenditures rose from $918 million to $2.8 billion. Guaranteed student loans expanded from 1.3 million to 4.8 million recipients, and from $1.8 billion to $11.4 billion in loan amounts.

The stated goal, however, of the national administration of the 1980s has been to reduce the federal role in education. President Ronald Reagan's first Secretary of Education, Terrel Bell, recalls then chief of staff Ed Meese's determination to "persuade the new president to 'cut to the bone' and eventually eliminate all federal financial assistance to education."[9] Bell's successor as secretary, William Bennett, charged that the U. S., while outspending the rest of the world on education, was getting an insufficient return on its investment. This charge was made despite the fact that the U. S. education spending, as a function of the GNP, is in the middle range of developed nations. Other countries with far more homogeneous populations spend more than the U. S., in terms of the proportion of the total GNP to each country, including Japan (6.0 percent), the U.S.S.R (6.7 percent), the Netherlands (7.9 percent), and Sweden (9.0 percent).

The quality issue, however, has been a politically convenient way to shift public attention away from access. The crowning achievement of former secretary of education Terrel Bell was the establishment of a National Commission on Excellence in Education, under the leadership of David Gardner, president of the University of California. The commission's report, *A Nation at Risk*, attracted worldwide attention as much for its stirring rhetoric as for its content. Through statements like "the educational foundations of our society are being eroded by a rising tide of mediocrity that threatens our very future, as a nation and as a people,"[10] the public debate on education has dramatically shifted in the direction of quality.

This report and myriad others, especially Ernest Boyer's study of the American high school, focused on elementary and secondary education and laid the groundwork for similar reports on the quality of higher education. Secretary Bell established a Study Group on the Conditions of Excellence in American Higher Education. Led by Professor Kenneth Mortimer of Pennsylvania State University, the study group issued a report in 1984 titled *Involvement in Learning: Realizing the Potential of American Higher Education*. While this report was not nearly as critical as *A Nation at Risk*, nor as widely acclaimed, it has had an impact on higher education across the nation and has triggered a host of other reports, particularly studies and reports on undergraduate education. The *Involvement in Learning* study group argued that quality in higher education is a function of student involvement. If the teaching-learning process is to be strengthened, colleges need greater student involvement in the teaching-learning process, higher expectations of students, and first-rate assessment of learning procedures with regular feedback.

In 1987 Secretary of Education William Bennett felt so strongly that leaders of higher education were dragging their feet on implementing educational reforms, that he wrote the governors of all the states telling them that lack of accountability was one of the most significant problems in higher education and urging them to provide the leadership for requiring state-level college assessment programs.

A 1985 Association of American Colleges report, *Integrity in the College Curriculum*, generated a review of degree requirements. During the same period the Education Commission of the States released its 1986 report, *Transforming the State Role in Undergraduate Education*, and the National Governors' Association established a Task Force on College Quality under the chairmanship of Missouri governor John Ashcroft. This group issued its report, *Time for Results: The Governors' 1991 Report on Education.* One of the more influential reports is a Carnegie Foundation for the Advancement of Teaching study of four-year college undergraduate education authored by Ernest Boyer and called *College: The Undergraduate Experience in America.* Boyer asks how the quality of a college education and student learning should be measured:

> Today, the academic progress of students is assessed by each professor, course by course. Class grades are dutifully recorded. The final mark of achievement is the diploma, which presumably signifies an educated person. But good teachers are not necessarily good testers and the college has few ways to evaluate the quality of education overall.
>
> During our study we heard calls for a new approach to evaluation. Increasingly, state and national education officials, lawmakers, parents, and students are wondering just how much is being learned. How can college goals and the evaluation of student achievement be more closely linked? Should there be assessment beyond course grades? Are the testing procedures now used adequate to the task?[11]

From 1986 to 1988 Ernest Boyer also chaired a twenty-one person Commission on the Future of Community Colleges, appointed by the board of directors of the American Association of Community and Junior Colleges. This commission's report was published by AACJC in 1988 under the title *Building Communities: A Vision for a New Century.* Under the chapter title "Leadership for a New Century" five recommendations are presented for assessing student outcomes and institutional effectiveness:

- We urge that classroom evaluation be the central assessment activity of the community college. That process should be strengthened through faculty development programs which focus on the use of classroom evaluation to improve teaching.
- We recommend that each community college develop a campus-wide assessment of institutional effectiveness. Such a program should include a periodic reexamination of mission goals, specific programs, individual student outcomes, retention rates, and the performance of graduates.
- Faculty and administrators in each community college should be involved in defining in explicit terms the educational outcomes which the institution aspires to produce for its students. Those outcomes should be clearly related to the mission of the college and to an informed understanding of the educational needs and goals of the college's student population.
- College-wide assessment processes should be designed to ascertain the extent to which desired outcomes are achieved in a student's literacy skills, general education, and area of specialization. Care should be exercised in the selection and use of standardized tests. Innovation and creativity should be encouraged in collaborative faculty efforts to devise appropriate new assessment procedures, perhaps including locally-developed examinations, student projects, performances, portfolios, and oral presentations.
- Every college should consider further evaluation of the impact of its programs by conducting periodic interviews or surveys of current students, graduates, and employers of graduates.[12]

In 1985 the board of directors of the American Association of State Colleges and Universities appointed a commission, led by Secretary of Education Terrel Bell, to study the role and future of public state colleges and universities. This report, released in late 1986 and titled *To Secure the Blessings of Liberty*, also underscored the need for institutional student outcomes and determining institutional effectiveness.

However, it has become abundantly clear that the internal

debates of the academy are quickly being appropriated by external political forces. Even though the reports warn against political interference and prescriptive legislation, political leaders are maintaining a great interest in this subject and keeping the pressure on college and university leaders to develop better indicators of institutional effectiveness.

Persistent themes run through the reports, particularly the governors' reports. One theme calls for clarification of the mission of individual institutions. Another theme calls for the development of indicators of institutional effectiveness and an evaluation of program quality. The governors have carried their call for assessment to the various accrediting agencies, urging them to require demonstrated levels of performance in granting institutional accreditation. The governors also call for the accrediting community to require that colleges and universities collect information about student outcomes and to use this information in the evaluation of college programs.

In reviewing recent developments in higher education, the amount of political and public interest in the quality of undergraduate education stands out. In past years the primary motivation for access to higher education came from forces external to the institution. Concern about civil rights, the economy, jobs, social mobility, and human resource development came from sources largely outside the academy, while the primary impetus to discuss quality in higher education came from inside the institution, from the academic community. That trend has now been reversed, with federal and state government leaders expressing an increasing interest in the quality of higher education; and it does not appear that interest will decrease in the decade ahead. Political leaders in the 1990s will insist upon maintaining access to higher education, but they will also insist that institutions clarify the indicators utilized to judge institutional effectiveness.

The 1980s experience of three collegiate institutions can be instructive in understanding how different kinds of higher education institutions are dealing with the persistent tensions between access and quality. These three minicase studies have been chosen not because they are the best illustrations, but because they are representative of work in the field and because their assessment process has been consistently monitored and recorded.

Miami-Dade Community College

Miami-Dade Community College is one of the largest community colleges in the country. The majority of students represent ethnic minorities: 50 percent are Hispanic, 17 percent are Black, and 45 percent of the students indicate that English is their second language. Almost two-thirds of the students attend college part time and all are commuting students. Nearly one out of three students qualifies as a disadvantaged student according to federal Pell Grant guidelines. Miami-Dade operates on four primary campuses and a number of smaller centers, offering 180 different certificate and degree programs. If the twin ideals of access and quality can live comfortably together in this college, it is likely they can do so in any other college.

A decade ago Miami-Dade president Robert McCabe and his colleagues began asking themselves if their college was a revolving door for students rather than the intended open door to success. They began to wonder out loud how they could maintain access and still provide high-quality programs. Their questioning and study led to a number of reforms.

Students are now assessed carefully upon admission, with required college preparatory developmental courses provided for those with deficiencies. Students must show a proficiency in reading, mathematics, and written English expression before being allowed to take college-level work. Students with English as a second language must also demonstrate proficiency in reading, writing, and speaking English.

Student progress is continually monitored, utilizing a system called standards of academic progress. It is a program of warnings, probation, and suspension. If a student's grade point average falls below 1.5, or if the student withdraws from over half of his or her classes, the academic progress standards take effect and the student is warned, put on probation, or suspended. Students are not just warned; they are also notified of ways to improve or change their situation and offered help.

A process called academic alert and advisement gives all students feedback on academic progress. A computerized letter is sent to all students about six weeks into the semester, informing them of their academic and attendance progress. If a student is experiencing problems, the letter serves as an early warning system and indicates how the student can get help. This letter also advises students what they need to do to meet degree requirements or what to choose for courses for the next term.

A quality college preparatory developmental program is offered to all students deficient in the basic skills of reading, writing, and computation via an array of computerized and individualized programs. The emphasis in the basic skills program is upon achievement and success and not on the length of time required to move upward.

Miami-Dade requires a core curriculum aimed at specific curricular objectives for every degree-seeking student. The core curriculum represents the collective vision of the academic community about the competencies of an educated person and the knowledge, skills, and values expected of any individual awarded a Miami-Dade degree.

A vigorous and well-supported faculty and staff development program is in operation at Miami-Dade. Faculty committees constantly review the quality of the core courses and are given the time and training to make appropriate curriculum changes. Curriculum review and updating is considered a dynamic process involving the faculty on a regular basis. Faculty regularly audit each other's classes, or team teach, to understand the other's teaching methods and disciplines. Considerable work is done to individualize instruction wherever possible. All of this requires a vibrant and involved staff development program and open communication.

If test results can be any indication of quality, Miami-Dade has a success story to tell. In 1982 the state of Florida initiated a statewide testing program (CLAST) required of all students at the end of their college sophomore year. Students must pass all of the subtests in reading, writing, essay, and computation in order to be awarded an associate degree or advanced to junior standing. In 1985 the 88 percent of the Miami-Dade students who passed all of the CLAST tests scored higher, on an average, than did the students who took the tests from the two local and selective universities. This record is all the more remarkable, considering that at least one-third of the Miami-Dade students would not likely have been admitted to

148

more selective universities as freshmen.[13] The Miami-Dade Community College story indicates that an open-door college can emphasize quality along with access.

Northeast Missouri State University

Northeast Missouri State University (NMSU) has developed a "value added" assessment program aimed at determining academic quality and an assessment of the students' educational experience at the university. Traditional university indicators of quality have focused on the most degreed and decorated faculty, the size of the financial resources, and the quality of students upon entry. NMSU has taken another approach in defining quality, based upon the institution's impact upon student learning from entry through program completion.

The cornerstones of the NMSU value-added approach come from the results of the ACT and ETS external national examinations available to all colleges and universities, along with national and longitudinal comparisons of student performances in specific disciplines gathered from the Graduate Record Examinations, and other preprofessional and pregraduate exams. In addition, the NMSU faculty have developed extensive attitude and self-assessment tests that measure personal and individual changes in student attitudes and achievement as a result of the college experience.

Students are surveyed and tested upon entry, at intermediate points, and upon graduation. A sample of alumni are also surveyed each year in order to determine the long-range aspects of the university experience.

Charles J. McClain, who served as the university's president for seventeen years, was actively involved in the evolution of the fifteen-year-old value-added program. He points to five principles that have led to the success of NMSU's value-added program: (1) assessment must have a guiding purpose related to the mission of the institution, which in NMSU's case has been to provide a curriculum and program that ensure that the university's graduates are nationally competitive; (2) the value-added assessment model was initiated at the macro-level for the overall qualitative improvement of the university and has gradually evolved through academic divi-

149

sions, disciplines, and major states to the micro-level of focusing specifically on improving the achievement of an individual student; (3) the faculty must not only buy into a value-added assessment model for it to be truly successful, but they must also assume ownership of the program; (4) a program of such magnitude—a comprehensive collegewide assessment program that attempts to measure as accurately as possible changes in a student and determine the value of those changes—will unfold incrementally and follow an initially meandering course, which allows the institution to discover what is best for its mission and its students; and (5) perhaps the most important aspect of the value-added assessment program has been its impact on organizational culture and climate. An atmosphere of excellence seems to pervade the NMSU campus.

The key to the value-added assessment program appears to be the use of national external examinations. It is difficult for institutions to demonstrate quality without some comparative information that also reflects important knowledge in a particular academic discipline.[14]

Alverno College

Alverno College in Milwaukee, Wisconsin, is a private women's liberal arts college with a long and distinguished record of developing assessment-based teaching and learning experiences. The administration and faculty at Alverno asked themselves a couple of fundamental teaching-learning questions some fifteen years ago. If the components of effective student performance are known, why can't the college systematically teach toward these knowable and learnable components? Rather than wait for the end of a course or the end of a program to assess student progress, why can't the college insist upon a related, continuous assessment of learning in individual classrooms?

The Alverno faculty and administration developed an institutional culture that promotes dynamic questioning and introspection about assessment and feedback that promotes student learning. The Alverno faculty have moved their highly successful assessment experiences off campus to corporate trainers and faculty in other colleges, explaining the Alverno "assessment as learning" approach.

The key to the Alverno approach is in specifying performance levels for eight competencies, with student achievement monitored by faculty teams. External examiners are used to assess overall learning beyond the level of individual courses. In addition, students receive consistent feedback.

In each Alverno classroom, faculty identify the particular competencies the course is intended to develop, convey that information to the student, and arrange classroom instruction and student involvement toward learning that can be demonstrated, observed, judged, and related to overall institutional goals. The feedback program is designed to help students see increments of improvement and to help students develop the ability to self-assess learning. Even though the Alverno assessment-as-learning curricular program is unique, individual faculty members practice what every effective teacher does. They establish and communicate clear expectations, insist upon student involvement in learning, assess learning, and provide continuous feedback to the student.

The Alverno faculty and administration indicate that what they are doing is not particularly new. They have just applied what is known about effective teaching and learning to a systematic and institutionwide assessment-as-learning program. What is different at Alverno is that the performance assessment program has systematically been applied across the entire college curriculum. Alverno College gives the public and its own students some clear signals that it will be accountable on an institutionwide basis, that it cares deeply about student learning and educational quality, and that students are performing at consistently high levels.

The TASP Program

The states of Florida, New Jersey, and Texas are leading the way in mandating, from the state level, some type of academic assessment program. As an example, the Texas Academic Skills Program (TASP) is designed to ensure that all public college and university students pass basic tests in reading, writing, and mathematics. If a student does not pass all these sections of the TASP, the student must take developmental college preparatory courses until he or she can pass that particular tests. There is a stringent penalty attached to the TASP tests. A student may not receive a baccalaureate or associate degree without passing this battery of tests. Of the 17,000 students who have now taken the tests, 81 percent have receive a passing grade of seventy or better on the first try.

Dan Angel, president of Austin Community College in Austin, Texas, and an early proponent of the TASP program, indicates that TASP is pushing the Texas schools, colleges, and universities closer together into an "all one system" approach to education. He also feels that more college students will be successful in their college experience because of better high school preparation and because of the regional remediation, monitoring, and reporting procedures.

However, all is not smooth with TASP. The Mexican American Legal Defense in Education Fund has challenged the TASP program on five counts: (1) the lack of lead time allocated for developing remedial courses; (2) the impact of TASP upon minority students; (3) the accuracy of the tests; (4) insufficient dollars to administer the program; and (5) lack of multiple criteria to make judgments about academic proficiency.

Regardless of the challenges, it appears that accountability and the testing issues are here to stay and leaders in higher education must learn to deal with them.[15]

Questions Related to Quality

At least seven questions seem to run through all of the reform reports and discussions having to do with accountability and improving the quality of higher education, and these same themes or questions are applicable to all kinds of colleges and universities:

- How clearly are the goals and purposes of the college, and of the college program, communicated to students and to the public? Do students understand the "why" of their learning?
- What is the congruence between the objectives of individual courses and the overall educational goals of the institution?
- How can colleges and universities help students develop a greater sense of belonging, and a deeper involvement in

the teaching-learning process, without overwhelming an already busy faculty?
- How can colleges and universities improve the quality of internal communications and consistent feedback among students, faculty, staff, and administration?
- How can colleges and universities best identify and help students having problems early in the term without reducing academic standards? How can college dropout and failure rates be reduced?
- How can colleges and universities best use instructional technology to enhance the quality of learning without losing the warm human touch?
- How can colleges and universities best evaluate the quality of student learning and the overall effectiveness of the institution?

Accreditation

The national Council on Postsecondary Accreditation in its statement on "Educational Quality and Accreditation" reduces the discussion of quality to three fundamentals:

> The quality of an educational process relates to (1) the appropriateness of its objectives, (2) the effectiveness of the use of resources in pursuing these objectives, and (3) the degree to which objectives are achieved. Without a clear statement of what education is expected to provide, it is not possible to determine how good it is. . . . Primary emphasis [has moved from] process and resources to increased concentration on results and learning outcomes. . . .[16]

Quality in higher education will continue to be an issue of national debate and local college implementation well into the decade ahead, and regional and national self-regulatory accreditation agencies are likely to lead the way. The major purpose of the accreditation associations is to bring together educational leaders in a network of common interest to reach the shared goal of quality education in schools and colleges. This sounds simple, but it is a complex process. Developing quality education and a favorable

153

economic and political climate in which quality education can flourish is difficult. No school, college, or university lives in isolation; each is part of a national and regional network and cannot be divorced from it. That is why the voluntary accreditation associations and process will take on added importance in the decade ahead.

Accreditation associations require self-study and peer review in making judgments about programs and institutions. Self-regulatory accreditation associations have the power to shape the arguments and the environments that are favorable to good practice in education. Essentially, the accreditation process is a key tool to help educational institutions in their unending quest for educational quality.

Unfortunately, some college faculty and leaders do not see the accreditation process as a vehicle to achieve excellence. One of the challenges in the decade ahead will be to help educational leaders clearly see the accreditation process as vital to the cultivation of excellence. Some educators participate little in the work of the accreditation enterprise and tend to operate alone. At the same time, they enjoy the benefits of the extensive work stimulated and coordinated by other school and college leaders without providing much participation or support. That will change in the 1990s. The pressure will be on all institutional leaders to make the voluntary accreditation process work.

Accreditation associations will likely lead in developing institutional effectiveness indicators. They are the most likely and appropriate vehicles through which school and college leadership can represent broad educational interests and debate tough quality-indicator questions. An energetic and effective accreditation association can have a major impact on the process of cultivating excellence in education because it is about the only overall networking organization with the capacity to formulate and represent the composite of college views and concerns about institutional quality on a national or regional basis.

The Commission on Colleges of the Southern Association of Colleges and Schools states the challenge this way:

A self-evaluating organization has been described as an organization constantly in conflict with itself. Such tensions are worth enduring only if, as a result, institutions overcome their resistance to change and provide positive incentives for faculty members and administrators alike to become involved in using evaluation results to improve programs and services.[17]

Assessment

Overall internal and external concerns about quality in higher education focus on the outcomes, the results of the investment in higher education. The effort to get a handle on the quality issue has triggered considerable assessment action at state government and campus levels. Assessment is generally used as an umbrella term to describe a variety of measurements of student learning and/or institutional effectiveness in the teaching-learning process. Assessment moves beyond the time-honored continuous classroom grading procedures.

As generally used in higher education today, the term "assessment" describes a collegiate information system with four primary purposes: student course placement; program or course evaluation; some kind of certification often taking the form of external exams; and determining overall institutional effectiveness.

Assessment in colleges and universities looms as a major force in the decade ahead. As recently as 1984 only eight states admitted to having any kind of formal collegiate assessment policy. Today that number approaches thirty-five states, with more states added each year to the list. At least three views about assessment predominate, all revolving around the question, What should students know in order to be awarded an associate or baccalaureate degree?

One view is that the sheer diversity of objectives among the over 3,000 accredited colleges and universities makes it difficult, if not impossible, to apply one assessment instrument to all institutions of higher education. The assessment instrument will vary with institutional missions and students' aspirations, it is argued, and decisions about assessment practices and procedures should be left to the local college.

1987 State Assessment Policies for Public Institutions of Higher Education

Requires Degree Qualifying Tests	Requires Academic Progression Tests	Requires Screening Teacher Ed.Tests	Requires Placement Exams for Freshmen[1]	Requires Program Be Established	Encourages Program Be Established	Conducts Alumni and Follow-up Surveys	No Formal Policy for Assessments[5]
California[2] Georgia*	Florida* New York[4]	Arizona* Arkansas* Connecticut* Kansas* Michigan Minnesota* Mississippi* North Carolina* Oklahoma* Oregon* Texas* West Virginia*	California Connecticut Florida* Georgia* Hawaii* New Jersey* New York[4] Tennessee Texas Wyoming	Colorado[3] Connecticut Illinois Missouri New Jersey South Dakota Tennessee Virginia	Alabama Georgia Louisiana	Alaska Maryland North Carolina Rhode Island	Delaware Idaho Indiana Iowa Kentucky Maine Massachusetts Montana Nevada New Hampshire New Mexico North Dakota Ohio Pennsylvania South Carolina Utah Vermont

Notes:
1. Defined as "basic skill" placement examinations for entering students.
2. California State University System only (19 campuses).
3. Institutions not in compliance by 1990 may have up to 2 percent of their state appropriation withheld.
4. City University of New York only.
5. Some of these states have policies under consideration, others have pilot programs, and still others confine formal assessment programs to precollegiate and college admissions processes.

* Same assessment instrument mandated in all higher education institutions.

Source: Carol M. Boyer et al., *Assessment and Outcomes Measurement: A View from the States* (Denver: Education Commission of the States, 1987).

A second view holds that a certain base level of knowledge and academic skills should be required of all college degree holders. The implications for colleges and universities under this view are that all students must demonstrate a certain level of uniform competence as a condition for receiving a college certificate or degree. Proponents of this view would require some form of statewide, or even national, standard testing.

A third, and more complex, view of assessment focuses on the value that has been added to individuals' lives as a result of their

1986 Assessment Methods
(by percent)

Tests	Community Colleges		Four-Year Colleges		Universities	
	Appro-priate Method[1]	Method in Use[2]	Appro-priate Method[1]	Method in Use[2]	Appro-priate Method[1]	Method in Use[2]
1. College-Level Skills Tests	61	23	70	26	55	19
2. Test in General Education	48	15	71	13	51	15
3. Comprehensive Exams/ Major	46	7	82	26	67	25
4. Higher Order Skills in:						
Critical Thinking	69	15	89	26	79	17
Quantitative Skills	74	14	88	27	83	24
Oral Communication	83	26	88	29	82	23
Writing	85	40	91	50	87	43
5. Placement Tests in:						
Mathematics	95	98	95	74	89	82
English	95	97	88	79	89	79
Reading	93	89	78	52	71	52
Other Skills	75	38	59	34	64	36
6. Pre- and Post-Tests:						
Remedial	85	69	78	63	67	58
7. Value-Added Measures	62	9	80		64	9

Notes:
1. Opinions of campus administrators (percentage agreeing with each type). Weighted survey data from 365 institutions (125 two-year, 71 baccalaureate colleges, and 165 universities).
2. Either for all or some students.

Note: "Appropriate Method" refers to the proportion of administrators surveyed who felt the method in question was appropriate for their institution.

Source: Elaine El-Khawas, *Campus Trends, 1986* (Washington, D. C.: American Council on Education, 1986).

investment in college education. This "value added" assessment program means taking into account prior learning and student characteristics, involving some form of pre- and posttesting. The major argument in favor of value-added assessment is that students enter college today from widely varying socioeconomic and educational backgrounds, and it is not enough to assess what they know when they leave the college environment, but to assess their progress. This view asks, Where was the student at the beginning of the college experience and where is the student when he or she exits that experience?

At this point in history there appears to be little consensus among these three points of view about overall collegiate assessment practices and the uses of the results. However, there does seem to be growing agreement that programs that assess individual student learning should target four primary areas of concern: cognitive development, skill development, attitudinal development, and after-college performance.

There is broad agreement that basic-skills placement tests must be used to screen students into appropriate programs, and such testing is currently standard practice in most colleges and universities. But after that, assessment practices and tests currently in use are widely varied. Assessment preaching seems to be well ahead of assessment practices.

Unfortunately the term "assessment" has become synonymous with testing in the minds of many. Here are just a few examples of other assessment indicators:

Access Assessment Indicators

1. The number of students completing certificate and degree programs based upon initial college entry aspirations.
2. Overall institutional student retention rate.
3. Percent of feeder high school graduates attending college.
4. Proportion of students from low-income families attending college.
5. Student opinions about the registration and course placement process.

Quality Assessment Indicators

1. Analysis of student academic achievement and progress.
2. Analysis of student affective development.

3. Analysis of job placement rates.
4. Securing opinions about program quality from students, alumni, and employers.
5. Analysis of performance after transfer from a two- to four-year college or from a four-year college to graduate school.

In the Carnegie study of the undergraduate experience, Ernest Boyer made this observation about assessment:

> In the measuring of college outcomes we reject paper and pencil tests that focus on simple recall and measure that which matters least. Rather, a quality undergraduate college is concerned about outcomes that transcend what students derive form separate courses. Students need to think clearly, be well informed, be able to integrate their knowledge, and know how to apply what they have learned.[18]

Recognizing the limitations of assessment and the responsibility of colleges and universities to ascertain quality, presents higher education with a challenge for the next decade. Whether higher education leaders trivialize or deify assessment processes, diminish or enlarge the assessment effort, or enrich or stultify assessment of learning experiences, one thing is certain: the subject of assessment will not be leaving the higher education scene soon.

Access and Quality: Persistent Tension in Higher Education

The nation has given higher education two agendas: access and quality. Finding the proper balance between these two will likely dominate policy-level discussions about higher education well through the 1990s. The arguments go something like this: Fail at the quality business and colleges will also fail to meet the competitive needs of our country. Fail at the business of access and America will fail to develop its most precious resource, the human resource.

Given the force behind these two agendas, many colleges and universities face a serious contradiction in mission and in priorities. Access and quality are not mutually exclusive. There is a considerable linkage between the two, particularly in open-door colleges. But at the same time, they are not mutually supportive in program priorities, or resource allocation, or public understanding of the college identity. Opening the college doors of opportunity to a diverse array of talent and individuals from a variety of socioeconomic backgrounds is not likely to raise the scores on the Scholastic Aptitude Test or the Graduate Record Examinations.

Since many decision makers and influential observers of the higher education scene view test score results as the priority indicator of quality, that reality must be a starting point for understanding the persistent tension between access and quality. The answer for some educational leaders is to limit sharply who gets into college. If one were assigned the singular task of improving test scores, it could be done quickly and easily by simply limiting the number and kind of individuals who take the tests. Test scores would rise overnight and the particular educational elixirs advocated by that leader or that college might be acclaimed as the panacea for all the ills of higher education. Fortunately, most education and political leaders have rejected push-button accountability in the search for quality. Political pronouncements about test results are not likely to improve the quality of higher education. Rather, the word gets around and such political rhetoric tends to close the college doors for many uncertain and unsure individuals who have not experienced much success in education.

One of the most insightful comments on high admission standards and emphasis upon prestige comes from British educator Michael Brock:

> Taking into account the fact that the drop-out and failure rates are minuscule in a university such as Oxford, and very low by international standards throughout British higher education ... many British employers seem almost skeptical about the country's higher education.... In short, people are saying: "It may be a high class product; but it is not the product we need."[19]

Even the language of educators adds to the tension between

access and quality. It is not uncommon to hear school and college personnel talk about the pursuit of excellence as though excellence were an object to be caught. The dictionary indicates that the word "pursue" means to follow for the purpose of overtaking, or capturing, or chasing something. How many leaders in higher education are breathless from chasing an elusive goal called "excellence"?

Perhaps a less sophisticated but more descriptive word like "cultivate" would be more appropriate for the decade ahead. The word "cultivate" means to prepare for growth, to improve the growth of something by labor and attention. Is higher education primarily a process of pursuing the academically talented and sorting them out from the not-so-academically-talented? Can one definition of "excellence" be applicable for all aspects of higher education and for all students? Rather, is not higher education in a democratic society a process of empowering people and helping as many individuals as possible grow to their full potential?

Whether a college stresses the liberal arts over professional courses, whether the curriculum is upside down with career courses coming first in the sequence, or whether the students are old or young, black or white, full time or part time, is not the crucial issue in helping individuals develop their full potential. What does matter is how faithfully the college community cultivates excellence, and systematically involves the whole college in seeking the best in students. If colleges and universities cannot, or will not, assess student outcomes and institutional effectiveness, and if the United States does not fully develop its human resources, we become a wasteful society regardless of what else we do. It cannot be access or quality in American higher education in the decades ahead, it must be both, and for better or worse it will be both. This observation means that assessment will vary depending upon the mission of the institution. It will be necessary to develop access indicators of effectiveness as well as quality indicators.

Dateline 2000 Forecast

1. There will not be one set of indicators that will fit all of higher education institutions any more than one suit of clothes will fit all sizes and shapes of individuals. During the decade of the 1990s different sets of effectiveness indicators will be developed for different types of colleges, and so recognized by the media and political decision makers.

2. Student outcome assessment practices will be separated in the assessment debate from institutional effectiveness indicators.

3. Institutional effectiveness measures will be separated between access indicators and quality indicators. Examples of access indicators might include an analysis of the proportion of ethnic minority individuals enrolling in colleges, retention and graduation rates. Examples of quality indicators might include student surveys a year or so after graduation, or program completions, or employer surveys.

4. It will become the norm for student outcome and student success measures to be developed by surveying and analyzing attitudes and goals of students entering college, following student progress toward these goals, and developing attitudinal, occupational, and educational follow-up information after the student leaves the college. As an example, by examining the attitudes and records of students after receiving bachelor's degrees from four-year colleges, researchers might provide some much-needed insight into the contributions of community colleges to baccalaureate degree education.

5. The role of the institutional researcher will be greatly strengthened and enhanced in colleges and universities, providing much better information to be fed into the planning process. Answers to key collegiate questions often rest upon spurious assumptions because of inadequate data collection and analysis.

6.   Assessment will be taken seriously on and off the campus as assessment findings are reflected in collegewide decisions about the budget, academic policies, and program priorities.

7.   As colleges and universities develop better and more universal indicators of institutional effectiveness, and more reliable student-success tracking systems, the political decision makers and public opinion molders will move away from the current emphasis upon testing.

8.   Testing will again become a tool for faculty to utilize in assessing student progress and/or program success. The program evaluation experience of the faculty at the University of Tennessee, Knoxville, will become widely recognized and utilized by all college faculty, whereby item analysis of student performance on locally designed major field examinations have led to many faculty-initiated changes in curriculum structure, course content, and teaching approaches.

9.   Accrediting bodies, through the self-study process, will move with considerable speed in the 1990s toward implementing a full-blown institutional effectiveness-assessment accreditation process. Work on this is already well under way in various parts of the country.

10. Colleges and universities all across the country are beginning to institutionalize the assessment process, to gather hard evidence that the college mission is being accomplished, to utilize the outcomes assessment information to make a difference in the delivery of educational services, and to communicate the assessment information effectively to the external audiences.

Executive Summary

Tradition in higher education has pinned the blue ribbon upon those colleges and universities with the toughest admission standards, the most Ph.D.'s among the faculty, and the greatest financial resources. These are known as "quality" colleges. However, an increasing volume of decision makers are rejecting that approach and calling for colleges and universities to discuss student outcomes rather than inputs when talking about quality. Specifically, many people are asking about the institutional impact upon student learning. What value has been added to the life of the student?

Will the value-added student learning assessment program emerge as a key instrument for colleges to prove their comparative worth in the 1990s? Is the college degree a quality-assurance credential for employers? Do universities increasingly view completion of the associate degree as an important credential for transfer to the upper division?

There is persistent tension between access issues and quality issues in the discussions about the effectiveness of higher education institutions. The public seems to be caught between these polemic arguments, unable to make solid judgments about the quality of the college and university product.

Politicians are responding to funding pressures and public questions by pushing for more accountability in the higher education enterprise. For many leaders the accountability problem can be handled by developing more and better tests to assess student achievement.

Educational leaders are taking the accountability questions seriously and are developing many new and innovative approaches to assess student outcomes and to determine institutional effectiveness. There are no simple approaches, nor can there be push-button accountability, but answers are being framed and college assessment practices and procedures significantly changed and improved.

The strength of the American higher education system is that its diversity nearly guarantees access to a college or university somewhere in the country. A glaring weakness is that with all that diversity quality is variable, difficult to assess, and even more

164

difficult to describe. In this diverse system of colleges and universities, institutional effectiveness measures will relate more to institutional mission and student population standards than will any national testing program.

Notes

1.   Betsy Jane Becker, review of *The Case Against the SAT*, by James Crouse and Dale Trusheim, *Thought & Action* (Spring 1989).
2.   *Parade* (4 June 1989).
3.   American Association of Community and Junior Colleges, statistical reports, 1989.
4.   U. S. Department of Education, National Center for Education Statistics, *The Condition of Education, 1989* (Washington, D. C.: GPO, 1989).
5.   American Association of Community and Junior Colleges, Policy Statement on Access, adopted 1987.
6.   American Association of Community and Junior Colleges, *Statistical Yearbook of Community, Technical, and Junior Colleges 1987/88* (Washington, D. C.: American Association of Community and Junior Colleges, 1987).
7.   *Statistical Yearbook.*
8.   College Entrance Examination Board, Advisory Panel on the Scholastic Aptitude Test Score Decline, *On Further Examination* (New York: College Entrance Examination Board, 1977).
9.   Terrel H. Bell, *The Thirteenth Man: A Reagan Cabinet Memoir* (New York: Free Press, 1988).
10.   U. S. Department of Education, National Commission on Excellence in Education, *A Nation at Risk: The Imperative for Educational Reform* (Washington, D. C.: GPO, 1984).
11.   Ernest Boyer, *College: The Undergraduate Experience in America* (New York: Harper & Row, 1987).
12.   American Association of Community and Junior Colleges, Commission on the Future of Community Colleges, *Building Communities: A Vision for a New Century* (Washington, D. C.: American Association of Community and Junior Colleges, 1988).
13.   John E. Roueche and George A. Baker, *Access and Excellence: The Open-Door College* (Washington, D. C.: Community College Press, 1987).
14.   Charles J. McClain, *In Pursuit of Degrees With Integrity: A Value-Added Approach to Undergraduate Assessment* (Washington, D. C.: American Association of State Colleges and Universities, 1984).

15. Dan Angel, "The Academic Skills Program," unpublished paper, 1989.

16. Council on Postsecondary Accreditation, *Educational Quality and Accreditation: A Call for Diversity, Continuity and Innovation* (Washington, D. C.: Council on Postsecondary Accreditation, 1986).

17. Southern Association of Colleges and Schools, *Resource Manual on Institutional Effectiveness* (Decatur, Ga.: Southern Association of Colleges and Schools, 1989).

18. Boyer, *College: The Undergraduate Experience.*

19. Michael Brock, "Who Gets to the University," unpublished paper, 1986.

Chapter VI

Revitalizing Civic Learning

I know no safe depository of the ultimate powers of society but the people themselves; and if we think them not enlightened enough to exercise their control with a wholesome discretion, the remedy is not to take it from them, but to inform their discretion by education.

Thomas Jefferson
Letter to William Jarvis
September 28, 1820

I f one agrees with Thomas Jefferson that for democracy to work
education is essential, then education at all levels has an awe-
some responsibility. But why not just leave the matter of civic
education to the elementary and secondary schools? After all, isn't
that where our society educates the mass of our population? Furthermore, isn't the tired old "civics" instruction out-of-date and less
important than the other more sophisticated interests of higher
education?

There are at least five major reasons as to why colleges and
universities of all kinds will give new priority attention to the subject
of civic learning and civic responsibility in the decade ahead: (1)
citizen alienation from their leaders and distrust of government at all
levels has increased significantly over the past twenty-five years; (2)
the civic knowledge of the U. S. population has declined to a level
that weakens the fabric of our democratic society; (3) the teachers of
tomorrow, the college students of today, must have a clear, coherent
conceptual framework and point of reference regarding the problems of public policy determination and the service obligations of a
citizen in a democratic society; (4) experiential service learning is
finding a new priority place in higher education; (5) education for
citizenship in a complex democratic society must become a lifelong
process.

Colleges and universities have a special obligation to educate the policymakers of our democratic society, and a parallel
obligation to systematically provide lifelong civic learning programs for adults. How well this is accomplished could, at least in
part, determine the future civic and political health of our nation.

Citizen Confidence and Efficacy

Over the past twenty years citizen alienation has substantially increased. A significant percentage of the American popula-

Percent of the American Population with
High Confidence Ratings in Leaders

Leadership Groups	1966	1973	1986
The Military	61		36
Colleges	61		34
Medicine	73		33
Supreme Court	50		32
Organized Religion	41		22
Congress	42		21
Local Government		29	21
State Government		22	19
The Press	30		19
The White House		18	19
Executive Branch	41		18
Major Companies	55		16
Law Firms		24	15
Labor Unions	22		11

Percent of American Population Feeling Loss of Efficacy

General Feeling of Powerless (Alienation from the power structure)	29		60
What I think does not count much any more	37		60

Source: Louis Harris, *Inside America* (New York: Vintage Books, 1987).

tion do not have much confidence in our nation's social, business, education, and government leaders. The Lou Harris public opinion polls of 1966, 1973, and 1986 reveal a dramatic loss of confidence in leaders of all kinds over a twenty-year period. Even though college leaders, and higher education in general, stand at the top of the confidence scale at 34 percent, they are well below their peak of 61 percent recorded twenty-four years ago.

It is significant that all leadership groups fell so far below the confidence marks of a quarter of a century ago. Nearly two out of three adults in the population indicate a sense of powerlessness and feel alienated from the power leaders of the country. This alienation seems to stem from a feeling that there are two levels for justice. The rich and powerful seem to "get away" with things for which others are penalized.

An "attitude" study of American youth conducted by Peter D. Hart Research Associates provides a detailed look at young people's (ages fifteen through twenty-four) values and goals, their ideas about citizenship, and their interest in civic learning. In reviewing the survey results, Arthur J. Kropp, president of People For the American Way, the organization that commissioned the study, said:

> This study sounds the alarm for America's democracy. It paints a troubling portrait of a generation that is—for very understandable reasons—turned off and tuning out politics and citizen participation. . . . Politicians, the media and all Americans need to take a good look at our failure to get our young people thinking positively about our political process. Our neglect is chipping away at the very foundation of our democracy: our next generation's preparedness to take on the awesome task of self-government.[1]

Among the study findings:

- When asked to describe a good citizen, most young people neglected to name any citizenship responsibilities beyond being honest, a good friend, trustworthy. Only 12 percent of the youth surveyed volunteered voting as a basic tenet of good citizenship.
- When asked to grade the importance of various life goals on a scale of one to ten, less than a quarter (24 percent) highlighted being involved in helping in the community. When asked if they had ever volunteered for any community service, nearly two out of three young people said no. Sixty percent said they probably would not volunteer to work in a political campaign. At the same time of these

negative findings, an overwhelming 89 percent of the youth said they would support a community service program in a high school that offers extra credit to students who volunteer.

- Nearly two out of three young people said they know "just some" or "very little" about the way our government works. An overwhelming 70 percent of the students felt that "sometimes politics and government seem so complicated that a person like me can't really understand what's going on."

College students have similar attitudes as the younger people, and have moved from a sense of involvement in 1966 to a sense of indifference, detachment, and mistrust. This attitude is best illustrated in the decline in numbers of eighteen- through twenty-four -year-olds voting in elections. Since 1971, when the eighteen-year-olds gained the constitutional right to vote in federal elections, there has been a dramatic decline in the eighteen- to twenty-year-old voter participation. In 1972, 58 percent of the eighteen- to twenty-year-olds reported that they had registered to vote in the presidential election, and that fell to 47 percent in 1984. But even more dramatic, in 1972, 48 percent of this age group reported they had actually voted for president, and this fell to 36 percent in 1984. This means that in 1984 less than half of the eighteen- to twenty-year-olds had even bothered to register to vote, and nearly two out of three of those registered failed to exercise their voting franchise for president of the United States.[2]

It is shocking in examining the Harris poll and related information that citizen confidence in, and knowledge of, state and local government is so low. The government closest to the people, the government they rub shoulders with every day, seems distant and unresponsive to a majority of the people. Have textbooks and teachers paid so much attention to the federal government that students gain little knowledge of their local justice system, or local tax system, or state governance issues? Isn't it paradoxical that 92 percent of the seventeen-year-olds could correctly locate the Soviet Union on a map of Europe, but only 36 percent could find the region on a U. S. map of the territory acquired from Mexico in a war?

174

The voter turnout in local and state government elections is almost always lower than the turnout in a national election. Voting in our democratic government is considered the fundamental act of self-governance. The citizen is provided an opportunity to make a judgment and to express a choice. Yet, a pitifully small minority of citizens choose to participate in local government elections.

Here are a few key questions for education leaders at all levels to consider: How long can our country, including colleges and universities, continue to ignore one hundred million adults who say they feel alienated from their leaders and the organizations they represent? How long can we ignore the problems of voter apathy among young people? Are we as a nation becoming civically illiterate and uninterested in public policy issues? What responsibility do colleges and universities have to educate for citizenship and for improved civic learning?

It has become painfully obvious that even though we share in the benefits and rights of local community life and our democratic society, we feel little overall responsibility to participate in the political process. But more importantly, the majority of our citizens do not seem to even understand the basic foundation principles of the United States government.

What Do They Know and Value?

The most extensive assessment of learning among young people has been conducted by the National Assessment of Educational Progress in 1969, 1972, 1982, and 1986. Tests on history and literature were administered in 1986 to a large sample (8,000) of seventeen-year-old students across the country. These are the folk who will be aged thirty or thirty-one in the year 2000.

In most cases these students were taking, or had recently taken, courses in U. S. history and American government, which are normally given in the junior year of high school. Keep two facts about these tests in mind: First, the test was given to in-school students. This means that we do not have a gauge for what that host of high school dropouts may know. Second, the test was offered to students who are one year away from voting age and exercising their basic civic rights and responsibilities.

Out of the 141 questions about history and civics learning knowledge, the national average was 54.5 percent correct answers. Out of the 141 questions, 19 probed for knowledge of the United States Constitution, important amendments, and Supreme Court decisions interpreting the Constitution. With an average score of 54.4 percent correct on the Constitution, students scored above 80 percent on only two questions.[3]

Top Five Civic Learning Scores

1. Thomas Jefferson was the main author of the Declaration of Independence?- 84.4%
2. Guarantee of free speech and religion is found in the Bill of Rights? - 81.3%
3. Abraham Lincoln wrote the Emancipation Proclamation? - 68.0%
4. The Declaration of Independence marked the colonies break with England? - 67.6%
5. *Brown* decision of 1954 ruled school segregation unconstitutional? - 63.7%

Bottom Five Civic Learning Scores

1. Reconstruction refers to readmission of Confederate states after the Civil War? - 21.4%
2. Magna Carta is the foundation of the British parliamentary system? - 30.6%
3. The Articles of Confederation failed to provide adequate taxing power? - 36.8%
4. The Three Fifths Compromise in the Constitution defined the status of slaves? - 37.7%
5. The Emancipation Proclamation freed slaves in the Confederacy? - 38.2%

It becomes quickly apparent that the seventeen-year-old knowledge of some key civic learning principles is inadequate. As an example, a basic concept in our federal government is the system of checks and balances that divides power among the three branches

176

of government, yet two out of five students (40 percent) could not answer correctly the question "Checks and balances divides power among branches of the federal government?" Only about half of the students could identify the statement "Give me liberty or give me death" with Patrick Henry. Less than half (43.8 percent) understood that the Constitution divides powers between states and the federal government.

In a 1988 unpublished study by Clifford Adelman of the Office of Educational Research and Improvement of the U. S. Department of Education, it is revealed that college students who take the Graduate Record Examinations do poorly on the political science speciality subject tests. The math and science scores have been going up, but political science scores are now the lowest mean scores of any of the specialty subject tests. So, the problem with civic learning is not just the problem of the schools but also of colleges and universities.

One of the most precious words in the English language is "liberty." The events of Tiananmen Square in Beijing, China, galvanized attention on the subject of liberty as have few other events in recent history. The brutal oppression by the Chinese government of the students seeking only a few freedoms, and the opening of the Berlin Wall, that dramatic movement of people in Eastern Europe toward freedom, have caused some reflection upon our own system of government.

Liberty is the foundation stone of the United States government that all citizens must feel and understand. It was the aim of the founders of the country to emphasize liberty by limiting the power of leaders. The basic principle was brilliantly established in two ways: by listing certain political liberties (or rights) that leaders cannot abridge, and by establishing constitutional checks and balances.

The health and vigor of our democracy depend in large measure upon the ability of schools, colleges, and universities to transmit to each new generation the political vision of liberty and equality that unites the nation. It goes beyond knowledge, to commitment, and it is not commitment to some kind of propaganda or knee-jerk patriotism, but a commitment based upon factual knowledge that has been critically analyzed. Ernest Boyer has stated the challenge this way:

> The undergraduate experience at its best will move the student from competence to commitment.... Our abiding hope is that, with determination and effort, the undergraduate college can make a difference in the intellectual and personal lives of its graduates, in the social and civic responsibilities they are willing to assume, and ultimately in their world perspective.[4]

It might be useful if more college students attended a citizenship naturalization ceremony. Persons seeking United States citizenship repeat the Pledge of Allegiance and take an oath to support our Constitution. Those of us who are second-, third-, and fourth-generation Americans take the rights and responsibilities outlined in our Constitution for granted. It is sad, but true, that most new citizens in our country have a better grasp of civic knowledge than do the native-born Americans. It might be important for all students to review the oath of American citizenship from time to time.

Oath of American Citizenship

> I hearby declare, on oath, that I absolutely and entirely renounce and adjure all allegiance and fidelity to any foreign prince, potentate, state, or sovereignty of whom or which I have heretofore been a subject or citizen; that I will support and defend the Constitution and laws of the United States of America against all enemies, foreign and domestic; that I will bear true faith and allegiance to the same; that I will bear arms on behalf of the United States when required by law; that I will perform work of national importance under civilian direction when required by law; and that I will take this obligation freely without any mental reservation or purpose of evasion; so help me God.

Teacher Education and Civic Learning

Probably the most influential report completed in the 1980s on how to "fix" teacher education was the Holmes Report developed by a group of deans of colleges of education who began meeting in 1983 to consider how best to reform teacher education. Their report, issued in 1986, was widely accepted, and by the end of 1986 over one hundred schools and colleges of education had joined in a coalition to work toward implementing the report's recommendations. However, there was little mention in this influential report about the civic learning of future teachers.

The long-range health of the elementary and secondary schools of the nation is inextricably tied to the quality of the teacher coming out of the collegiate teacher education institutions. The concerns of the leaders of teacher education seem to focus, with a few exceptions, on how to improve the instructional competencies of the classroom teacher. The critical public purposes of teacher education, to help schools carry out their civic mission and prepare responsible and knowledgeable citizens for a democratic society, go largely undiscussed in the Holmes Report.

The American Association of Colleges for Teacher Education (AACTE), under the leadership of David Imig, has endeavored to keep the subject of civic learning alive among teacher educators. The November/December 1983 *Journal of Teacher Education* was devoted entirely to the revitalization of civic learning. The AACTE board of directors established a special task force on civic learning, but by and large the recommendations of this group have yet to be implemented in the teacher education institutions.

The cross-campus liberal arts faculties have, for the most part, taken little interest in helping develop the teacher force of the nation. One can only wonder how future teachers gain an understanding of comparative political and economic systems, of physical and human geography, of the beliefs that have shaped our democratic values and culture.

The idea of a liberal education originated largely from the "polis" of democratic Athens and the "civitas" of Rome preparing people to live in a political community. The phrase "liberal education" meant the education of a free man or woman in preparation for citizenship. Benjamin Franklin called for a civic purpose in higher education at the College of Philadelphia. Thomas Jefferson proposed a program of civic arts at the College of William and Mary and the University of Virginia.

The new National Board of Professional Teaching Standards has drawn up a list of tentative categories that will provide the knowledge base of teaching for which national certificates might be issued. There is no mention (at least to date) in this list of what civic learning should be included in the education of teachers.

In the twentieth century the civic learning aspect of liberal education has been reduced by emphasis upon disciplinary specialization. The civic learning purpose of preparing people for their role as citizens has become lost in survey courses, in the narrow interest of the discipline, or in pressures of career preparation. It has only recently moved up into the forefront of discussion about strengthening civic learning in the liberal arts in undergraduate education and developing a core curriculum. The 1990s will likely see the leaders of liberal education coming together with the leaders of teacher education to declare that preparation for citizenship in a democratic society should be a priority goal for schooling, for liberal education, and for teacher education.

There are signs that civic learning is becoming a priority concern of the rank-and-file teacher. The American Federation of Teachers (AFT), in joint sponsorship with Freedom House, a human rights monitoring organization, and the Education Excellence Network of Teachers College, Columbia University, launched an Education for Democracy project. This coalition of interests developed a "Statement of Principles" aimed at strengthening the teaching of democratic values. This document has been endorsed by over 150 prominent citizens and has received broad praise from teachers. The AFT calls for the development of new approaches to pre-service and in-service teacher education to help teachers present a revamped social studies curriculum built around a core of history and geography.

Service Learning

It has been said that we are living in an information-rich but experience-poor society, and that is ever so true in education at all levels. In the agricultural age, and to some extent in the industrial era, people received most of their information from books, teachers, neighbors, and churches, but they were also involved in all kinds of experiences. Most children had chores at home and most had a pretty fair idea about the work of a mother or father.

Today we live in a society where we are overloaded with

information. Children have little real understanding of the work of their father or mother, and they see the brutal scenes of murder and terrorism before they have experienced the loss of a pet dog. When they enter a classroom they are confronted with more information that is generally less interesting than the information on television, on videotapes, or on the new interactive compact discs.

The challenge for educators at all levels is to provide educational experiences that will enable students to relate classroom learning with real life. Can higher education be as rich in experience or in information? There are many leaders in higher education who are answering that question in the affirmative.

Campus Compact is a coalition of nearly 200 college and university presidents working to foster civic and service learning in higher education. Under the leadership of Frank Newman, president of the Education Commission of the States, and President Donald Kennedy of Stanford, Howard Swearer of Brown, and Timothy Healy, formerly of Georgetown University, Campus Compact was established in July of 1986 and headquartered at Brown University with Susan Stroud as the executive director. Newman states the case for the Compact this way:

> The college experience should . . . develop within each student a sense of country and community service and a desire to help others. Patriotism in the best sense means a willingness to believe in and work for improvements in the country. This must not be a by-product of a college education, but a central, urgent, conscious purpose.[5]

The Compact proposes to help colleges and universities address the issue of civic responsibility through the curriculum and through the development of college programs that allow and encourage students to experience civic learning by way of community or national service. Here are a few examples of recent collegiate activity in service learning:

- Martien Taylor, a Yale University student, organized a National Teach-In on Homelessness, which took place on fifty college campuses in the fall of 1987. Students were motivated by this event to initiate new programs for the homeless, to strengthen community commitment for providing more affordable housing, and to be advocates for legislation.

- Georgetown University has developed an English-as-a-second-language program in cooperation with the public schools. The purpose of the program is to involve university students as tutors to provide public school students with general academic assistance, particularly to help students learn English.
- The Lambda Sigma sophomore honor society at Lawrence University in Wisconsin places student volunteers in local literacy programs. Lawrence students work with students from nearby Fox Valley Technical College to assist in learning labs and in the adult basic education program.
- Graduates of Berea College in Kentucky and Mount St. Mary's College in California now receive a diploma that certifies that students have participated in community service activities. These two colleges represent a growing number of colleges requiring community service for graduation.
- Thiel College, a small private liberal arts college in western Pennsylvania, operates a campus-based community service center. Action teams of faculty, students, and community volunteers work together to solve community and regional problems. The Thiel College project stresses involvement in learning, applied academics, civic learning, and community service in a coordinated collegewide program.
- The state of Washington legislature has directed the Higher Education Coordinating Board to establish community service programs employing the use of work-study funds and State Student Incentive Grant funds. Community service programs aimed at literacy, mentoring, and minority student outreach have been developed under this program.
- Brevard Community College in Florida has established a

community service office to coordinate collegewide service learning activities. Students at the college are now involved widely across that region of Florida in literacy programs, youth service programs, and volunteer programs.

- Baylor University has launched a campus chapter of Habitat for Humanity, and scores of other higher education institutions are following suit. The purpose of college habitat chapters is to build simple, decent houses in partnership with low-income families.

- Many states are developing a state version of the national Campus Compact: California Compact, Pennsylvania Compact, Michigan Compact, Wisconsin Compact, Minnesota Compact, and Florida Compact are all in the development stages.

- The Maricopa County Community College District in Phoenix, Arizona, involving seven colleges, has developed a broad-based community service effort. As an example, Rio Salado College has established an adult literacy program in cooperation with the Black Family and Child Services Center.

- A new law passed in the state of Illinois requires the twelve public four-year colleges and universities to provide students with the opportunity to participate in thirty hours of community service each college year. This law also encourages community colleges and private colleges to make similar efforts.

In many ways volunteerism is somehow ingrained into the American character and habits. Literally millions of individuals, about half of the adult population, are involved on a weekly basis in some sort of volunteer service activity. Churches, hospitals, schools, community organizations, and many more all depend upon volunteers. Yet, it is strange that this spirit of volunteerism, indeed the subject of volunteerism, has not found its way into much of the citizenship education programs of schools and colleges. Much is being done, but we have a long way to go, particularly to involve the other half of our society that remain uninvolved.

Educators and lawmakers across the country are sensing a new stirring of interest among college students of all ages in community service activities. College students are increasingly saying that it is easy to get caught up in the nonreal world of a college campus where the individual is surrounded by the same kind of people doing the same kind of things, and where learning is not generally applied to real-life situations.

Since 1961, an estimated 125,000 individuals have served our country around the world as Peace Corps volunteers. It is clear that when people serve others, compassion and commitment begin to become a part of their lives. If you don't believe that, just talk to a Peace Corps alumnus.

By Dateline 2000 it is safe to say there will be some sort of voluntary national community service program involving millions of college students. Our country has enormous needs in caring for the very young and the very old, in education and literacy efforts, and in health programs. These needs are merging with the collegiate community service mission to offer college and university students some rich new ways to apply learning.

The notion of enacting a new federal program to encourage every young person to perform some form of national-community service is also gaining momentum in the U. S. House and Senate. Many bills along this line have been introduced, the latest by Senator Edward Kennedy, chair of the Senate Labor and Human Resources Committee, combining the best features of the numerous community service bills that have been introduced in Congress:

- *Voluntary National Service and Education Demonstration Program (Pell-Garcia).* A $30 million pilot program offering educational benefits, up to $7,200 per year, to a limited number of sixteen- to twenty-five-year-olds enlisting for two years in the military or in state-approved community service programs.
- *Citizenship and National Service Act (Nunn-McCurdy-Kennelly).* A large-scale program of military or civilian service, earning vouchers valued at $10,000 to $12,000 each year for one or two years of military or community service. The vouchers would replace existing federal

student aid. (The Kennelly bill would not affect current programs.)

- *Youth Service Corps Act (Dodd-Panetta-Udall-Martinez)*. Paid opportunities for up to two years of service in conservation or state or community projects, primarily for disadvantaged youth aged fifteen to twenty-five.
- *National Community Service Act (Mikulski-Bonior)*. A National Guard-type program enabling citizens to volunteer for at least three years of community service two weekends a month and two weeks a year, or on a part-time weekly basis. Vouchers worth $3,000 could be used for education, job training, or purchase of a home.
- *Service to America Act (Kennedy-Ford)*. Grants to encourage schools, colleges, and universities and community agencies to create part-time service opportunities for schools and college students and out-of-school youth.

President George Bush announced in the summer of 1989 the establishment of a Points of Light Foundation, a public-private partnership encouraging all Americans to volunteer some time to community service activities. A major part of the foundation effort will be centered in the Youth Engaged in Service (YES) initiative. This program involves motivating young people, up to age twenty-five, in full- or part-time community service, helping to foster a lifetime service ethic and to develop a new sense of civic responsibility.

Civic Education and Lifelong Learning

By Dateline 2000 it is estimated that nearly one-third of the U. S. population will be over the age of fifty. Between the years 1970 and 1986 the over-age-thirty-five group of college students grew from 823,000 to 1,885,000. The over-age-thirty-five students now comprise 16 percent of the college enrollment. Continuing education has become a booming business for colleges and universities. But scant attention has been given to the idea that civic learning is a lifelong responsibility.

As long ago as the early 1920s Walter Lippmann was sending

up warning flares to indicate that public ignorance of increasingly complex civic problems would be democracy's greatest challenge.[6] As political power continues to shift toward older Americans, reflecting demographic changes, will the political and civic choices of Dateline 2000 be made upon the basis of knowledge and understanding? If so, how will this understanding be developed? Painful choices must be made and the gap between civic issues and civic understanding continues to grow wider.

By Dateline 2000 the success of a college or university is likely to be measured, at least in part, by how often its students return to college, and never will that be more important than in the civic education of adults. Will colleges and universities lead the way in civic learning for adults by developing a new adult education "civics" program based upon discussion of public policy and contemporary issues? To date the jury is still out in answering this question.

Leonard Oliver, of the Kettering Foundation, makes this observation:

> As interstitial institutions between secondary schools, that offer pap as "civics," and four year colleges and universities that assume it is the students' personal responsibility to gain the skills necessary for effective participation in civic and public life, the community colleges may be our only educational institution with the mission, resources, and interest to systematically and effectively infuse concepts of civic values and the civic arts into their educational program.[7]

Oliver lays down the gauntlet for all colleges and universities to fulfill the adult education civic learning mission. Of course, many colleges sponsor contemporary-issues lecture series, and occasional weekend seminars, but few have developed coherent civic learning programs for adults.

In 1981 Ernest Boyer and Fred Hechinger recommended a new adult education degree program in civic education, but few colleges have even seriously discussed the proposal:

Specifically, we propose that the nation's colleges and universities become systematically engaged in the civic education of adults. We do not propose that adult education be reduced to endless seminars on world affairs. . . . What we need, perhaps, is a new adult education in civic education . . . to give this new priority the stature and credibility it deserves.[8]

However, all is not bleak in the higher education civic learning endeavor. The Commission on the Bicentennial of the U. S. Constitution, led by former Chief Justice Warren E. Burger, has motivated many colleges and universities to revitalize the study of history and civics. This emphasis upon studying the Constitution has truly been an educational commemoration.[9]

The American Historical Association and the American Political Science Association jointly sponsored Project 87, aimed at improving school and college civic learning. They sponsored conferences, scholarly research, and publications. Other groups like the National Endowment for the Humanities, the National Council for the Social Studies, and the Council for the Advancement of Citizenship (CAC) have contributed in significant ways to the revitalized interest in civic learning and responsibility. The CAC, in particular, holds the promise of doing even more in this area. Under the leadership of Diane Eisenberg, this group is widely representative of over eighty interested and contributing member organizations.

There are many other individuals, such as R. Freeman Butts, professor emeritus of Teachers College, Columbia University, recently a senior scholar of the Kettering Foundation, and a visiting scholar at the Stanford University Hoover Institution, and Ernest L. Boyer, president of the Carnegie Foundation for the Advancement of Teaching, who have kept the civic learning flame burning for many years. Many other organizations have as well, such as the American Federation of Teachers, under the leadership of President Al Shanker, who continues to press for more and better civic learning.

Communities are beginning to question their civic infrastructure, examining everything from community leadership, to citizen participation, to long-range planning efforts, to the complex interaction of people and organizations. This effort, led by the National Civic League (NCL), headquartered in Denver, Colorado, is designed to help a community assess its civic health. The NCL sponsors the All American City program and Civitex, a computer-based set of case studies of successful community problem-solving efforts, and administers the National Civic Index.

The NCL has had extensive experience, and great success, in applying its Civic Index to local communities, and is now beginning to move the process into a broader context involving colleges and universities. The Colorado Community College System is piloting the Civic Index program with Morgan Community College in Fort Morgan and with Morgan County leaders. The significant feature of this project is that it recognizes higher education as an equal partner in assessing the civic infrastructure of a rural county.

There are ten components to the Civic Index and they serve as a description of the types of infrastructure factors that must be present for a community to deal with civic concerns. The Index components include an examination of citizen participation, community leadership, government performance, volunteerism and philanthropy, intergroup relations, civic education, community information sharing, capacity for cooperation and consensus building, community vision and pride, and intercommunity cooperation.

The Index is intended to be a tool local leaders can use for evaluating the civic infrastructure of their community. Colleges and universities have, in this program, an important real-life process providing students with some new kinds of civic learning experiences. So often, civic problems must be resolved in the heat of conflict. Colleges and universities can make significant contributions to civic vision and pride by helping communities solve community issues in a rational problem-solving mode rather than in a crisis situation.

The decade ahead will see colleges and universities of all kinds revitalizing their historic civic learning mission. The responsibilities, as well as the rights of citizens, will be emphasized and activated by student participation in a service learning experience. It is a major force moving across the national landscape.

Dateline 2000 Forecast

1. Three forces will intersect in the 1990s: the needs of children and youth, societal pressures such as the drug crisis and literacy needs, and national self-interest. These pressures will swing the country behind a massive collegiate community service program. Community service will not be required of every eighteen-year-old, as some are predicting, but it will become so popular that nearly all college and university students will have experienced some form of community service activity by Dateline 2000.

2. Colleges and universities, along with the public schools, will launch widely successful efforts revitalizing interest in civic education for all students.

3. Service learning will become commonplace in college and university degree requirements, with long-lasting impact and profound benefit to the nation.

4. Liberal arts faculties and teacher education faculties will work together to design new interdisciplinary courses, or series of courses, aimed at improving the civic learning of future teachers.

5. Many colleges and some universities will design and offer new civic education degree programs aimed at the adult population.

6. College and university students will be actively engaged in helping communities across the nation examine their civic infrastructure by utilizing the Civic Index.

7. By Dateline 2000 the civic learning of students at all levels will have made significant improvements.

8. As schools, colleges, and universities give greater emphasis to civic learning, the Roper Confidence/Efficacy Poll of Dateline 2000 will move upward to approximate those of the 1966 ratings.

9.   The voter turnout of the eighteen- to twenty-four-year-old age group will move upward as colleges and universities make great efforts to register students and mount voter turnout campaigns among students.

10.   Volunteerism will increase among all ages of the population.

Executive Summary

As the United States is celebrating the bicentennial of the Constitution, a strange unease has spread across the land about the quality of civic learning in schools, colleges, and universities. The voices of criticism are being heard and the citizenship education reform forces are building new strength. Colleges and universities are giving new priority attention to the subjects of civic learning and community service.

Citizens' alienation from their leaders and a general distrust of government at all levels, along with a general decline of civic knowledge among young people, have motivated many leaders and many interested organizations to mount campaigns to improve civic learning in schools, colleges, and universities.

Teacher education institutions are moving out to improve the civic learning of teachers and looking for ways to better fulfill their historic civic education mission in the preparation of teachers.

New attention is also being given to adult and continuing education civic learning programs. Formal and informal "civics" courses and programs are being developed to help adults gain knowledge and understanding about the complex political issues of our times.

Service learning, whereby college students participate in community and/or national service programs, is gaining ground each year. It is likely that a voluntary community-national service program will become the law of the land during the 1990s.

Notes

1.   People For the American Way, *Democracy's Next Generation* (Washington, D. C.: People For the American Way, 1989).
2.   U. S. Department of Commerce, Bureau of the Census, *Statistical Abstract of the United States, 1989* (Washington, D. C.: GPO, 1989).
3.   Diane Ravitch and Chester E. Finn, Jr., *What Do Our Seventeen-Year-Olds Know? A Report on the First National Assessment of History and Literature* (New York: Harper & Row, 1987).
4.   Ernest Boyer, *College: The Undergraduate Experience in America* (New York: Harper & Row, 1987).
5.   Frank Newman, *Higher Education and the American Resurgence* (Princeton: Carnegie Foundation for the Advancement of Teaching, 1985).
6.   Walter Lippmann, *Public Opinion* (New York: Harcourt-Brace, 1922).
7.   Leonard P. Oliver, "Teaching Civic Value and Political Judgment in the Community College," in *Colleges of Choice: The Enabling Impact of the Community College,* ed. Judith Eaton (New York: Macmillan, 1988).
8.   Ernest Boyer and Fred Hechinger, *Higher Learning in the Nation's Service* (Princeton: Carnegie Foundation for the Advancement of Teaching, 1981).
9.   For additional information on the study of the U. S. Constitution, see *Selected Bibliography on the Constitution,* Commission on the Bicentennial of the U. S. Constitution, 808 17th Street NW, Washington, D. C. 20006.

Chapter VII

They Aren't Acting Their Age

College education is being reshaped by the forces of limited financing, economic change, shifts in life-style and life expectations, and the demographics of our population. At the same time, a call is emerging for new leaders with new ideas to adapt our institutions to changing external forces.

Judith Eaton
Vice President
American Council on Education

I mages in the mind form the reality for most of us. This is certainly true with certain phrases like "college student." The national media tends to image a college student as an individual about twenty years old, going to college full time, living on campus in a sorority, fraternity, or dormitory, and preparing for a career in one of the professions. This image is accurate for some college students but not for the majority of college students today.

As an example, a *USA Today* news article stated, "A sharp decline in high school graduates completing college in four years is raising the specter that the USA's education level is falling for the first time."[1] This observation is based upon follow-up surveys conducted by the U. S. Department of Education on high school graduates (this ignores the millions of high school dropouts who pass the GED tests) of the classes of 1972 and 1980. In this study it was found that approximately 24 percent of the class of 1972 had obtained a college bachelor's degree, while only 19 percent of the class of 1980 had done so. While some of this difference may be explained by variations in the methodologies used to survey the two graduating classes, other factors were at work. The vast majority of college students today find it financially necessary to work full time or part time while attending college. Much to their credit, college students have developed their own scholarship program called W. O. R. K. As a consequence there are many more college students attending college classes on a part-time basis and completing a baccalaureate degree program in nine or ten years. Furthermore, the "stop-out" phenomenon is more extensive than ever before. Fewer and fewer college students attend only one college or go by way of a straight line from high school to college to obtain a bachelor's degree in four years. The typical college student today will attend two or three or more colleges.

In a dramatic twenty-year enrollment shift, today nearly half of all public college students are classified as part-time students.

Public College Enrollments				
Year	Full Time	% Full Time	Part Time	% Part Time
1966	2,967,259	68	1,413,827	32
1976	5,640,169	58	3,672,465	42
1986	5,168,400	53	4,553,174	47
Private College Enrollments				
1966	1,502,512	73	554,879	27
1976	1,762,920	73	645,872	27
1986	1,798,269	70	772,773	30

Source: American Council on Education, *1989-90 Fact Book on Higher Education* (New York: American Council on Education and Macmillan Publishing Co., 1989).

Even in the private colleges, where there are normally more full-time students, there has been some increase of part-time students.

Do these statistics signal an overall decline in the percent of the population holding college baccalaureate degrees, and does that decline signal anything about the quality of the educational program? The answer is an unqualified no to both sides of that question. There has been a steady upward trend of adults earning a bachelor's degree, from 4.6 percent of the adults (twenty-five and over) in 1940 to 20.3 percent in 1988. What will the 1990 census reveal? Experts are predicting a 23 to 24 percent bachelor's degree figure for the over-age-twenty-five population for 1990 when all of the figures are complete. This issue is so complex in terms of college-going behavior that only something like the decade census can give us the facts. It must be noted that even in 1990 three out of four of the adult U. S. population will not hold a bachelor's degree. With the growing demand for higher-level competencies for most of the U. S. workforce, one must ask about the kind of quality higher educational experiences available to this largely neglected majority of the population. However, it is encouraging to note that an increasing number of these adults are finding their way into college classrooms.

The trouble with defining a "college student" today as someone obtaining a baccalaureate degree in four years at the age of twenty-one or twenty-two is that college students are no longer acting their age. Age and time (seat time spent) are no longer reliable predictors of college behavior. An increasing number of young people are going to college part time, while an increasing number of adults (twenty-five and over) are going to college full time.

Respected economists David Breneman and Susan Nelson completely missed this trend toward part-time college attendance in 1981 when they stated:

> In our analysis of the National Longitudinal Study of the High School Class of 1972, we found that only 16 percent of two-year college students enrolled in academic programs had earned a bachelor's degree four and one-half years later, compared to 44 percent who began in a four-year college or university. . . . These findings raise an important question for state educational policy in the 1980s, particularly for those states where excess capacity is anticipated in the higher education system. Should states continue to encourage transfer enrollments in community colleges or instead pursue policies to assist as many full-time degree-seeking students to enroll directly in four-year colleges?[2]

It is not uncommon today for many individuals, particularly those who work part time, to take eight to ten years to complete a college baccalaureate degree program. This trend will grow in the 1990s as people move in and out of the collegiate experience during a lifetime. The age of lifelong learning has indeed arrived.

Answer these two multiple-choice test questions to see if you can determine where to place these "college students":

> Terry is working full time and goes to the local college part time in the evenings and on weekends and lives at home. Is Terry:
>
> a. An eighteen-year-old single male and recent high school graduate?
> b. A thirty-year-old married female?
> c. A forty-year-old divorced female?
> d. A fifty-year-old married male seeking a job change?

Andy is working part time, goes to college full time during the day, and lives off campus in an apartment. Is Andy:

a. An eighteen-year-old single male and recent high school graduate?
b. A thirty-five-year-old female divorcee?
c. A forty-five-year-old married female?
d. A sixty-year-old retired male?

The answer to these two questions should be "all of the above." There simply is not a typical "college student" today. College students come in all sizes, shapes, ages, nationalities, and ethnicity.

College Enrollment by Age
(in thousands)

Age	1972	%	1982	%	1986	%
24 and under	6,553	72.0	7,931	64.4	7,714	61.3
25 and older	2,542	28.0	4,378	35.6	4,788	38.7
Totals	9,095	100.0	12,309	100.0	12,402	100.0

Source: U.S. Department of Commerce, Bureau of the Census, *Statistical Abstract of the United States, 1989.*

The twenty-five-and-older age group in 1986 made up 38.7 percent of the total college student bod, as opposed to 28 percent in the fall of 1972. In terms of sheer numbers, this means that the over-twenty-five-age group increased by 2.2 million students over the fourteen-year period from 1972 to 1986. The increase for the under-twenty-five age group during this same period was 1.1 million students. It is clear that college enrollment increases have been fueled by the baby boomers and others of the adult population returning to college.

More than sixty-one million baby boomers in the U. S. population were between the ages of thirty-five and fifty-four in 1989, and that figure is projected to be over eighty-one million, or nearly one-third of the population by the year 2000. The leading edge of the baby boom generation will then be fifty-three years old and empty-nesters with money and time to spend. Publishers have already figured this aging trend by developing new magazines for the age-thirty-five-plus reader, like *Moxie*, *Lears*, and *Mirabella*.

The percentage of men between the ages of fifty-five and sixty-five who remain in the workforce has fallen from 90 percent in 1960 to 75 percent in 1989. At the same time, more men are living longer and have more free time. All of this means that more and more older people will find their way into college classrooms to train for a new career, to sharpen skills, or just for personal growth and development.

One of the ironies of individuals not acting their age as related to traditional college-going behavior is that an estimated 15 percent of the total community, technical, and junior college enrollment are individuals already holding a college degree. DeAnza College in the Silicon Valley of California reports that 33 percent of its 27,000 students already hold a bachelor's degree or higher.

Henry Brickell, president of Policy Studies in Education, framed the adult education paradox in this tongue-in-cheek way in a 1987 lecture at the Harvard University Institute for the Management of Lifelong Education:

> All graduate schools in the United States are adult schools. If all adults 25 and over withdrew from college tomorrow morning, virtually every graduate school in America would close. . . . It's a curiosity. Adults are widely known to be marginal students with soft interests, rusty skills—not our best. Graduate schools, on the other hand, are known to be our best, our most demanding, taught by our highest prestige, most capable faculty members. What a curiosity that the very best, our most demanding, most challenging programs are dominated by our weakest, most rusty, (largely part-time) marginal students. It could change your mind about what an adult student is.[3]

It appears that community college leaders, in particular, have developed these institutions into colleges that by and large fit the organization to adult lifestyles and learning patterns. While many four-year college and university undergraduate programs still mainstream the adult into the traditional youth-culture college environment, saying in effect that adults must adjust to the university culture rather than ask the university to adjust to adults.

There will be a new definition of "college student" in the decade ahead to include adults as well as young people, those attending part time as well as full time, those employed as well as those preparing for a career, and those developing new competencies as well as those maintaining present competencies. Perhaps it will no longer be necessary for colleges to maintain separate divisions for adult and continuing education classes.

Women in College

The dramatic story in the past fifteen years of higher education enrollment has been the large increase in women over the age of twenty-five attending college classes. The under-age-twenty-five female enrollment grew 70 percent from 1970 through 1985. At the same time, the over-age-twenty-five group jumped 300 percent, from 879,000 to 2,895,000. The over-age-twenty-five group now comprises 45 percent of the female collegiate enrollment. It was about 25 percent in 1970.

While there can be no question that women over the age of twenty-five have helped colleges and universities maintain or increase enrollment over the past ten years, it must be pointed out that the male population aged twenty-five and over has also increased. In 1970 males over age twenty-five made up nearly 30 percent of the collegiate enrollment, and this number increased to 38 percent in 1985.

It appears that the big increase in the over-age-twenty-five female enrollment is about over. The catching-up phase, where older women have been attending college at about twice the rate of men, also seems to be slowing down. But even if the over-age-twenty-five college-going rate of women drops to that of the male population, this will still amount to significant increases, certainly sufficient to balance the drop in the eighteen-to-twenty-four age group.

Where Are the Eighteen-Year-Olds?

Colleges and universities have, for the most part, maintained or increased enrollments during the 1980s, against predictions of declines, by attracting an increasing number of older students to the campuses. By the mid-1990s there will be about as many individuals over the age of twenty-five in the college population as under twenty-five. But for those colleges relying exclusively upon the traditional college-age population of eighteen- to twenty-four-year-olds, they will find severe competition for a decreasing number of people.

Ages 18-20 Population and Projections
(in thousands)

Year	Age 18	Ages 18-24
1980	4,340	30,350
1985	3,692	28,749
1990	3,431	26,140
1991	3,311	25,694
1992	3,187	25,061
1993	3,257	24,699
1994	3,195	24,195
1995	3,299	24,281
1996	3,281	23,511
1997	3,409	23,461
1998	3,610	23,747
1999	3,635	24,183
2000	3,681	25,231

Source: U. S. Department of Commerce, Bureau of the Census, Current Population Reports, Series P-25, No. 1018, 1989.

There were 6.1 million fewer seven- to thirteen-year-olds in 1985 than in 1970. This is a 21 percent decline in the number of individuals who will be turning age eighteen and older in the 1990s. There will be 5.1 million fewer eighteen- to twenty-four-year-olds by the year 2000 than in 1985, with the lowest year coming in 1997. The lowest years for eighteen-year-olds will be between 1992 and 1996.

There is no mystery to the vanishing eighteen-year-olds. The high school graduates of the year 2000 entered the first grade in 1988. Unless significant changes are made in the high school dropout rate, we can predict with fair accuracy how many of the eighteen-year-olds in the 1990s should be attending college. But the competition for them will be fierce.

The military is now developing recruiting strategies, backed by significant dollars, to gain its share of the eighteen-year-old crop each year. Predictions are being made by military leaders that it will be necessary to recruit one of four able-bodied male eighteen-year-olds if the all volunteer military is to be maintained at current levels during the 1990s. Of course, world events, particularly in Eastern Europe, could allow for the reduction of the size of the U. S. military force.

Employers, public and private, are facing significant shortages of workers in most parts of the country. They are increasing their advertising and recruitment efforts, and are attracting many young people who feel making money is more important than college attendance, at least for the moment.

There is increasing competition among colleges, universities, and proprietary schools for the eighteen-year-old market. It is the opinion of some researchers that the current decline in black males attending higher education institutions can be tracked to the increases of student recruitment efforts by proprietary schools offering short-term training, to the military offering good financial incentives along with training and education benefits, and to a workplace suffering from worker shortages.

The New Seniors

In 1980 the median age of Americans moved up to an all-time high of 30.6. It is estimated that by the year 2000 the median age will move up to 36.6 years. The nation is aging rapidly. The older population of those sixty-five and over will increase significantly, from twenty-seven million in 1982 to thirty-five million by the year 2000. The American Association of Retired Persons has an annual budget of $145 million to support its work in Washington, D. C., and in statehouses across the country. It has become one of the most im-

202

portant legislatively powerful groups in the country.

Given the new "gray power" of society at large, colleges and universities are also feeling the impact. Many new programs are springing up on college campuses to better serve the over-age-sixty-five group. The most popular program and probably the best known is the Elderhostel program. It has grown rapidly, with more than 100,000 individuals enrolled in over 800 Elderhostel programs on college campuses in 1985. Many colleges and universities offer free or reduced tuition to persons over sixty-five, encouraging them to enroll in regular colleges classes. Some colleges are establishing special senior citizen programs in nursing homes and at other off-campus locations.

San Joaquin Delta College in Stockton, California, has joined with the Senior Service Agency to offer a low-cost luncheon on campus each day for senior citizens. The luncheon is followed by a schedule of afternoon classes called the Emeritus College. The classes are often designed specifically by the over-age-sixty-five group itself.

The role of higher education in serving an aging population is certainly changing, but as one senior citizen taking college classes said, "I have been waiting all my life to really begin my liberal education . . . and why not? I have gladly paid my taxes to support education all my life for younger people, and now it is my turn."[4]

Ethnicity

Next to age and gender, the most important trend in the changing U. S. population is the growth of the Black, Hispanic, and Asian populations. In 1987 ethnic minorities comprised 22 percent of the overall population; by the year 2000 they will be about 28 percent. New entrants into the workforce by Dateline 2000 will be 43 percent minorities or immigrants, 42 percent female, and 15 percent White males. This statistic, compiled by the Hudson Institute in its study *Workforce 2000*, has been widely misquoted as applying to the total makeup of the workforce. The overall workforce in 2000 will be about 45 percent white males. The Hudson Institute figures are only for new entrants to the workforce.

> The blacks fertility rate is over 30 percent higher than whites and expected to remain so; the rate for Hispanic immigrants is even higher than for blacks. If total immigration averages a million a year between now and 2000, our population then will be 72 percent White American, 13 percent Afro American, 11 percent Hispanic American, and just over 4 percent Asian American and other.[5]

Thirty years ago seventeen workers were supporting the Social Security fund for each retiree. In the year 2000 it is projected that three to four workers will be supporting the fund per each retiree, and most importantly, of those three workers one will be nonwhite. Many observers are saying that if for no other reason than sheer economics, it is increasingly important to pay close attention to the education and socioeconomic condition of the ethnic minority population.

In many of the major city school districts of the nation the minority student population has become the majority student population, but the teaching force remains largely white, and the education achievement of students remains low and uneven. The speed of the changing mix of ethnic minorities in urban schools is breathtaking. The Boston Public Schools have moved in a little over a decade from a 27 percent minority student population to 70 percent. In Texas 46 percent of the public school population is nonwhite, and in California the majority of the elementary school population is now nonwhite. The 1984 birth rate, the lowest in a decade, brings the population change into sharp focus. The birth rate of Whites was 64 per 1,000 females, for Blacks it was 72, and for Hispanics it was 86. Seventeen states plus the District of Columbia now have more than 25 percent ethnic minority enrollment in the public schools. These states are on the eastern seaboard, in the southeast, and in the southwest.

Many colleges and universities, particularly urban colleges, have also experienced a dramatic shift in the ethnic minority enrollment pattern. The Los Angeles City College has gone over a sixty-year period from being a 100 percent white student body to being a rich and balanced ethnic mix of Hispanics, Blacks, Asians, and White students.

Los Angeles City College Enrollment Shifts

This chart dramatically portrays the shifts in the ethnic background of students at the Los Angeles City College during the sixty years of its existence. The influx of new students of widely differing backgrounds presents a significant challenge to urban colleges:

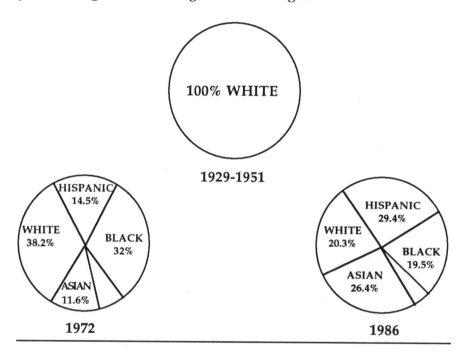

All ethnic minorities are continually increasing their participation in higher education except the black population. In the black population it is the black male participation in higher education that has fallen from 35 percent in 1976 to 27 percent in 1986 for the eighteen- to twenty-four-year-old age group, despite an increasing number of black male high school graduates. The eighteen- to twenty-four-year-old black female participation rate has also fallen, but to a lesser degree, from 32 percent in 1976 to 29 percent in 1986; however, the overall black female participation numbers have remained stable during the decade of the 1980s.

At the same time as a static black student participation in

Statistics on Black Population
Participation in Higher Education

Year	Black High School Graduates		Black Enrollment in Higher Education	
	Female	Male	Female	Male
1976	1,302M	936,000	563,000	470,000
1978	1,384M	956,000	601,000	453,000
1980	1,425M	1,055M	643,000	464,000
1982	1,572M	1,171M	644,000	458,000
1984	1,613M	1,272M	639,000	437,000
1986	1,576M	1,225M	645,000	436,000

Source: American Council on Education, *1989-90 Fact Book on Higher Education* (New York: American Council on Education and Macmillan Publishing Co., 1989).

higher education, the Hispanic, Asian, and Native American populations have significantly increased their enrollment in colleges and universities. In fact, the University of California at Berkeley reports an increase in Asian students, making up 26 percent of the 1987 freshmen class.

Even though much remains to be done, there are many encouraging signs that the education of ethnic minority students is improving. The portion of Black twenty-five- to twenty-nine-year-olds completing four years of college has continually increased to a new high of 15 percent in 1987. The percentage of Black eighteen- to twenty-four-year-olds attending college has increased, with some ups and downs, between 1970 and 1986 from 17 percent to 22 percent. Future gains, particularly for Black and Hispanic males, will depend in large part upon increasing the high school completion rate. The college-going rate for the eighteen- to twenty-four-year-old Hispanic has remained unchanged at 18 percent for the decade of the 1980s.

During the decade of the 1980s the number of Black high school graduates increased, from 69.7 percent in 1980 to 75.6 percent in 1986, while the percentage of White high school graduates remained relatively unchanged. The percentage for Hispanics rose

Participation in Higher Education by Race
(in thousands)

Year	White	Black	Hispanic	Asian	American Indian	Non Resident Alien
1976	9,076	1,033	384	198	76	219
1978	9,194	1,054	417	235	78	253
1980	9,833	1,107	472	286	84	305
1982	9,997	1,101	519	351	88	331
1984	9,815	1,076	535	390	84	335
1986	9,914	1,081	624	448	90	344
Ten Year Percentage Increase 76-86	9%	5%	62%	126%	18%	57%

Source: American Council on Education, *1989-90 Fact Book on Higher Education* (New York: American Council on Education and Macmillan Publishing Co., 1989).

from 54 percent in 1980 to 60 percent in 1986.

The minority enrollment in community, technical, and junior colleges now approximates in most colleges the proportional minority representation in the population at large, with an even larger than proportional representation of Hispanics and Native Americans. Assuming two- and four-year colleges work hard on transfer rates for minority students, this should mean an increasing volume of minority students reaching four-year colleges and universities in the 1990s. Significant attention is being given minority student attendance in college by institutional leaders and national higher education associations, which augurs well for the future.

On the down side, racist attitudes, as characterized by racially motivated incidents occurring in several large cities during the 1980s, can also be found on college and university campuses. Where such racist attitudes and overt actions remain unchallenged, especially if minority students fail to see racial diversity in the faculty, or much of a supportive program, the performance of minority students is damaged. Studies have shown that perceptions of discrimination, poor peer relations, and attitudes of benign neglect from college administrators and faculty are closely related to levels of performance for minority students.[6]

The education of ethnic minorities is beginning to receive the attention of leaders all across the nation, including governors. A 1971 interstate compact agreement established the Southern Growth Policies Board involving the governors of twelve southern states. The compact calls for the board to prepare a statement of regional objectives every six years recommending strategies for solving regional problems. The process for developing this report has become known as the Commission on the Future of the South. The 1986 commission report outlines ten regional objectives, with a priority objective of "strengthening society as a whole by strengthening at-risk families."

Under the leadership of the governor of each state, the commission issued its 1986 report under the title *Halfway Home and a Long Way to Go*. Governor Bill Clinton of Arkansas summarized the 1986 report this way:

> In Hot Springs, Arkansas, twenty-three years ago, as a boy of seventeen I saw Dr. Martin Luther King, Jr. make his "I Have A Dream" speech on television. I will never forget one thing he said that now means more to me than anything else. He said that he hoped one day his four little children would be judged not by the color of their skin but by the content of their character. I would like to see the people who live in my state and in my region be judged by the content of their character, but it will never happen until every child, by dint of his or her effort, can get a decent education and a decent, nationally competitive set of economic opportunities. And that is why we ought to do our best to chart the future of the South in 1986.[7]

The 1990s will likely see significant increases in disadvantaged school-age youth (commonly called at-risk youth), particularly of Black and Hispanic ethnic origins. The Charles Stewart Mott Foundation recently asked MDC, Inc., a private, nonprofit research organization, to conduct a study of how at-risk youth are faring in education today. It concluded that one in three of school-age youth could be called "at risk" because they are at risk of emerging from school unprepared for work of the kind there is to do, or unprepared for college. In too many cases they are prepared only for a permanent underclass life in U. S. society, and the underclass has begun to form: Mean earnings of twenty- to twenty-four-year-old Black male high school dropouts declined 41.6 percent, from $11,210 to $6,552, between 1974 and 1984. The decline for Hispanic background young men for the same period was 38.6 percent.

At the same time the at-risk population is increasing, the Bureau of Labor Statistics is predicting that by the mid-1990s the large majority of good jobs will require some form of education and/or training beyond high school. Bluntly put, the United States must rapidly find some new, more effective ways to educate and to train the at-risk population of this country. It is likely there will be a job for anyone who wants to work in the 1990s, if he or she is qualified. The key current question is, how will that person become qualified?

Ethnic Minority Leaders

There is an increasing number of well-educated and politically sophisticated Black and Hispanic leaders emerging across the country. In 1988 there were nearly 300 Black mayors in U. S. cities, up from 240 in 1970. The 1989 elections of a Black governor in the southern state of Virginia, a Black mayor of New York City, a Black mayor of Seattle, Washington, and a Hispanic mayor of Miami, Florida, have broken down the racial barriers in the world of politics probably forever.

The groundbreaking character of the 1989 elections sets the stage for the development of a new political mosaic, blurring the racial colors of the 1980s with new color patterns. Minority citizens are increasingly representing as broad a socioeconomic range as the remainder of the population. Blacks in particular are increasingly moving from the inner cities to the suburbs as they move higher into the economic mainstream.

College Child Day Care

A related question to the education of ethnic minorities and who attends college today is the question of who cares for the children while mom or dad is attending college classes? In a survey of 278 mayors and city managers conducted by the National League of Cities, child care was listed as the number one 1984 concern. Mayor James Moran of Alexandria, Virginia, states the situation this way:

> It's not that women want to be out to work or that men don't want to stay home. Nobody has that option any-more. Anybody who is educated and able to fill a job really has to fill that job to maintain his or her place in society. It's becoming something of a crisis. . . . It's going to get worse. There will be very few women with high school degrees, or college degrees, who are not going to be working full-time. And already, 45% of the need for licensed child-care slots is not being met. People are putting their children into deficient situations. They find relatives, friends, or who-ever they can out of necessity, but it's not what they want for their children and, often, it's not what their children need.[8]

Colleges and universities all across the country are establish-ing child care and early childhood development centers to help solve the child care problem for parents attending college classes. By the year 2000 predictions are that two out of every three families, ac-counting for ten to eleven million children under the age of six, will have working mothers outside the home.

Some Facts to Ponder

Here are some demographic trends and facts to ponder when considering the demographic forces that will impact higher educ-tion in the 1990s.

- All who will be in colleges and universities by the year 2000 are alive today.

210

- Twenty-seven percent, or one out of four, of high school students do not currently complete their high school program. That figure has remained fairly constant for the past twenty-five years. If this rate continues, some ten to eleven million students will not complete the high school program during the decade of the 1990s.
- Conservative estimates place the number of adults who are unable to functionally read or write at about twenty million individuals.
- The national college-going rate of recent high school graduates has remained nearly constant, at 34 percent, over the past twenty years, with the female rate increasing and the male rate decreasing.
- The number of individuals eighteen to twenty-four years old will decline from 30.3 million in 1980 to 25.2 million in the year 2000. This is a loss of five million college-going-age students over a twenty-year period.
- The number of forty-five- to fifty-four-year-olds will increase during the 1990s by 46 percent, from 25.4 million in 1990 to 37.2 million in 2000. This is an increase of 12.1 million individuals in this age category in one decade.
- It is now estimated that 70 to 75 percent of all job classifications will require some form of postsecondary education or training for entry by the mid-1990s.

A Diverse Enterprise

The American education enterprise is large and incredibly diverse. Over 25 percent of people in the United States are students, or employed by the schools, colleges, and universities. The sheer size and scope of the U. S. enterprise makes it difficult to understand and even more difficult to effect changes. American schools and colleges operate almost upon the "cottage industry" basis. Decision making is widely dispersed among 112,000 different publicly and privately operated schools and colleges. Thus, the problem of marketing new ideas and exemplary practices to the U. S. educational institutions is compounded by a highly decentralized deci-

The U. S. Education Enterprise

Education Population	1987-88 Number
Number of Students	
Elementary and secondary	45,900,000
Postsecondary	12,544,000
Teaching Staff	3,352,000
Nonteaching Staff	3,500,000
Total Education Participants	65,296,000
Total U. S. Population	244,100,000

Source: U. S. Department of Education, National Center for Education Statistics, *The Condition of Education, 1989.*

sion-making process. An estimated sixty-five million students and staff are scattered throughout a greatly diversified system of educational institutions, including public, private, and proprietary schools, colleges, and universities, plus day care centers, nursery schools and kindergarten, vocational schools, graduate schools, seminaries, and research centers.

Local control is the hallmark insignia of education in the United States. Fifty states and a myriad of schools and colleges have the most to say about all facets of education. Education is pluralistic in terms of governance, curricula, and decision making. Even the academic calendar in colleges and universities is not uniform. About one-half of the institutions are on an early semester system, one-fourth on the quarter system, and the other quarter use a scattering of different systems, like the 4-1-4 plan.

Some 83,000 public elementary and secondary schools are operated by 15,700 school districts or separate governing bodies. Approximately 25,600 elementary and secondary schools were privately operated in the 1985-86 school year. There were 3,389 public and private colleges and universities in the 1986-87 college year, enrolling 12.3 million students, staffed by 750,000 full- and part-time faculty members. In addition to colleges and universities, an estimated 8,956 privately operated postsecondary institutions of all kinds and descriptions were operating in 1987.

College Enrollment Trends

Public elementary and secondary school enrollment declined during the fifteen-year period from 1970 to 1985, while higher education enrollment increased. However, the elementary school enrollment began rising in 1985. The fact that there were 6.1 million fewer young people aged seven to thirteen between 1970 and 1985 means there will be a 21 percent decline in the number of young people turning age eighteen in the 1990s. After 1995 the number of eighteen-year-olds will begin to grow again, albeit at a much slower rate than the boom years of the 1960s and 1970s. The number of young people aged sixteen to twenty-four represented 23 percent of the population during the late 1970s; by 1995 they will comprise only 16 percent of the total population, offering further evidence that the typical college student of the future will be different than the college student of the 1960s and 1970s.

Enrollment in Institutions of Higher Education and Numbers of Institutions, by Type and Control, 1987

Type of Institution	Enrollment (thousands)			Number of Institutions		
	Total	Public	Private	Total	Public	Private
Total	12,301	9,457	2,844	3,389	1,548	1,841
Doc.-Granting Inst.	3,429	2,655	774	213	134	79
Research U. I	1,579	1,258	321	70	45	25
Research U. II	630	541	89	34	26	8
Doc.-Granting U. I	680	495	185	51	30	21
Doc.-Granting U. II	540	361	179	58	33	25
Comp. U. & Clgs	3,303	2,377	926	595	331	264
Comp. U. & Clgs I	2,971	2,280	691	424	284	140
Comp. U. & Clgs II	332	97	235	171	47	124
Liberal Arts Colleges	584	44	540	572	32	540
Liberal Arts Clgs I	214	5	209	142	2	140
Liberal Arts Clgs II	370	39	331	430	30	400
Comm., Tech., & Jr. Clgs	4,518*	4,250*	268*	1,367	985	382
Specialized Inst.	467	131	336	642	66	576

*Figure excludes institutions with unavailable enrollment figures.

Source: Adapted from U. S. National Center for Education Statistics data by the Carnegie Foundation for the Advancement of Teaching.

Comparative Fall Term School and College
Enrollment Projections
(in millions)

	Actual			Estimated		
	1975	1980	1985	1990	1995	2000
Elementary (K-8)						
Public	25.6	24.1	24.2	26.2	27.3	27.3
Private	3.7	4.0	4.2	4.2	4.2	4.2
Secondary (9-12)						
Public	19.1	16.8	15.2	14.4	16.6	16.6
Private	1.3	1.3	1.4	1.4	1.4	1.4
Higher Education						
Public	8.8	9.4	9.5	9.8	9.4	9.8
Private	2.3	2.7	2.8	2.8	2.7	2.8
Total	60.8	58.2	57.3	58.8	61.6	62.1

Source: U. S. Department of Education, National Center for Education Statistics, *The Condition of Education, 1989*.

High School Dropouts

The education achievement level of the population increased steadily from the turn of the century up to about the mid-1960s. However, the high school dropout rate is a bit higher today than in 1965, when there were about seventy-seven high school graduates for each hundred persons seventeen years of age or older. At that rate, an estimated eleven to twelve million students will not complete high school during the 1990s.

However, it is important to point out that an increasing number of adults are earning high school equivalency certificates after passing exams such as the General Education Development (GED) tests. An estimated 750,000 different individuals take the GED tests each year with about 475,000 passing the tests to receive the GED certificate. The number of individuals taking the GED tests has increased tenfold over the past thirty years.

214

High School Completion Rates

School Year Ending	Total 17-year-olds (in thousands)	High School Graduates[1] (in thousands)	Graduates as % 17-year-olds
1910	1,786	156	8.8
1920	1,855	311	16.8
1930	2,296	667	29.0
1940	2,403	1,221	50.8
1950	2,034	1,200	59.0
1960	2,672	1,858	69.5
1970	3,757	2,889	76.9
1980	4,262	3,043	71.4
1981	4,207	3,020	71.8
1982	4,121	2,995	72.7
1983	3,939	2,888	73.3
1984	3,753	2,767	73.7
1985	3,658	2,677	73.2
1986	3,621	2,642	73.0
1987	3,696	2,693	72.9

[1]Includes graduates of public and private schools. For most years, private school data have been estimated.

Note: Includes graduates of regular day school programs. Excludes graduates of other programs and recipients of high school equivalency certificates.

Source: U. S. Department of Education, National Center for Education Statistics, *The Condition of Education, 1989.*

College Degrees Earned

Despite a leveling-out of the number of high school diplomas, the number of individuals earning college degrees continues to climb, with a few up-and-down years. The U. S. Department of Education estimates that 1.8 million college degrees of various kinds were awarded during the 1987-88 college year, as opposed to 1.75 million degrees awarded in 1978. There has been a definite leveling-off of degrees awarded during the past three to four years.

Over 1.8 million college degrees of various kinds were awarded during the 1987-88 college year as opposed to 1.39 million degrees earned in 1971.

College Degrees Earned

School Year Ending	AA/AS	BA/BS	MA/MS	Ph.D	First Profes- sional
1971	252,610	839,730	230,509	32,107	37,946
1976	391,454	925,746	311,771	34,064	62,649
1981	416,377	935,140	295,739	32,958	71,956
1986	446,047	987,823	288,567	33,653	73,910
1987*	435,000	987,000	291,000	34,200	73,700
1988*	450,000	989,000	290,000	33,500	74,400

*Estimated

AA/AS: Associate of arts, associate of sciences degrees
BA/BS: Bachelor of arts, bachelor of sciences degrees
MA/MS: Master of arts, master of sciences degrees
Ph.D: Doctor of philosophy degrees
First Professional: Chiropractic, dentistry, law, medicine, optometry, osteopathic medicine, pharmacy, podiatry, theology, and veterinary medicine

Source: U. S. Department of Education, National Center for Education Statistics, *The Condition of Education, 1989.*

The largest growth in degrees earned has occurred in the number of associate degrees and in such professional degrees as law, medicine, and pharmacy. However, it must be pointed out that the decade of the 1980s has experienced a leveling-out in number of degrees earned. Projections indicate that there will be slow growth in associate and baccalaureate degrees earned in the 1990s, and graduate degrees earned will remain fairly level or even decrease a bit. One of the significant shifts that continues to occur is for corporations to establish their own accredited degree-granting institution, particularly aimed at graduate education. If that trend continues, as some predict, then the graduate degrees awarded would significantly increase. A *U. S. News & World Report* magazine report predicts:

> Hundreds of corporations will grant degrees, most often in high technology, science, and engineering, where state-of-the-art equipment and research will surpass that on most campuses.[9]

However as more and more leaders of business and industry are embracing the idea of lifetime learning for their employees, colleges and universities have a window of opportunity to serve the employers of the nation in new and productive ways. Continuing education is now a fact of life in many corporations, and in many ways has become the bridge between academe and the business world. Cooperative programs between colleges, universities, and the employer world are becoming commonplace. Only time will tell if this results in more college degrees being awarded.

The Military and Higher Education

It is becoming increasingly apparent that world events will permit a downsizing of the U. S. military forces. Most of the individuals leaving the service will carry the educational benefits of the new Montgomery GI Bill with them. It is estimated that 450,000 veterans are expected to be using the new GI Bill each year in the first part of the 1990s. This represents a gain of over 100,000 veterans over the 327,000 enrolled in colleges in 1987. In addition to the GI Bill, servicemembers are substantially involved in pursuing college credit coursework through the Servicemembers Opportunity College and college programs. In 1987 military personnel were enrolled in more than 778,000 college-level courses, earning over 19,000 associate degrees, 6,000 baccalaureate degrees, and some 7,000 graduate degrees. It is anticipated that college enrollments of veterans could nearly fill the gap created by the decreasing number of high school graduates, at least in the first five years of the 1990s.

Dateline 2000 Forecast

1.   The number of ethnic students attending college and completing college programs will significantly increase by Dateline 2000. Graduate schools will have the largest problem in recruiting and retaining minority students because of the competition.

2.   The adult literacy rate will begin to increase, the high school dropout rate will begin to decrease, and many adults including returning veterans will return to college for upgrading and retraining. This will create a new demand for higher education services and replace the number of decreasing eighteen-year-olds.

3.   Part-time college attendance will increase and colleges and universities of all kinds will offer a broad spectrum of classes in the evening and on weekends to the expanding part-time and adult student population. It will be possible to complete a full four-year college program by evening and weekend class attendance in many colleges.

4.   Many colleges and universities will develop "a college within a college" to accommodate a growing number of adults attending college classes. The student services program will be different for adults from the program that serves the recent high school graduates, and will largely function in the evenings and on weekends. It will not be uncommon for adults to be involved in Evening College Student Senates and related activities.

5.   By Dateline 2000 each state will have developed coherent college transfer agreements, coordinated academic calendars, common course numbering and credit systems, and a modicum of sequential curriculum planning.

6.   An increasing number of colleges will work in partnership with employers, offering an array of short-term and long-term courses. Many of the workers of the future will have one foot in the workplace and the other foot in the learning place.

7.   The community service program of colleges and universities will increasingly be called upon to help solve communitywide problems by performing a convening function and serving as a common meeting ground for civic and cultural renewal.

8.   By Dateline 2000 there will be a commonly recognized new definition of a college student to include a much broader spectrum of individuals beyond the eighteen- to twenty-five-year-old age group.

9.   Dateline 2000 will see the development of more experimental colleges and universities to test strategies and develop creative new approaches to serving adults.

10.   Enrollments in colleges and universities will continue to grow at about the same pace as the overall population growth, but economic pressures will dictate that the largest growth will occur in the lower-cost institutions.

Executive Summary

An increasing number of young people are going to college part time and "stopping out" now and then, while an increasing number of adults (twenty-five and over) are going to college full time. The phrase "college student" needs a new definition. By the year 1992 there will be about as many individuals over the age of twenty-five in the college population as under age twenty-five.

In a dramatic twenty-year enrollment shift, nearly half of all public college and university students are now classified as part-time students, yet there continues to be a steady upward trend of more adults holding the bachelor's degree or higher. They are just taking much longer than four years to earn the degree.

College and university enrollments are increasing or are being maintained by attracting a large volume of older students to the campuses. There will be a 21 percent decline in the overall number of eighteen-year-olds in the 1990s. There will be 3.5 million fewer eighteen- to twenty-four-year-olds by the year 2000 than in 1985. The lowest years for eighteen-year-olds, and consequently the most competition for their attention, will be in the four-year span between 1992 and 1996.

All ethnic minorities are continually increasing participation in higher education except the black male population. There is evidence that the young black male has selected the military, proprietary schools, and full-time work at a higher rate than his counterparts. With increased attention to the education of ethnic minority students at all levels of education, the number of ethnic minority students entering and completing college programs in the 1990s should increase significantly.

The strength of the American higher education system rests in the diversity of its colleges and universities. A rich array of institutions serve a huge variety of student and societal needs. It would be a mistake to try to establish a hierarchy among the different classifications of colleges and universities. Excellence can be found in the diversity. Diversity in American higher education is to be celebrated and each classification of institutions respected. The fast-changing nature of the college student, and the needs of a fast-changing technological society, will require the resources of all different types of colleges and universities.

220

Notes

1.   *USA Today*, 5 August 1989.

2.   David W. Breneman and Susan Nelson, *Financing Community Colleges: An Economic Perspective* (Washington, D. C.: Brookings Institution, 1981).

3.   Harvard Institute for the Management of Lifelong Education, Annual Report, 1989.

4.   Personal communication with a senior citizen student at San Joaquin Delta College.

5.   Kiplinger Washington Letter Staff, *The New American Boom: Exciting Changes in American Life and Business Between Now and the Year 2000* (Washington, D. C.: Kiplinger Washington Editors, 1986).

6.   Michael T. Nettles et al., "Comparative and Predictive Analysis of Black and White Students' College Achievement and Experiences," *Journal of Higher Education* (May/June 1986).

7.   Southern Growth Policies Board, Commission on the Future of the South, *Halfway Home and a Long Way to Go* (Atlanta: Southern Growth Policies Board, 1986).

8.   "Parents Are Facing a Child-Care Crisis," *USA Today*, 29 August 1989.

9.   *New York Times*, 9 May 1983.

Chapter VIII

The Search for Synergy

The student who can begin early in life to see things as connected has begun the life of learning. . . . The connectedness of things is what the educator contemplates.

Mark Van Doren

T he search for synergy, for combinations, for cooperation, for the correlated working together of different technologies, is pressing inward, outward, downward, and upward upon higher education institutions. There is an external explosion of knowledge and technology development causing an internal college implosion of interdisciplinary work. Different systems and different academic disciplines are increasingly acting together, with one accord, to produce results greater than the sum of the parts. As an example, experiments are under way in the space research program using the space shuttle, space technology, and eventually orbiting space stations to speed the development of new biotechnology pharmaceuticals for mass production on earth. ("Biotechnology" simply means the manipulation of organic processes to make new products.) This research program involves the disciplines of biology, chemistry, physics, pharmacology, electronics, aeronautics, aerospace medicine, health care, agriculture, engineering, environmental studies, computer science, and probably some others. The linkages among the disciplines and interdisciplinary work promise to produce an impact of significant proportions, with a growth curve that will take off early in the decade and keep going right through Dateline 2000.

William Aldridge, executive director of the National Science Teachers Association, comments on the traditional subject-by-subject approach and need to better coordinate subject matter learning by helping students understand the connectedness of things:

> The fundamental problem with high school biology, chemistry, and physics courses is that they are not coordinated, are highly abstract and theoretical, do not spend enough time on each subject, and do not use correct pedagogy. In short, we never give students the chance to *understand* science. . . . Most people are able to learn physics, chemistry, biology, geology, and other related subjects. People

can learn how these subjects apply to their lives and to society's problems. If we teach science to *all* students in a coordinated way from the concrete to the abstract, with practical applications, our future citizens will be more evidence-oriented. They will know how and when to ask questions, how to think critically, and then how to be able to make important decisions based on reason rather than on emotion or superstition. Science made understandable and accessible to all will also mean more and better scientists and engineers—and a different mix among them, including larger numbers of such now underrepresented groups as women and minorities.[1]

Interdisciplinary Education

The search for synergy emphasizes the importance of an interdisciplinary education and the development of broad skills. College-educated workers of the future must be able to handle projects from start to finish, from the definition of system requirements through project management. This will require "hands on" managers and project leaders able to roll up their sleeves and help with the work in practical ways. Manufacturers are now predicting a rapid shift from assembly line production to smaller units with smaller suppliers involving fewer workers with the abilities to do more complex things.

Richard Lindgren, president and CEO of Cross and Trecker Corporation of Michigan, says that business will experience a full quota of "gut-wrenching" changes as the latest technological advances move business and industry toward Dateline 2000. The key for competitive manufacturing success in the United States will be the development of multitalented personnel:

> There's a critical shortage of trained personnel in manufacturing. We are already seeing instances where new technology is failing because the skills are not available to design, build, install and operate state-of-the-art equipment.
> We need to revamp our training capabilities to give

our younger employees skills in computer-aided design, computer programming, electronics repair, systems design and a wide expanse of new skills that only a few years ago were not required of our factory personnel.[2]

The new U. S. manufacturing system will be based upon smaller units that tie everything together, from the order through the production process and delivery. The result of this change will mean fewer individuals trained to perform specific tasks, fewer mistakes, smaller inventories, and shortening the time between an order and delivery.

Rapid technological changes are motivating fundamental shifts requiring a workforce that is well educated, highly skilled, and highly adaptive. The National Research Council now estimates that the occupational half-life, the time it takes for one-half of workers' skills to become obsolete, has declined from seven to fourteen years to three to five years. Workers at all levels of the workforce will need basic literacy skills and cognitive skills enabling them to be lifelong learners and adjust to new work situations.

A Merging of Media

The 1990s will see a synergistic merging of various media and processes. Food and pharmaceutical companies may be uniting to form "pharmi-food" companies. Agricultural researchers, immunologists, cancer researchers, and others may be uniting to create foods that can treat viruses and cancer.

Telephone networks are generally being transformed into multimedia networks enabling users to communicate in combinations of video, text, and voice. Telephone companies are being changed into comprehensive communications companies combining the functions of telephone, data networks, video conferencing, and cable television. As fiber-optic cable is installed throughout local and interstate transmission networks, end users such as colleges, businesses, homes, and individuals will be able to communicate anywhere, anytime, in any medium through visual, voice, data, or image media.

When the country is fully wired and networked with fiber-optic cable and miniature video cameras installed in many places, or made more portable and more economical, virtually anything, anywhere, can be recorded. Video programming and messages can be presented live, or stored and accessible to users in the same fashion as electronic mail is transmitted today. Personal computers will be able to carry full-motion video signals, making it more and more feasible for individuals to work at home or in places other than a home office.

Will the TV industry and the cinema industry disappear over this next decade and be replaced by some new type of video-film company? It is possible that by Dateline 2000 the two will become one. Both industries are already moving in that direction as aspects of the electronic image dominate because of speed and efficiency. The technology now exists to beam a film into a thousand theaters via satellite (like the prizefights), eliminating the need for a thousand film prints.

Will the textbook of the future be the interactive video disc? The video disc technology has been around for ten years or so, but has been slow developing, because it takes an interdisciplinary approach to branching, and development of full-motion technology has been difficult. The development of the interactive video disc is a prime example of the search for synergy, bringing together individuals with an unusual array of knowledges, skills, and values. CD-I (compact disc interactive) combines the digital audio disc with full-motion video and other visual elements, and with computer capabilities to permit easy-to-use interaction.

Bernard Luskin, president of American Interactive Media, and a leading force in the development of CD-I, says:

> The most critical obstacle to development of a critical mass of CD-I titles has been a dearth of individuals with appropriate skills. We must continue to develop and implement training methods that expand the pool of experienced CD-I designers, programmers, and others. . . . The creation of successful CD-I discs requires the efforts of a team of producers, directors, visual and audio artists, and technicians, interactive and multimedia designers, and subject matter experts in a variety of fields.[3]

Imagine the consequences in teaching and learning if most textbooks included a CD-I on the back cover that would simulate and illustrate the difficult concepts presented in the text. For the first time, in one medium, educators will be able to meet the individual learning patterns and styles of each student.

The space program is also an illustration of the search for synergy. In many ways, the byproducts of space research programs may be as important as the findings about space travel itself. Space flights have spawned everything from cordless tools to food warmers. The development of lightweight materials for orbital and moon structures could produce new ways to build affordable homes and improve earthbound construction. From the "tinkertoy" assemble-in-space idea could flow new methods and machines for new commercial applications. The space program also requires a new synergistic cooperation among engineers, scientists, astronauts, managers, computer operators, technicians, assembly personnel, and even security personnel.

The Computer

The history of the computer, now about forty years old, also reveals a search for synergism. The computers of today are smaller, and many times faster, than they were ten years ago. In another ten years they will be even smaller and faster. But the key to advances in computer design and capability rests in sophisticated software design and development. Writing computer programs requires basic intelligence, a sense of logic, mathematics competency, communication skills, knowledge of computers and computer science. Some of the advances in computer design and software development can be traced to space research and flights into space. On the other hand, the space program would not have been developed without the computer.

Researchers are now developing a single silicon chip the size of a postage stamp containing as many as one hundred million memory bits that will incorporate all the power of a 1986 mainframe computer. This development will shrink the size of the personal computer, allowing it to perform billions of instructions per second and replacing the linear one-step-at-a-time operation.

Artificial intelligence now has come into view in the computer world, leading to the creation of "thinking" robots patterned after human intelligence. It will likely be a long while before a computer is developed that can react to rapidly changing conditions, or develop the human feel of nuance, or be clever enough to solve complex problems with little or no human instruction. Expert systems are probably the best we can expect for a decade or two. But advances will be made. Even now the race is on in this country, in Japan, and in other countries to produce a memory chip capable of storing a million pages of text on a single postage-stamp-size chip. The voice-activated computer is just around the corner, and "talkwriters" will begin to replace the typewriter and word processor. Voice input-output systems already exist, but they can recognize only a few hundred words presented by a single speaker, and they are expensive.

All of the progress in the development of the computer is an example of the way various disciplines and various technologies come together in a synergistic way to improve the way we work, communicate, and live.

The Impact of Technology

There can be little question that the world is in the midst of a technological revolution, moving from chemical processes to electronic ones, from an industrial age to a learning age, from manual labor to automated labor, from analog to digital, from the cow chip to the potato chip to the silicon chip with the potential capacity of containing one hundred million memory bits. The technological revolution is proceeding at an explosive pace. College professors can now efficiently organize and develop their own tailor-made textbooks for each college course. With virtually all publications written and typeset electronically, it is only a short step to distribute them on compact discs or digital tapes. This book is being developed by way of desktop publishing.

Michael Schulhof, vice chair of the U. S. Sony Company, makes an insightful comment about the current pace of change:

> If I had to pick a similar period when society was funda-
> mentally changed, I'd pick the 1880s with the introduction
> of the telephone and electricity.[4]

The development of "user-friendly" educational telecommunications programs will create a new kind of synergy problem,
blurring institutional identities. Students will have more and more
options in the selection of higher education programs. Students in
Alpena, Michigan, or Salem, Oregon, may be selecting coursework,
via fiber-optic cable to their homes, offered by a community college,
a state college, or a national university located far away from their
homes.

Most of our system of higher education has been based upon
institutional autonomy and geographic placement. How will autonomous institutions respond to the rapid transit of college courses
via telecommunications over state lines, or easy rental of first-rate
college courses from the local ComputerLand store?

As long-distance learning increases, via satellite expansions,
and as the CD-I is fully developed in textbook fashion and available
at the local library or computer store, it will become less important
who sponsors that particular college course. By Dateline 2000 higher
education institutions of all kinds will be discussing and redefining
the traditional definition of a college or university.

The households of one hundred years ago had no toasters,
mixers, electric washing machines, dryers, electric lights, central
heating, electric motors, or apartment house elevators. Five out of
six houses had outdoor plumbing. Gas lighting, in one form or
another, was universal. When Thomas Edison invented the incan-
descent electric lamp in 1879, and the electric power generating
plant in 1882, those inventions opened the way to energize the world
in a new way.

When Alexander Graham Bell invented the telephone in
1876, he provided a new form of human communication that is still
being refined and expanded today. By 1880, 50,000 telephones were
in use; by 1900, 750,000 were in use; and today there are 86,000,000
telephones in the United States alone, serving 93 percent of the
households.

Look at some of the technological inventions of the latter part

231

of the nineteenth century:

- 1877   Telephone
- 1879   Electric Lamp
- 1882   Electric Power Generating Plant
- 1885   Automobile
- 1886   Phonograph
- 1888   Electric Motor
- 1891   Motion Picture Camera

Every so often a special technological breakthrough comes along in a culture to change the way people work, live, and even think. The invention of the printing press opened the knowledge of the world to anyone who wanted to read, and it certainly opened the doors of education to the masses. However, the Gutenberg Bible, the first book printed in movable type, was not welcomed by the scholars of 1457, when it first appeared. The sacred book lacked page numbers, consistent punctuation and grammar, and was difficult to read. The new high technology of that day was certainly not "user-friendly," even as much of the high technology of today is not user-friendly.

The Automobile

The first practical gasoline-powered four-wheeled cars were produced by two German engineers, Gottlieb Daimler and Karl Benz, in 1889. By 1900, when American automobile makers were beginning to develop the horseless carriage, twelve companies turned out about 4,000 machines. Henry Ford produced his first Model T in 1908 and soon had developed an assembly line approach to building the automobile. By 1910, 187,000 automobiles were built by sixty-nine automobile manufacturers. But not everyone was enthusiastic about this new invention. The president of Princeton University, Woodrow Wilson, warned his students, in 1907, about the evils of that newfangled invention called the automobile:

> Nothing has spread socialistic feeling in this country more
> than the use of the automobile. ... To the countryman they
> are a picture of arrogance of wealth, with all its independ-
> ence and carelessness.[5]

During the early days of the automobile it was largely the plaything of the wealthy. It was expensive, made loud noises, smelled bad, and certainly frightened the horses. In short, the automobile was not user-friendly. However, no technological invention has impacted our economy and way of life as the automobile. Much of the U. S. economy is driven by the automobile, in gasoline sales, traffic control, road construction, auto repairs, auto manufacturing, and auto sales. The automobile has also brought a downside, in auto accidents, deaths, traffic gridlocks, commuter life, air pollution, insurance and repair expenses. What at one time was considered a luxury item for the rich has today become a necessity for the masses.

Imagine for a moment what the world economy will be like when an alternative fuel is developed to operate the internal combustion engine, or when hydrogen becomes the common fuel for engines rather than gasoline. The economy of the world will dramatically change. Until that happens six or seven countries in the world will control the worldwide oil price and supply: Saudi Arabia, Iraq, United Arab Emirates, Kuwait, Mexico, Venezuela, and possibly Iran. When market power and control is concentrated in a few countries, literally a few individual leaders, the world economy can easily be held hostage. Over 70 percent of the oil reserves in the world are controlled by four Middle Eastern countries. Remember the oil embargo of 1973 after the Arab-Israeli war when the United States experienced severe oil shortages and booming price increases?[6]

Advances in technology and the creation of new inventions often offer the possibility of improving life for millions of people, but these same advances carry with them new challenges and create a new set of problems to be solved.

The Airplane and Space Travel

In 1903 Wilbur and Orville Wright developed a flying machine, using the power of the gasoline engine, that flew briefly over the sand dune beaches of North Carolina. But unlike the swift development of the automobile, many years would pass before the airplane would broadly impact the lives of the average citizen. However, the impact of this technological breakthrough is felt widely around the world today. The world has certainly grown smaller, indeed the universe has grown smaller, with the development of jet airplanes and space shuttles. The airplane has even become a political weapon, with whole plane-loads of passengers blown up or held hostage by some political terrorist group.

The airplane has had a terrific impact upon the economy, in manufacturing, ticket agents, airplane crews, and swift travel. By the end of 1988 airliner manufacturers indicated that their manufacturing assembly lines had a record backlog of orders, backed up into the mid-1990s. Billions of dollars change hands with airline merger activity. In the one year of 1986 there were four large airplane mergers: United Airlines bought the Pacific Division of Pan Am, Northwest Airlines bought Republic Airlines, Delta Airlines bought Western Airlines, and Texas Air bought Eastern and Continental Airlines with much ensuing labor strife.

Space exploration and development, motivated by the Soviet Union with the launch of *Sputnik* in 1959, has been the most dramatic technological breakthrough in the late twentieth century. The Soviet Union put the first man into space, made the longest flights, and led this effort until July 20, 1969, when American astronauts stepped upon the surface of the moon. The public marveled at the ability of the computer to guide a space vehicle down to a landing on the moon. At the same time they were cursing computers when they tried to correct a computerized billing error.

The U. S. government-financed space program took a giant step backwards with the *Challenger* disaster of early 1986. During this lull in government-sponsored space program development, the commercialization of space began to take shape around the world. Venture capitalist and aerospace companies began to form new consortiums and limited partnerships, helping the commercialization of space to progress and become a profitable commercial venture. As an example, the country of France launched a computerized satellite in October of 1989 capable of handling 120,000 simultaneous telephone calls.

Integrated Telephones, Computers, and Electronics

Integrated Services Digital Network (ISDN), which allows users to send images, voice, text, and data over a single telephone line, will be widely used by Dateline 2000. ISDN and broadband ISDN will make it simple to conduct a simultaneous telephone conversation using textual material, graphics, images, and live video all on the home computer screen. Broadband ISDN is now moving out of the research laboratories into experimental hookups. The fiber-optic technology is moving so fast that a cable installed between Washington, D. C., and Boston is already obsolete. Scientists say that the potential of fiber optics is such that in theory every individual in the United States could have at least one voice channel on a single fiber as thin as a human hair, and that a transatlantic phone conversation could be conducted with no echo, no lag time, and no noise interference.

Satellites will continue to serve hard-to-reach places and will probably retain the worldwide television market. However, fiber-optic cable and satellites will work together in a mixed system even as cable television and satellites now work, or do not work, together. Replacing the copper telephone connections that now go into nearly every office and home in the country will take time, but it will happen, and will be well on the way by Dateline 2000.

Miniaturization

The first digital computer, called the Electronic Numerical Integrator and Computer (ENIAC), was developed at the University of Pennsylvania in 1944. It weighed approximately thirty tons, required a thirty-by-fifty-foot space, and needed 200 kilowatts of electricity to power 18,000 vacuum tubes. In 1954 the first commercial computer was sold by the Universal Automatic Computer Com-

235

pany (UNIVAC). It was expensive and also a monster in size compared to the inexpensive, small microprocessor of the late 1980s. The computer of the 1980s become the king of technology, leading technological developments, even as electricity became the king of technology in the 1880s and laid the synergistic foundation for thousands of other technological advances.

The fastest supercomputer of 1990 can perform 1.2 billion arithmetic calculations in one second. Even the workhorse small personal computer can perform 1,000 arithmetic operations per second. The International Business Machines Corporation (IBM) produced its first personal computer in 1981. In four years it had sold 1.7 million personal computers, producing nearly $4 billion in revenues.[7]

At this writing, microprocessor circuitry has been reduced to one micron (the human hair measures seventy to one hundred microns in diameter), and a single chip can process ten million instructions per second. As this kind of compression continues on toward Dateline 2000, it will lead to the development of expert machines becoming machine assistants to a large assortment of occupations. The miniaturization of technology is on the verge of a new leap into the future. A report to the National Science Foundation in 1988 listed hundreds of potential developments in the new microtechnology. Among them:

- Minature machines to drive tiny computers, camcorders, tape recorders, and Dick Tracy wristwatch videos;
- Tiny scissors to assist doctors in performing microsurgery;
- Micro-optical systems required for fiber-optic communication.
- A silicon motor not much wider than a eyelash.

In 1980 there were 303,000 individuals employed in the computer and data processing business. By 1986 that number had nearly doubled, jumping to 554,000. In 1981 there were 2.1 billion personal computers in public use, and six years later, in 1987, there were 37.7 million in use, with half of the increase being home use.

The rapid growth of the computer industry has been re-

Computer and Information Science Degrees Awarded

	1971	1981	1983	1986
Associate	NA	11,000 est.	12,970	13,307
Bachelor's	2,388	15,121	24,510	41,889
Master's	1,588	4,218	5,321	8,070
Doctorate	128	252	262	344
Total Computer Degrees	4,104	30,591	43,063	63,610

Source: U. S. Department of Commerce, Bureau of the Census, *Statistical Abstract of the United States, 1989.*

flected in the dramatic jump of college computer science degrees awarded, from 4,000 in 1971 to 63,000 fifteen years later in 1986. In the public schools, 18 percent of the schools had at least one microcomputer in 1981. Six years later, in 1987, 96 percent had microcomputers.

Artificial Intelligence

Voice-activated computers will become commonplace, handling vocabularies of five to ten thousand words. But the real technological breakthrough will occur when machine intelligence and human intelligence begin to interact on a technical basis and complete the search for synergy between humankind and machines.

Will this happen? The answer is certainly, at least to some degree, but building human intelligence into a machine will likely require some different approaches than the familiar digital computer. Machines have been developed that can approach brainlike speed but they lack vision, the ability to physically see, and they lack the ability to deduce and reason. Researchers are now hooking brainlike transistor circuits together called neuronets. They are finding that these circuits can produce something called associative memory. Shown a picture, the neuronet can place that picture into memory and instantly recognize it when shown from any angle. If researchers can find the synergy between digital circuits and neuronets, the possibilities are mind-boggling. Cetron and Davies, in their book *American Renaissance*, postulate on the synergistic possibilities of new technology this way:

> Small computers will become a routine fixture of everyday life, helping more and more students—of all ages—to learn at their own pace both at home and in the classroom. . . . Here's one idea: Talking dolls could engage in full-blown conversations. . . . Slip the doll into a Cossack costume, stick in a matching "smart card" and the doll would become a Russian language tutor and playmate.[8]

It is estimated that the large majority of the Ivy League college faculty now use computers regularly; at Yale University it is 90 percent of the faculty. About twenty-five to thirty colleges and universities across the country now require all entering students to purchase a computer, allowing for the full integration of computer use in all cross-campus courses.

The Impact of Technology Upon Higher Education

For education the technological breakthrough of the century will likely arrive in the form of simulated learning utilizing a new technology like the interactive compact disc (CD-I). The laser-read video disc, introduced early in the 1980s, has struggled in development, and continues to compete with the digital video interactive developments of huge companies like Intel. The branching and development is complex and time-consuming, and incorporating full-motion pictures onto the disc has been difficult and expensive. But these problems are being overcome. CD-I is moving through these difficulties and is ready to emerge upon the consumer and education scenes with enormous potential. It appears to be one of the more important user-friendly technological-educational developments of the decade.

238

Agreements have been reached by major video disc producers around the world to standardize terms, players, and production processes. There is not likely to be a VHS or Beta or MS-DOS or OS-9 controversy in this industry. The race is on to produce the lowest cost, user-friendly, effective CD-I in the world and the competition is keen, but there promises to be compatibility among the various CD-I players and the software.

The CD-I development combines new, powerful microchip computer-driven players with "student-friendly" software. In the search for synergy, the CD-I developers have combined computers with video, motion pictures, text, graphics, and with simulations. The technology has been developed and CD-I has now moved to the state of developing software that lets the user set the pace and control the sequencing utilizing, voice, video, text, and graphics.

Yet to be fully developed, but on the way, is the large, flat, high-definition, color-television screen monitor that will cover an entire wall. Small colored TV monitors will still be used, but the green CRTs will be gone with their crowded and unappealing screen designs. The large, flat, full-wall monitor will be most useful in large groups and classrooms, and more natural, like talking with someone face to face.

Simulation

The development of the optical video disc promises to offer educators a literal shelfful of affordable interactive learning systems, techniques never before available for classrooms (or homes) simulating real-life situations. Examine just one application of learning utilizing the CD-I. Some students learn best by hearing, others by seeing, others by doing, and others require all these mediums. But one general weakness of most of education is in helping students understand the application of knowledge—to become application literate.

Visualize a time when textbooks will be accompanied by a video disc illustrating and simulating some of the most difficult concepts in the text. The student can privately and interactively review this material as many times as needed to master the subject

239

in a simulated situation.

Simulation is not a futuristic dream. It is a part of the education and training program of many employers, particularly the military, but it is not widely used in higher education. The thrust toward utilizing technology to enhance education and training is being widely shared by such companies as General Electric, McDonnell Douglas, Boeing, Sperry, Singer, the military, and the airlines.

With the introduction of the "link trainer" in the late 1950s the aviation industry took the lead in simulation education and training. Today the dramatic refinements in flight simulation technology have made zero "real-plane" time for training a reality in many situations. For certain seats in a commercial airliner cockpit, simulation methods have totally eliminated the real airplane as a training tool. The Air Force is experiencing the same situation in the simulation training of pilots for transport-type aircraft.

Simulation duplicates exactly the control-feel dynamics of the airplane during the take-off, cruise, bad weather, windshears, icy runways, landings, brake and tire failures. If simulators were not used for copilot training, the airlines indicate it would cost an additional $900,000 in airplane cost to train a minimum of 300 new pilots each year.

The Army National Guard has developed a Synthetic Flight Training facility in Pennsylvania to train helicopter pilots. Simulation is accomplished by using UH-1 Huey helicopter cockpits and by programming in them the required environments, via computer, with full-motion systems. Opened in 1977, this simulator, it is estimated, has saved $3.6 million and 1.5 million gallons of aviation fuel in just the first three years of operation. Of course, an undisputed advantage of the simulator is the ability to program emergency procedures without endangering the life of the pilot.

The Defense Science Board issued a report in 1982 warning that military training was falling dangerously far behind the operational requirements of new high-tech weapons. This report indicated that there was a disconnect between the skill-performance requirements for operation and maintenance of new weapons systems and the aptitude of the available and projected manpower to meet those requirements.

The military has moved with considerable speed to address

240

this situation by installing simulator systems and including them as integral parts of the education and training programs. The Air Force Academy has developed a new concept in foreign language instruction using individually self-paced interactive video disc instruction coupled with regular classroom instruction. The video disc instruction brings the foreign language and the culture together in a synergistic way, allowing the student to interact with the material.

Student workstations are arranged in groups of four or five and student stations are networked to a main computer to track student activity. As an example, a lesson will simulate the student being in a French restaurant and ordering from the menu in French. If the student needs help, he or she can call up a glossary showing the English translation of each word. This is just another example of how CD-I can help a college simulate a learning situation by applying the knowledge to a real-life experience.

A User-Friendly Future

A CD-I system has its own built-in computer, equipped with all the processing power of any microcomputer or personal computer. But N. V. Phillips, the Dutch company developing the CD-I players and the moving force behind American Interactive Media, is downplaying the computer capability of CD-I. It wants the system to be as easy or easier to use as a VCR and look like a stereo component rather than a computer. Richard Bruno, the Phillips researcher who helped develop CD-I, indicates that Phillips wants the CD-I to be so simple to use that it will not intimidate anyone.

Probably the most ambitious and futuristic of all technology developers is Ted Nelson, author of the 1987 book *Computer Lib–Dream Machines*. Nelson has developed something he calls the Xanadu Project in cooperation with the California-based Autodesk Company. Nelson dreams of designing a supernetwork that would bring published text material and sound and film material into every home in the world. When questioned about the possibilities of his dream ever becoming reality, he asks, how would people have reacted in 1876 if Alexander Graham Bell had announced that by 1976 his gadget would be used in most homes and businesses and people could use it to talk with anyone in the world?[9]

Futurists have been predicting for years that technological breakthroughs will allow millions of individuals to work full time at home. So far that prediction has been slow in being fulfilled. Most jobs are still not that flexible, and employers generally still want to see their employees personally now and then. But moving the work to the workforce is coming. The state of California, in an effort to combat gridlock, urban congestion, and lost productivity, is experimenting with telecommuting in several state agencies, involving over 150 people. Their occupations range from lawyers, appraisers, accountants, researchers, to secretaries and word processors. They report to the office on a part-time basis and the remainder of their work is done at home. It is estimated that over 100,000 individuals are now working at home as telecommuters in jobs like insurance claims, word processing, systems analysis, telephone order taking, and data entry.[10]

Over the past fifteen years banks have nearly universally installed user-friendly automated teller machines. Coin-operated vending machines proliferate, and employers of all kinds are quickly automating processes in order to extend limited resources through technology.

Faculty and administrators in higher education institutions have waxed and waned over the past twenty years in their enthusiasm about the potential of technology. It has probably been the development of the microcomputer that has rather quickly brought a new gleam of possibility into the eyes of educators. They have been led down the technological garden path before, only to find the technology difficult to use, expensive, not accessible, and often not very functional for the purposes of teaching and learning. However, technology has had a significant impact upon the curriculum. One hundred years ago one would not have found college-university programs in electrical engineering, x-ray technology, automotive engineering and computer science. Even fifty years ago there were no computer science and information programs in colleges. There are literally hundreds of examples to be found in college catalogs as to how the college and university curriculum has changed because of technological developments.

In an unpredictable sort of way it has been word processing

that has motivated many college and university faculty to use technology. Teaching writing with such software as Writer's Workbench, Word Bench, or Writer's Helper has become the norm for many college English professors. English faculty indicate that the pedagogical methods of teaching writing have changed dramatically in the last twenty years. Faculty members are increasingly playing the role of coach as well as lecturer.

Many higher education institutions are finding that technology has made it possible to better serve handicapped students. The availability of the liquid crystal display (LCD) hooked up to a computer and used with the overhead projector empowers faculty to illustrate and simulate abstract concepts.

Distance learning has removed geographical barriers for many individuals. Now a college can extend the expertise of highly qualified faculty to multiple sites. Many colleges have installed interactive telecommunications systems linking several teaching sites. Colleges and universities have found that distance learning works best when it is student-friendly and interactive, when faculty control the classroom, and when substantial faculty development programs are available.

The American Association of Community and Junior Colleges initiated a Community College Satellite Network in 1989. The network was established as a way for colleges to share resources concentrating on the four areas of teleconferencing, telecourses, training for business and industry, and cable programming. Other organizations like the National University Telecommunications Network, National Technological University, PBS Adult Learning Service, and the Learning Channel have been offering successful distance learning programs for several years.

Application Literate

One curricular program that is being developed across the country as a result of the rapid technological changes is the tech-prep/associate degree program, aimed particularly at serving the two academic middle quartiles of a typical high school student body. Training and education have become integral to most "wide-technology" workers, whether they be nurses, law enforcement person-

243

nel, electronic technicians, or marketing representatives.

Beginning with the junior year in high school, students select the tech-prep program (even as they now select the college-prep program) and continue for four years in a structured and closely coordinated high school-college curriculum. They are taught by high school teachers in the first two years, but also have access to college personnel and facilities when appropriate. Starting with a solid base of applied science, applied math, literacy courses, and technical programs, the high school portion of the career program is intentionally preparatory in nature. Built around career clusters and technical-systems study, such a tech-prep approach helps students develop broad-based competence in a career field and avoid the pitfalls of more short-term and narrowly delineated job training. It is the responsibility of the high school to open up the world for the high school student rather than close it down through narrow and specific job training.

Based upon locally developed agreements, the tech-prep/ associate degree program is developed with many options for the student. The usual scope and sequence of the tech-prep/associate degree program indicates leaving the highly specific areas of the technical education program for the college two years. However, it is not so important where, or even when, the student gains the required learning. What is important is that the student see the program spelled out and see the "gestalt" of the entire four years.

This high school tech-prep program dovetails with specific technical education programs at the collegiate levels. More intense technical specialization is developed at the college level, always in tandem with broad technical and broad educational understandings aimed at working in a wide-technology society. The college technical education programs include law enforcement, nursing, electronics, computers, business, marketing, entrepreneurship, agriculture, electron microscopy, construction trades (usually in cooperation with the apprenticeship program), mechanical technologies, health occupations, and many others. The tech-prep/associate degree program requires close curricular coordination. Most of all, it requires high school and college leaders and faculty members to talk regularly with one another and with employers.

The tech-prep/associate degree concept is providing a dramatic model for educators wishing to avoid slippage and loss of continuity in learning. Most important, it brings program structure and substance to the ordinary student. Here are some advantages of this program:

- Students are developing sound basic skills and knowledge.
- Students are obtaining a first-rate technical education preparation.
- High schools are motivating more students and perhaps losing fewer students between grades ten and eleven because they can see a future—a why for their efforts.
- Colleges are gaining better-prepared high school graduates.
- The tech-prep/associate degree program is encouraging more high school students to continue their education in meaningful ways.
- Employers are gaining better-prepared employees to work in a wide-technology society.

School superintendent Douglas James of the Richmond County Public Schools in North Carolina has implemented the tech-prep curriculum in cooperation with the Richmond Community College. Superintendent James states about this program:

> First, I would have to say that the program has had the greatest impact on secondary education in Richmond County since high school consolidation in 1971. Previous to Tech Prep, 25 percent of our high school students were enrolled in our pre-college program and 75 percent in the general academic/vocational curriculum. Now, over 30 percent are enrolled in the pre-college curriculum and another 30 percent in our Tech Prep program which involves a more rigorous academic and technological course of study.
>
> Enrollment in Algebra I has increased 42 percent over our 1985-86 enrollment with an associated increase in our average end-of-course test scores. Algebra II enrollment has increased 57 percent with a slight decrease in average

245

end-of-course test scores. A significant increase has also been experienced in student enrollment in more advanced English, social studies, and science courses. . . .

Since the beginning of our Tech Prep program, our average SAT score has increased 46 points, the dropout rate declined from 7.2 percent annually to 4.8 percent and the percentage of graduates choosing to attend a community college increased from 24 percent to 46 percent.[11]

The Tension of Transition

Our country is currently in the tension of transition, even as one hundred years ago society was moving from an agricultural economy to a manufacturing-industrial economy. That age counted upon the factors of low-cost labor, low-cost energy, abundant national resources, and the ability to lead the world economy. Today we are in the transition to the technological-learning age where knowledge, skills, and information are the products. This transition will require a shift in attitudes and a shift in behavior. The learning age counts upon well-educated, well-trained people, individual empowerment, and creativity. Learning takes place at any time, in any place, on any topic, and in any sequence. Learning also is best enhanced as individuals become application literate as well as knowledge literate. Thomas Hope, president of the Hope Reports, comments on the challenges this way:

> By the year 2000 there will be over six billion people in the world. All those babies will need to be educated and trained to work. A lot of that will depend on the media, and most of that will center on video. The botton line: Communication is fast becoming the most important thing in the world.[12]

IBM now requires each technician, marketing representative, and systems analyst to spend twenty days a year in education and training programs. And IBM is not alone in requiring such programs of its employees. Such widely diverse companies as State Farm Insurance, Southwest Forest Industries, Manufacturers Hanover Trust Company, Abbott Laboratories, Central Illinois Light Company, Citicorp, Steelcase Inc., Valley National Bank of Arizona, and Caterpillar Tractor Company all are moving education and training programs into high-priority positions in terms of strategic planning for economic growth. California superintendent of public instruction Bill Honig has summed up the challenge for schools and colleges this way:

> Don't be misled by advocates of a low-tech future. These modern Luddites have historically underestimated the extent and pace of change in the economy. They cite only a portion of the data from the Department of Labor, neglecting statistics that demonstrate substantive growth in jobs requiring high levels of preparation. They are out of step with the people who are hiring our graduates.[13]

It is estimated that more than $30 billion is spent annually by U. S. public and private employers for employee education and training programs. This figure does not include costs for training in the military. The Department of Defense estimates that some $50 billion is spent on education and training per year when all DOD education and training costs are included. Public and private employers are concluding that the competencies and related performance of the workforce are the major factor in determining the economic and social health of their enterprise. In fact, the skills gap between job needs and unskilled people may be the most important problem facing the United States in the decade ahead.

Clearly, more and more secondary schools and colleges are waking up to the reality of shifting the curriculum to match the needs of a technological world. They have no choice, as John Young, president of Hewlett-Packard, sees it:

> The growing pervasiveness of technology—and the certitude of ongoing technical advances—demands that we provide our young people with the solid base of scientific knowledge they will require. It is not only those who create technology who should have a competency in math and science. Those who use technology should also have a degree of understanding about the tools they use. They

247

must also be able to adapt to changes in technology and the new skill requirements they bring them.[14]

No longer can the debate of the importance of the liberal arts or career programs be allowed to degenerate into an either/or argument. They are both important, balance is needed, and the technological-learning age demands it. Educational excellence at all levels must be defined in terms of connectedness and applicability. The liberal arts and technical education need each other.

In the search for synergy, employers, labor, and colleges must find better ways to work together. But even more importantly, colleges and universities must find better ways to work with elementary and secondary schools. Educational technologies can be powerful tools to improve education, as vehicles to extend the teaching and learning process. The task of expanding basic research into the science of human learning and ensuring equity in access to collegiate learning for all learners falls largely upon the shoulders of colleges and universities. The task of developing the appropriate software, the productive simulation, the training of educators for their new role in managing technology, also falls largely upon colleges and universities. But no single sector of the economy or of education can make much progress alone. It must be done together in the search for synergy.

Dateline 2000 Forecast

1. Many major college textbooks of Dateline 2000 will be printed with the accompaniment of an interactive video disc. The publishing business will change dramatically, with the phrase "publish or perish" taking on a whole new meaning.

2. Doing more with fewer people will be at the heart of institutional survival in the decade ahead, and the wise use of technology will aid that process.

3. As telecommunications capacity increases, students will have a great diversity of options in selecting education courses and programs.

4. Telecommuting will become standard collegiate practice, with students taking some classes at home, some on campus, and some in an employer setting.

5. Each college and university will develop and maintain a comprehensive plan for use of technology across the institution.

6. The educational simulator will be developed similar to the aircraft "link trainer" to help students become application literate.

7. The skills gap will be greatly narrowed by Dateline 2000 primarily due to superb education efforts that fully utilize technological breakthroughs to individualize teaching and learning.

8. Technological advances will require colleges, universities, and schools to work more closely together in the search for synergy.

9. There will be a significant increase in multidisciplinary and interdisciplinary teaching and research in colleges and universities.

10. The 1990s will see a synergistic merging of various media to better serve the diversity of the higher education enterprise.

11. The fiber-optic cable will become a commonplace connection to most schools, colleges, businesses, and homes by Dateline 2000.

12. The interactive video disc will become a powerful tool to improve teaching and learning to help meet the different learning styles of students.

13. Faculty will routinely be developing their own textbooks utilizing graphics, text, video, and voice from many different sources.

14. The liberal arts and technical education will move closer together to help develop the flexible, well-educated, and technically competent individual required to meet the needs of the new learning age.

Executive Summary

There are striking similarities between the technological advances made around the turn of the twentieth century and those predicted for the turn of the twenty-first century. Advances in technology and the creation of new inventions offer colleges and universities many exciting new possibilities, but these same advances carry with them some new challenges. Rapid technological developments are pushing higher education institutions of all kinds into a search for synergy, for systems and disciplines to work together. There will be a merging of media utilizing voice, video, text, and graphics.

By Dateline 2000 higher education institutions of all kinds will be discussing and redefining college credit and college coursework. How will autonomous institutions respond to national and worldwide distance learning, the easy rental of college courses from the local video store, and the telecommuting student who takes some college classes at home via fiber-optic cable?

Colleges and universities will be giving much greater attention toward creating application-literate as well as knowledge-literate students. Simulators and simulation experiences will be designed to help the process. Rapid technological change is making the workplace more complex. This fundamental shift in the nature of work requires a worker, at all levels, who is well educated, highly skilled, and highly adaptive, fully able to apply learning in most situations.

Notes

1.   National Science Teachers Association, *Essential Changes in Secondary School Science: Scope, Sequence, and Coordination* (Washington, D. C.: National Science Teachers Association, 1989).
2.   Richard Lindgren, "Gut-Wrenching Changes Loom Ahead," *Michigan Business* (July 1989).
3.   Personal communication.
4.   *Wall Street Journal*, 7 June 1989.
5.   Ralph K. Andrist, *American Century: One Hundred Years of Changing Life Styles in America* (New York: American Heritage Press, 1972).
6.   *Washington Post*, 23 October 1989.
7.   Reader's Digest Editors, *Reader's Digest Almanac & Yearbook, 1986* (New York: Reader's Digest Association, 1986).
8.   Marvin Cetron and Owen Davies, *American Renaissance* (New York: St. Martin Press, 1989).
9.   *Wall Street Journal*, 7 June 1989.
10.   Jeffrey R. Kosnett, "Telecommuting Is Finally Coming," *Changing Times* (November 1989).
11.   Personal communication.
12.   "Video 1990," *Corporate Video Decisions* (April 1989).
13.   Bill Honig, "The Education Excellence Movement: Now Comes the Hard Part," *Phi Delta Kappan* (June 1985).
14.   *Washington Post*, 5 May 1985.

Chapter IX

Some Misperceptions About Cost

Higher education is not just another family obligation to be financed, a charity to be paid, or a function of government to be supported. It is indeed all these things, but it is plainly and simply the future.

Robert Atwell
President
American Council on Education

A re you prepared for the doom-and-gloom stories about the high cost of higher education? As we move into the 1990s you can expect a plethora of reports alleging that college costs are out of control, putting higher education out of reach for large numbers of individuals. The October 1989 *Changing Times* magazine gave front-cover feature to this issue, with the headline "How to Pay a $150,000 Tuition Bill." That kind of headline will certainly give prospective college students, particularly low- and medium-income students, a good scare, and cause politicians to wring their hands and make public pronouncements about uncontrollable college costs. However, the facts do not support the headline for the vast majority of college students.

In recent years the press has regularly put the issue of the high cost of college into headlines and these articles have certainly influenced public opinion. In a 1987 poll conducted by the *Chronicle of Higher Education*, the average person guessed that a typical college student budget (tuition, fees, room, board, books, and transportation) would be about $9,100 for a year at a public college, when the average figure was $6,000 at a four-year college and $5,000 at a community college.

A 1988 survey of 1,000 young people, ages thirteen to twenty-one, conducted by the Gallup Organization for the Council for Advancement and Support of Education revealed significant misperceptions about the costs of higher education. Generally, the young people of America have been led to believe that college costs are about twice as high as the reality. Compare the costs of tuition, fees, and books developed by the College Board with the responses given by the survey respondents.

The average tuition and fee charges are also all well below public perceptions. In short, the full story is not being told about college costs. If a student attended a community college for two years and transferred to a public four-year college for two years,

College Cost Perceptions
(Tuition-Fees-Books)

	Actual 1989 Average Costs (a)	Survey Mean (b)	Survey Median (c)
Public two-year community, technical, or junior college	$1,158	$ 3,519	$2,000
State four-year college or university	$1,977	$ 6,841	$5,000
Private four-year college or university	$8,120	$10,843	$8,000

Note: Although survey mean and median price perceptions included the cost of books and supplies, the College Board figures did not. An additional $391 for two-year public, $411 for four-year public, and $427 for four-year private institutions were added to the tuition and fee costs of $776, $1,566, and $7,793.

(a) Figures, obtained from the College Board, are enrollment-weighted to reflect the experience of the average student.
(b) The mean is the average cost estimate, computed as the sum of all the cost estimates given by respondents, divided by the number of respondents.
(c) The median is the mid-point in the distribution of estimated costs. Approximately one-half of the respondents (50%) gave lower cost estimates than the median value, and one-half of the respondents (50%) gave higher cost estimates than this figure.

Source: Council for Advancement and Support of Education, college cost perception survey, 1988.

graduating in 1992, the average tuition and fees paid would amount to about $5,300 for the total four years. In a low-tuition state like California, with a couple of million students, the four-year tuition and fee costs would be around $3,500 to $4,000 for four years.

Robert Atwell, president of the American Council on Education, views the overstatements on college costs this way:

> By focusing almost entirely on the highest-priced schools, where the competitive pressures are most intense, the

media have obscured the reality that over 90 percent of college students attend either public institutions, where the average annual tuition is something on the order of $1,200, or substantially lower-priced private institutions.[1]

It is interesting to note that only 5.6 percent of the full-time undergraduate college students attend colleges where the tuition-fee cost is $8,000 per year or more, while 72 percent, nearly three out of four of all college students, attend colleges where the tuition-fee cost is under $2,000 on an annual basis.

College Distribution of Undergraduate Students by Tuition and Fees, 1987

Annual Tuition/Fees	Percent of Students Attending
$1,000 or less	34.6%
1,001 - 2,000	37.4
2,001 - 4,000	11.1
4,001 - 6,000	5.6
6,001 - 8,000	5.6
8,001 and above	5.5

Source: An extrapolation of College Board statistics.

The high-cost tuition scare is consistently fed by fuel from the banking and financial institutions. It is not unusual to receive in the mail appeals to put more savings into IRA accounts or various college savings plans, based upon the tuition costs of 5 percent of the colleges. Here is a typical appeal that appeared in a respected financial institution newsletter:

What Costs $14,326?

One year's tuition, room, board and expenses at a ... four-year college. And that's just the *average* bill. The price is steeper at many colleges, and getting higher all the time. For a free brochure on ways to meet the growing cost of college, mail the coupon below, or ask your Account Executive for a copy of "Saving for Your Child's Education."[2]

One cannot criticize those efforts that encourage students and parents to save for college. More must be done in this area. But truth-in-advertising would dictate that parents and students be given the range of college costs rather than only the high end of the scale, particularly when three out of four college students will be attending the lower-cost colleges. One must be quick to add that low- and middle-income individuals and families increasingly are struggling to pay college costs, even in the lower-cost institutions. But presenting misleading information about college costs exacerbates the problem.

Former secretary of education William Bennett brought the matter of college costs to the public attention in the mid-1980s with broad brushstrokes of rhetoric, to the effect that colleges and universities are basically greedy and unproductive. In his lecture at the 350th anniversary celebration of Harvard University, he stated:

> I have never seen a greater interest in *money*—money, cash, bucks—among anybody.... There is an extraordinary gap between the rhetoric and reality of American higher education. The rhetoric... is often exceedingly pious, self-congratulatory, and suffused with the aura of moral superiority.[3]

In a 1987 paper, sent by Secretary Bennett to the nation's governors, he bluntly stated that college and university tuition prices go higher and higher simply because college administrators can raise them, and because federal student aid continues to increase. He urged the governors to develop a cost containment program to control college expenditures and develop programs to make college administrators and faculty more productive.

Bennett may have set off the initial artillery in criticizing college costs, but governors, who in many ways have become the chief state school officers of the states, are carrying on the battle. In the news reports on the historic 1989 education summit meeting between President George Bush and the governors, higher education came in for criticism. Governor Thomas Kean of New Jersey, now president of Drew University, said he was surprised by the vehement statements that governors made about the greed of university officials:

> There is a good deal of feeling among the governors that higher education is not accountable—that what is driving it is not accountability, either academic or fiscal. I was surprised, really, about the consensus on that and the vehemence of some of the feelings led by a number of governors, who felt very, very strongly that there had to be greater accountability, that the goals had to be changed a bit, and it wasn't just a game of every year coming and asking for either higher tuition, more state support, or both.[4]

Governor Neil Goldschmidt of Oregon stated:

> I don't know of any group that says in response to the question about quality, that the issue is money. You ask any university president or faculty what the answer is. The answer is money.[5]

Some university students have become so concerned about the relationship of college costs to the quality of education that they have formed a national organization known as Undergraduates for a Better Education. In its second national conference in October of 1989 fifty students from thirteen universities attended. The organization is being assisted by three Syracuse University faculty members, William Coplin, Michael O'Leary, and Charles Sykes, who authored the book *Profscam: Professors and the Demise of Higher Education*. Professor Sykes states the case for the students this way:

> There's no way universities can expect students to pay $15,000 a year and be presented with huge, impersonal lecture classes, tests graded by scanners, and T. A.'s who can't read.[6]

Some College Attendance Options

Average Tuition and Fee Charges for Baccalaureate Students (using average charges for 1988-89 and inflated 6% per year)				
	Option I	**Option II**	**Option III**	**Option IV**
	Two Years at a Community College and Two Years at a Public 4-Yr. College	Two Years at a Community College and Two Years at a Private 4-Yr. College	Four Years at a Public 4-Yr. College	Four Years at a Private 4-Yr. College
1988-89	$ 730	$ 730	$1,400	$7,070
1989-90	773	773	1,484	7,494
1990-91	1,570	7,940	1,573	7,943
1991-92	1,664	8,416	1,667	8,419
Total	$4,737	$17,859	$6,124	$30,926
Average Total College Expense Budget (using average charges for 1988-89 and inflated 5% per year)				
1988-89	2,760**	2,760**	6,380	12,780
1989-90	2,900**	2,900**	6,710	13,640
1990-91	6,701	14,560*	7,060	14,560
1991-92	7,036	15,288*	7,483	15,288
Total	$19,397	$35,448	$27,633	$56,268

* Total college expense includes tuition and fees, books, transportation, room and board, and incidental costs.
** These two-year college costs are commuter student costs with students residing at home. All other costs are for students residing on campus.

Source: Based upon information extrapolated from *The College Cost Book, 1987-88* (New York: College Entrance Examination Board, 1987) and *1989-90 Fact Book on Higher Education* (New York: American Council on Education and Macmillan Publishing Co., 1989).

Students are beginning to ask if they are getting their money's worth. As college costs go higher and it becomes increasingly difficult to pay higher tuition fees, college administrators can anticipate a new kind of student activism motivated primarily by the cost factor.

What Colleges and Which Students?

In analyzing college and university costs, or the trends in students' ability to pay, a single question must always be asked: What colleges and which students? The institutions of higher education are so diverse, and the students attending those institution are so diverse, that one must always suspect the broad-brush statements about American higher education. As an example, the average yearly tuition and fee variance among the different college attendance options ranges from a low of $100 in California community colleges to a high of $16,495 at Bennington College in Vermont. The U. S. college student has a large number of options and choices in determining college attendance—and college costs.

In 1988 there were 3,389 accredited public and private two-year and four-year colleges and universities. On top of that number there are an estimated 8,000 postsecondary proprietary schools. In terms of the 3,389 colleges and universities, 1,367, or 40 percent, are community, technical, or junior colleges enrolling 37 to 40 percent of all college students. The two-year colleges are now the largest sector of higher education. The next largest sector is the comprehensive four-year colleges, primarily public, numbering 595 institutions and enrolling 27 percent of the students. There are 572 colleges classified as liberal arts colleges, primarily private, enrolling 5 percent of the students. The 213 doctorate-granting universities enroll 28 percent of the students, and 642 specialized institutions, like seminaries and law schools, enroll 3 percent of the students.

As would be expected, not only does this diverse array of institutions differ broadly in tuition charges, but they differ in significant ways in revenue sources and expenditure priorities. Tuition and fees support about 18 percent of the public college and university budgets, while one-half to two-thirds of the private college support comes from tuition and fees. The private colleges depend upon private giving and endowment funds to support about 20 percent of the college budget, while private giving represents a small portion of the public college revenue. However, public colleges of all kinds are placing increasing energy into private-giving efforts.

1987 Institutional Survey

Institution	Number of Institutions	Number of College Credit Students	Percent of Total Students
Community, Technical, and Junior Colleges	1,367	4,518*	37
Doctorate Granting Universities	213	3,429	28
Comprehensive Colleges	595	3,303	27
Liberal Arts Colleges	572	584	5
Specialized Institutions	642	467	3
Totals	3,389	12,301	100

* Figure excludes institutions not reporting 1987 enrollments.

Source: Carnegie Foundation for the Advancement of Teaching classification for the 1988-88 college year, and based upon U. S. Department of Education enrollment reports.

Revenue comes from so many different sources to support the various missions of colleges and universities that rational analysis is made complex. As an example, it is interesting to note that the public institutions account for 76 percent of the higher education headcount enrollment and 68 percent of the revenue and expenditures. Independent institutions account for 24 percent of the enrollment and 32 percent of the income and expenditures. However, as for full-time-equivalent (FTE) enrollment , the private institutions have 30 percent of the FTE students, indicating more full-time students than the public institutions show.

Higher Education Revenue Sources
1985-86

Institution	Amount in Thousands	Sources				
		Percent Tuition and Fees	Percent State and Local Appropriations	Percent Private Giving and Endowments	Percent Grants and Contracts	Other
Public 4 year & above	$41.9	17.9	54.5	5.8	16.4	5.4
2 year	10.6	18.1	69.2	0.7	4.9	7.1
Private 4 year & above	$24.7	51.8	1.3	20.3	16.6	10.0
2 year	.468	66.0	1.0	17.7	7.8	7.5

Higher Education Expenditure Functions
1985-86

Institution	Amount in Thousands	FTE Enrollment	Expenditure per FTE	Object of Expenditures		
				Percent Instruction and Academic Support	Percent Scholarships and Fellowships	Maintenance Operations and Other
Public 4 year & above	$39.7	4.2	$9,452	50.9	3.3	45.8
2 year	10.3	2.4	4,292	58.5	2.2	39.3
Private 4 year & above	4.1	2.0	12,050	44.1	10.4	45.5
2 year	467	.88	5,306	41.3	9.8	48.9

Source: U. S. Department of Education, National Center for Education Statistics, *State Higher Education Profiles, 1988.*

Another way to analyze the financial condition of higher education institutions is to look at the expenditures per FTE. Private four-year colleges spend $12,050 per FTE student, while public community colleges spend $4,291. However, analysis requires a deeper look than surface figures. Several questions come to mind. What is the faculty workload? What is the research and graduate education mission of the institution? Is there an economy of scale in terms of size of institution and size of classrooms? What is the community service component of the institutional mission? What capital outlay has been included in the expenditure figures?

It is possible to compare institutions with similar missions, but difficult, if not inappropriate, to compare institutions with different goals, purposes, and even those serving different populations. When the media talk about the high cost of higher education for all institutions, or when politicians lump all of higher education together when making pronouncements, this not only greatly oversimplifies the issues but misinforms people.

Major Factors Escalating College Costs

A variety of forces, most external to the institution, impact the way colleges and universities must do business. Some would argue that these forces impact all business and all governmental organizations, so there is nothing particularly unusual for institutions of higher education to face. That argument will hold up in some areas of college business but not in others. Colleges and universities are labor-intensive, social-educational institutions attempting to uphold the academic traditions of autonomy (free from politicization), academic freedom, and accountability. Higher education institutions are unique in the sense that they are held accountable in a political environment, yet they must remain free from those who would politicize colleges, and also must maintain enough autonomy to criticize the society that provides the financial support. Indeed, it is a persistent tension.

What are some of the forces that escalate college costs? First and foremost are the forces of inflation or sudden price increases. In the 1970s inflation outdistanced tuition increases and strained the financial ability of the institutions to the limit. The consumer price index (CPI) rose about 8 percent per year, while tuition and fees increased about 6 percent per year. There is always a two- or three-year time lag before colleges and universities can pass along some of the cost increases in the form of institutional cutbacks, or tuition and fee increases. Reports indicating that tuition increases in the 1980s have greatly outdistanced inflation rates are accurate for a few years but not over the long term. Over the thirty years between 1959 and 1989 the inflation rate has risen at a 5 percent annual rate, and tuition has increased at about a 6 percent annual rate for all institutions and at a much lower rate for some colleges, while the expenditures per each full-time-equivalent student have remained fairly level over the years when measured in constant dollars.

Operating Fund Expenditures

	Current Dollars	Constant 1980 Dollars	Full-Time Equivalent Enrollment	Expenditures per FTE in Current Dollars	Expenditures per FTE in Constant 1980 Dollars
All Institutions					
1969-70	$ 21,643,110,000	$ 47,287,888,000	6,283,658	$3,349	$ 7,526
1980-81	64,852,938,000	64,052,938,000	8,819,013	7,263	7,263
1984-85	89,951,263,000	72,192,025,000	8,951,695	10,049	8,065
Public Institutions					
1969-70	$ 13,249,546,000	$ 29,774,261,000	4,555,652	$2,908	$ 6,536
1980-81	42,279,806,000	42,279,886,000	6,642,294	6,365	6,365
1984-85	50,314,550,000	46,801,464,000	6,684,664	8,724	7,001
Private Institutions					
1969-70	$ 7,793,567,000	$ 17,513,634,000	1,728,006	$4,510	$10,135
1980-81	21,773,132,000	21,773,132,000	2,176,719	10,003	10,003
1984-85	31,636,713,000	25,390,620,000	2,267,031	13,955	11,200

Note: FTE for 1969-70 is estimated based on total enrollment.

Source: U. S. Department of Education, National Center for Education Statistics, *Digest of Education Statistics, 1987*.

The U. S. Department of Education has developed a higher education price index (HEPI) in an attempt to assess more accurately the price of the specific goods and services used by colleges and universities. When comparing the CPI and the HEPI with tuition charges over three decades, one can see that tuition increases are slightly lower than the HEPI and slightly higher than the CPI.

Comparison of Changes in Average Tuition Rates
The CPI and the HEPI

	Tuition	HEPI	CPI
1960-61 to 1970-71	3.3%	5.2%	2.9%
1970-71 to 1980-81	6.4%	7.5%	8.2%
1980-81 to 1987-88	9.8%	6.2%	4.3%
Long-term increases, 1960-61 to 1987-88	6.1%	6.3%	5.2%

Note: Average tuition charges weighted by undergraduate FTE enrollment. HEPI figures only extend through 1986-87. CPI figures adjusted to a school-year basis.

Source: Cathy Henderson, American Council on Education, 1988, an unpublished paper developed on the basis of data collected by the National Center for Education Statistics, Bureau of Labor Statistics, and Research Associates of Washington.

Sudden price increases certainly can impact a college budget in unexpected ways. As an example, health care and health insurance may be the earthquake social and financial problem of the 1990s. Health care costs are currently increasing at a 22 percent annual rate, four times faster than the rate of inflation. Our aging and longer-lived U. S. population, new and very expensive technology, and continually increasing medical fees are causing a dramatic and new "medi-flation." Employers, including colleges and universities, are caught in the middle. Employees and college staff members are also caught by being asked to bear more and more of the "medi-flation" expense. Then add to the employee-employer tension the insurance programs furnished to retirees by many colleges in recent years. It is now estimated that public and private employers of the U. S. paid out $9 billion in 1988 to fund insurance costs for retirees, and this cost is increasing at an estimated 15 percent annual rate. A most interesting class action suit has been filed in the Los Angeles U. S. District Court in 1989 on behalf of 84,000 retired General Motors workers. This suit alleges that GM illegally cut back "for life" insurance coverage of ex-GM workers. The settlement of this case could set a far-reaching precedent on providing benefits for college and university retirees.

Enrollment declines can also increase per student costs and dampen income projections. It is difficult for colleges and universities, where faculty are on contract or work under tenure agreements, to adjust quickly to income reductions. Enrollment declines can also greatly impact certain smaller college departments and the size of classes. The productivity of an institution of higher education goes up or down, primarily based upon three factors: the factor of faculty workload, particularly the faculty-student ratio; the factor of the large to small class ratio; and the factor of laboratories and lab equipment required to support programs.

The faculty member is a constant, the classrooms and laboratories are a constant, but the variable for controlling per student costs is enrollment.

Another aspect of the enrollment cost factor that drives up expenditures is the enrollment mix. In colleges that serve large numbers of low-income and disadvantaged individuals, more dollars will be allocated to student financial aid, to counseling, to developmental education programs, to tutoring, and to other student support services. The same set of circumstances applies to large increases of part-time students as full-time students. It is important when analyzing college costs to analyze also the enrollment mix of students, asking the question, which students?

College expenditures per student are related directly to facilities and geography. If a college has few large classrooms, forcing small classes, the costs will go up. If a college is geographically located in an urban environment, requiring heavy investment in security personnel and equipment, the costs will go up, often times dramatically. If a college is located in very cold parts of the country, requiring snow removal and extra heating, or in a hot part of the country, requiring air conditioning, the costs will go up.

High unemployment and economic recession tend to reduce growth in appropriations for public colleges and consequently drive up tuition costs for the students. At the same time, economic recession conditions also prompt more individuals to seek more education or seek job retraining to become qualified for a different job or career. This social phenomenon usually impacts the lower-cost colleges at the same time state and local funds are being reduced.

Economic recession also tends to reduce charitable giving for private colleges. Colleges and universities of all kinds are increasing efforts to raise dollars from the private sector, and a turndown in the overall economy only intensifies the competition for limited public and private dollars.

Shortages of any kind may drive up costs. Competitive salaries are essential to recruit and retain well-qualified faculty, and faculty shortages only drive the salaries higher. An undersupply of new faculty and an increasing volume of retiring faculty indicate that faculty salaries will continue the salary increases of the 1980s on into the 1990s. Faculty salaries are a significant portion of college and university expenditures. Since the early 1980s, faculty salaries have outpaced inflation. As program priorities shift, the faculty shortages become most acute in high-demand fields. As an example, in the mid-1970s, 15 percent of all baccalaureate degrees were awarded in business fields. By the mid-1980s the business portion of degrees awarded had risen to 24 percent. The average salary for a full professor in business was $57,628 in 1987-88, compared to $45,519 for a full professor in foreign languages.

Reduced federal or state commitment to student financial aid has forced institutions to devote more institutional funds for this purpose. Between the years 1980 and 1986 federal Pell Grants awarded to entering college freshmen fell from 31.5 percent of the total students to 16.9 percent. At the same time, local college grants increased from 12.8 percent in 1980 to 17.8 percent in 1986. In addition, more college freshmen were taking out loans to meet college expenses, and this loan burden has become a large concern to many people. Institutional aid has grown from $1.5 billion in 1977 to more than $5 billion in 1986.

The Pell Grant program, named after Senator Claiborne Pell of Rhode Island, is probably the closest the United States has come to sponsoring national education vouchers. They are completely portable and may be used at public and private colleges, universities, and proprietary schools. The federal appropriations for Pell Grants has gone up from $1.5 billion in 1976 to $3.5 billion in 1986, with the average grant going from $761 to $1,330. However, in terms of constant 1982 dollars, the average grant has gone down, from $1,414 to $1,214, over this same time period, with many more students participating.

An analysis of the growth in selected federal budget outlays over the decade of the 1980s presents a revealing picture, showing dramatic jumps in federal spending for defense, social security,

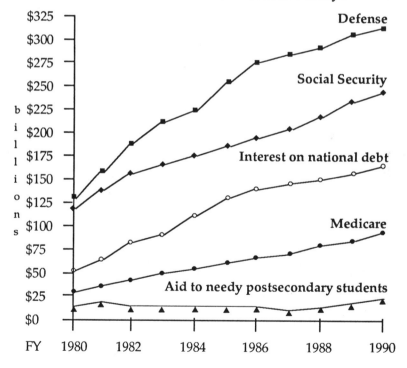

Growth of Selected Federal Outlays

Source: Budget of the United States government, fiscal year 1990.

interest on the federal debt, and Medicare, while aid for needy postsecondary students has remained relatively flat.

Another aspect of financing higher education is the problem of keeping up. It is difficult for most colleges and universities to keep up with the fast-changing state-of-the-art equipment. Increased budgets for computer hardware and software lead the list of reasons given for increasing college budgets. However, there are many other equipment needs. As colleges move into such areas as laser technology, electron microscopy, robotics, CAD/CAM, and a host of other technological developments, college budgets will be affected.

Percentage of All Institutions Reporting Larger Shares of Institutional Budgets Devoted to the Following Items (1987-88 Increase Over 1986-87 Levels)

	All Institutions	Public 2-Year	Public 4-Year	Independent
Computer Equipment and Operations	87%	85%	87%	88%
Faculty Salaries	72%	78%	65%	69%
Admissions and Recruitment	63%	54%	49%	75%
Institutional Student Aid	54%	35%	34%	78%
Renovations and Repairs to Existing Facilities	45%	48%	37%	47%
Student Support Services	43%	40%	24%	52%

Source: Elaine El-Khawas, *Campus Trends, 1988* (Washington, D. C.: American Council on Education, 1988).

Cost Containment Measures

In response to the criticism about the high cost of higher education, college and university leaders have generally assumed a defensive posture, citing some true but well-worn arguments. Deferred maintenance of campus buildings and equipment requires immediate attention or the costs will only go higher. New dollars are required to purchase state-of-the-art computers and scientific equipment, and to build facilities. Learning resources, library materials, supplies, energy costs, insurance, have experienced rapid increases. Salaries have increased rapidly to repair the faculty and staff salary losses due to the hyperinflation of the 1970s.

It is odd that, with an exception here and there, little is said about cost containment efforts. Much is being done in this area, but dollar-stretching activities have received little publicity. The general public seems to have little knowledge about college and university cost containment efforts. The public only knows about high costs.

Arnold Weber, president of Northwestern University, talks about the public perceptions of cost this way:

> The public will not—and should not—accept the inviolability of large tuition increases in the cause of "educational excellence" any more than it has accepted, or will accept, ever-increasing charges to obtain high-quality medical care. If the public, acting through Congress, has been unwilling to accept rising medical costs in the interest of extending human life, it is unlikely that it will tolerate what it perceives to be excessive tuition increases to attain that state of "excellence" that educators cherish. In both cases, the services involved are viewed as essential, or near essential, and consumers believe that they are being exploited by the fixed nature of the demand or by tacit collusion. . . .
>
> Our claim for special treatment by the public cannot be sustained without our displaying a sense of discipline and reciprocal responsibility to the society whose support we must ultimately earn through our actions.[7]

A healthy economy and sustained low-inflation rates certainly help colleges and universities contain costs. Increased state and federal support for student financial aid programs helps to relieve the pressure on institutions to provide locally funded need-based financial aid. Successful private fundraising campaigns can underwrite expensive capital outlay projects, local scholarship programs, distinguished teaching chair programs, and the procurement of state-of-the-art equipment. Growth in enrollment, and the related revenue enhancement, permit program development activities and increase productivity by filling vacant classroom chairs. These efforts certainly help to control college costs. But what has not received widespread attention are the efforts colleges and universities are making to stretch the available dollars.

The National Association of College and University Business Officers (NACUBO) and the USX Foundation have sponsored a program of college cost-reduction incentive awards since 1975. The awards (which generally receive the long-yawn treatment from the media) recognize innovative cost-saving ideas implemented by colleges and universities in a given calendar year. Even though the dollar savings are not massive for any single institution, a few examples of the winners over the years give a pretty good sample of dollar-stretching ideas being implemented in colleges and universities all across the country.

Vanderbilt University has developed a Professional Student Assistant Program. College students are placed into paraprofessional and entry-level college positions related to their individual field of studies. Under the mentor coaching of university personnel, students enhance their professional and educational development while at the same time providing support services for the Vanderbilt staff. Officials at Vanderbilt estimate that this program is not only helpful to students but saves the university an estimated $182,000 per year in personnel costs.

The University of Pennsylvania has cut costs by reconditioning laser printer toner cartridges. Entrepreneurial students run a student-operated business reconditioning and refilling toner cartridges at half the cost of replacements. The students pick up and return the recycled cartridges within twenty-four hours from more than 200 laser printers across the university campus. University of Pennsylvania officials estimate an annual $200,000 savings from this program, which requires no additional investment, and savings are realized immediately.

The University of Missouri at Columbia has solved the problem of duplicate mailing costs by creating the Automated Chargeback Manifest System. The purpose of the system is to combine mail from different departments going to the same address into a single package. The U. S. Postal Service and United Parcel Service give cheaper rates for postage with higher weights, and of course there is a savings in mailing one large package rather than several smaller packages. A nonregulated postage meter has been programmed to charge any pieces with a common mailing address to the mailing department's accounts without affixing postage. The pieces are then combined with others going to a common address. It is estimated that this system is saving the university $205,000 on an annual basis.

Lane Community College in Eugene, Oregon, has won the NACUBO-USX award twice in the last ten years. For its 1985 award this college simplified a cumbersome purchase order process by issuing bank credit cards to selected staff members for material and supply purchases under $100. The new system eliminates many complaints, saves staff time, and speeds the receipt of goods in many cases. The college puts its annual savings in processing costs at over $118,000. Complaints about the old system caused the president to call for a review of the process. An interdepartmental team found that 62 percent of all purchase orders were for less than $100 and constituted only 3.5 percent of the college's budget spent through purchase orders. To process a purchase order cost an estimated $75 in supplies and staff time. The credit card solution was tested for five months in seventeen departments and, after proving successful, was opened to all departments. Cards are used only for "petty cash" purchases of materials and supplies costing less than $100 and chargeable to a single departmental budget account number. A departmental budget administrator completes and signs an agreement setting forth the administrator's responsibility under the program and the conditions of use.

Here are some other examples of cost containment and prudent financial management outside of the NACUBO-USX awards program.

The Meramec campus of the St. Louis Community College develops a quarterly student financial aid report for institution-wide consumption. This report not only helps one to gain a better understanding of the total student financial aid program, but also helps to smooth the audit process for this program and eliminate audit problems.

Student Financial Aid Report
St. Louis Community College-Meramec

1. Number of Student Aid Applicants (Fall Term)	1,083
2. Number of Student Aid Applicants (Previous Term)	1,027
3. Number of Eligible Applicants	931
4. Number of Ineligible Applicants	96
5. Number of Pell Grant Recipients	687
6. Pell Grant Funds Awarded	$676,051
7. Number of College Work-Study Program Workers	150
8. College Work-Study Program Funds Expended	$57,829
9. Biweekly College Work-Study Payroll (Average)	$10,520
10. Number of Supplemental Grant (SEOG) Recipients	110
11. SEOG Funds Expended	$40,575
12. Number of Guaranteed Student Loan (GSL) Recipients	84
13. GSL Funds Expended	$100,360
14. Number of Short-Term Loan Recipients	150
15. Short-Term Loan Funds Expended	$46,859
16. Short-Term Loan Funds Collected	$11,755
17. Number of Part-Time Work Applicants	90
18. Number of Veterans Certified	187
19. Number of Scholarship Applicants	283
20. Campus Scholarship Funds Awarded	$55,204.25

The faculty and administration of San Joaquin Delta College in Stockton, California, have developed an exemplary salary and faculty load program that allows that college to maintain one of the better college salary programs in California and, at the same time, one of the lower per-student-expenditure levels. Based upon weekly student contact hours (WSCH) the faculty collectively bargained contract recognizes an institution-wide WSCH target, with certain laboratory classes and technical education classes excepted. Faculty are also provided readers and tutorial assistance in certain classes. Faculty members whose total WSCH load goes above the institution-wide WSCH target may receive additional pay, time off, or a reduced load the next term. Faculty below the institution-wide WSCH target must pick up an increased load the next term. In this college small classes are monitored carefully. When classes are canceled because of small enrollments, the college offers a series of midterm classes (four weeks later) to pick up those students from the canceled classes. This college has found that this combination of monitoring faculty workload and small classes lowers per student costs and increases productivity.

Colleges and universities are increasingly hiring risk managers to monitor all college insurance programs. If the college is small, it often allies itself with other community organizations, like school districts, to negotiate benefit packages and monitor insurance programs. Skillful risk management is saving colleges dollars as well as better serving their people. Some employers are even offering cash awards to employees who uncover physician, hospital, or other insurance-related overcharges. The Ryder System, which performs such a service, netted a $65,000 savings in 1988 by watching for too many second opinions and duplicate testing.

A cost containment trend is emerging for larger colleges and universities to establish self-insurance programs for fire, liability, error and omission, and even health insurance. Where self-insurance is not practical, co-insurance is becoming a common practice, with large deductibles and insurance companies only insuring major catastrophes or major medical benefits.

As insurance costs increase, college administrators are carefully explaining the benefits plan and related costs to the staff on a regular basis. Many colleges include a benefits explanation with the employee paychecks about twice a year. It is increasingly important to explain clearly the reasons for any change in the benefits package keyed to the employee's cost load as well as the cost load of the college. A recent Communications Workers of America strike against some telephone companies centered on the issue of whether to require the employees to pick up some of the increasing health insurance costs.

College leaders across the country are regularly exploring the limitation in benefits coverage, and other insurance programs, before announcing any changes. A growing number of colleges and universities now cover the spouse of an employee for health insurance only if the employee is the main wage earner of the family. Some colleges now offer a cafeteria benefits plan. If an employee has health insurance coverage through a spouse, some of the equivalent health insurance dollars can be applied to wages. Administrators are making sure that insurance plans have a "drop dead" provision that allows the college to cancel if coverage does not provide the staff with cost-effective and quality service.

Comparative Figures

In terms of comparative figures, there has been little change in college income and expenditure categories over the past several years. In 1969 student tuition and fees made up 23.6 percent of the total college revenue for higher education institutions. Fifteen years later that figure was nearly the same at 23 percent. Federal government contributions to higher education institutions were 16 percent of college revenues in 1969 and dropped to 12.4 percent in 1985. At the same time, state government contributions rose from 26.9 percent to 29.8 percent, making up for the shortfall from the federal government.

In the expenditure side of the budget, instructional salaries accounted for 32.7 percent of the budget in 1969 and 32.0 percent in 1985. Support services stood at 19.5 percent of the expenditures in 1969 and 19.4 percent in 1985. The largest shift in the expenditure categories was in university-operated hospitals, moving from 3.2 percent in 1969 to 8.9 percent in 1985.

Even in terms of college expenditures per full-time-equivalent student, there have been no dramatic shifts. In relation to constant 1980 dollars, expenditures per FTE have gone up over a fifteen-year period, from $7,526 to $8,065. Of course in terms of current dollars there are significant differences, from an average $3,349 per FTE in 1969 to an average $10,049 per FTE for all college students in all kinds of colleges.

Fifteen-Year Financing Comparison of Institutions of Higher Education in Current Dollars: Revenues and Expenditures

| | Percent Distribution of College Resources | | | | | |
| | 1969-70 | | | 1984-85 | | |
Current Revenue Fund	Total	Public	Private	Total	Public	Private
Student Tuition and Fees	23.6	15.1	38.6	23.0	14.5	38.7
Federal Government	16.0	14.6	18.6	12.4	10.6	15.9
State Governments	26.9	41.3	1.3	29.8	45.1	1.9
Local Governments	3.6	5.2	0.8	2.6	3.6	0.6
Private Grants and Contracts	4.7	1.9	9.5	5.3	3.1	9.3
Endowment Income	2.1	0.4	5.0	2.3	0.6	5.4
Sales and Services	16.7	15.7	18.6	21.3	20.0	23.7
Other Sources	6.4	5.7	7.5	3.3	2.6	4.5
Current Expenditure Accounts	Percent Distribution of College Expenditures					
Instruction	32.7	35.7	27.6	32.0	34.8	26.8
Research	10.2	9.6	11.2	8.4	8.8	7.7
Public Service	2.5	3.6	0.6	3.2	4.0	1.7
Academic Support	3.1	3.1	3.0	2.6	2.7	2.5
Operation and Maintenance of Plant	7.3	7.5	6.9	8.2	8.6	7.3
Scholarship and Fellowship	4.7	3.4	6.8	4.1	2.4	7.3
Auxiliary Enterprises	13.2	12.3	14.7	11.1	11.0	11.3
Hospitals	3.2	3.1	3.3	8.9	8.4	9.8
Independent Operations	3.6	2.4	5.6	2.1	0.2	5.6
Support Services	19.5	19.1	20.3	19.4	19.1	20.0

Source: Joel West, "Changing Patterns of Finance in Higher Education," unpublished paper, 1988.

Student Financial Aid

One factor that has not been discussed sufficiently in the public policy arena is the increasing number of college students who are working while going to college. In the 1986-87 college year more than 50 percent of all college students were employed, up from 40 percent in 1980. Increasing employment is most often a sign of increasing financial pressures on students. Younger students who do not have money to pay for a college education are working to help pay for it. Older students, whose priority is employment, are usually going to college to enhance a career or for enrichment experiences, and are nearly all working not only to pay for college expenses but to support a home and/or family.

Of the college students aged twenty-four and under, 87 percent of the part-time students and 43 percent of the full-time students were employed in 1986-87. American students finance higher education in five principal ways: working and self-contribution; parental contributions; state appropriations to public sector institu-

College Students (24 or Younger) Who Were Employed in 1986-87

	Full-Time	Part-Time	Total
Enrolled Full-Time	5.4%	37.6%	43.0%
Part-Time	62.8%	24.5%	87.2%

Source: Carol Francis, "Where Income Is Keeping Up," Carol Francis and Associates, unpublished paper prepared for the American Association of State Colleges and Universities.

tions and some private institutions; federal government contributions, primarily need-based student financial aid; and voluntary contributions from individuals and private sector businesses.

Families and students pay a much larger share of college costs, between 25 and 30 percent, than is the case in other first-world nations. The support from voluntary giving and from government appropriations is sizable, but it is the individual, the consumer, who bears the largest share of investing in a college education in the United States. The word has gotten around that the gap is widening between those individuals with a high school diploma and those with a college degree. In 1973 the earnings difference between the average male with a high school diploma and the average male with a college degree was 16 percent. By 1987 that gap had widened to 50 percent. Three out of four Americans say that even though the cost may be high, a college education is still worth the cost.[8]

In recognition of the tremendous investment individuals must make in securing a college education, and the difficulty low- and middle-income families have in helping fund a college education, federal and state government leaders have developed a government-sponsored student financial aid program that has now grown to $21 billion a year. Of this total an estimated $14.7 billion comes from federal sources, $2.1 billion comes from state sources, and nearly $4.2 billion comes from the institutions themselves, and this latter category is growing. Richard Rosser, president of the National Association of Independent Colleges and Universities, indicates the growing local college investment in student financial aid:

> Because federal aid in real dollars to students at independent colleges and universities has declined during the past decade, these institutions have had to make up the difference by giving out much more of their own money. In 1987-88, independent colleges and universities provided $2.3 billion in undergraduate financial assistance from their own funds, up from $397 million in 1970-71.[9]

The Pell Grant program is by far the nation's largest college grant program, making need-based awards to 2.6 million students involving $3.5 billion dollars in 1986. This figure is up from $1.4 billion serving 1.9 million students ten years earlier in 1976. An interesting shift has occurred in Pell Grants during the decade of the 1980s. The share of grants going to students in proprietary institutions increased from 13 percent in 1981 to 22 percent in 1986. Total Pell Grants to students attending proprietary schools rose from $300 million to $800 million during the same period.

The largest and most controversial source of student financial aid is the Guaranteed Student Loan (GSL) program. This loan fund has grown from $1 billion in the mid-1970s to over $8 billion in the mid-1980s. The legal assurance of receiving a full-value-interest subsidy and guaranteed default payments has encouraged lenders

Financial Aid to Undergraduates, Fall 1986

	Proportion of Students Receiving Financial Assistance, by Source			Proportion of Students Receiving Financial Aid, by Type of Assistance		
	Total	Federal	Other	Grants	Loans	Work-Study
By type of institution						
Public						
Doctoral	46.8	35.5	28.5	36.4	27.6	5.8
Other 4-year	47.3	38.4	30.0	38.1	24.9	8.1
2-year	28.5	19.9	18.1	25.4	7.8	2.4
Less-than-2-year	51.8	41.9	22.9	46.1	19.6	3.4
All	38.0	28.5	23.7	31.5	17.3	4.6
Private, not-for-profit						
Doctoral	61.8	45.7	50.8	52.2	39.5	13.0
Other 4-year	67.9	50.1	57.7	60.1	42.1	16.4
2-year	63.9	47.9	44.7	53.6	35.7	5.7
Less-than-2-year	66.2	59.4	35.5	55.5	40.4	5.0
All	65.3	48.4	54.1	56.7	40.7	14.3
Private, for-profit						
2-year and above	82.7	79.2	24.2	54.9	69.3	1.2
Less-than-2-year	84.8	81.4	13.0	63.5	71.5	0.5
All	84.0	80.6	17.2	60.3	70.7	0.8
By student characteristics						
Sex						
Men	44.5	34.1	27.8	36.5	23.9	5.6
Women	46.3	35.6	29.7	38.6	24.9	6.6
Racial and ethnic group						
American Indian	48.9	40.3	28.9	41.2	19.7	6.8
Asian	40.5	33.3	28.5	36.2	18.4	7.6
Black, non-Hispanic	63.8	55.7	33.2	56.6	35.0	9.8
Hispanic	47.8	40.9	27.2	41.1	24.0	5.8
White, non-Hispanic	43.3	32.0	28.4	35.1	23.6	5.6
Age						
23 or younger	50.0	39.0	33.5	41.2	28.7	8.4
24 to 29	42.8	34.2	21.9	34.4	22.5	3.6
30 and older	35.4	24.8	21.7	30.6	14.4	2.0
Attendance status						
Full-time	58.3	47.4	37.3	48.2	34.2	9.2
Part-time	24.4	14.4	15.0	20.3	8.4	1.1
All	45.5	34.9	28.8	37.6	24.4	6.1

Source: *Chronicle of Higher Education*, as developed from U. S. Department of Education data and reports.

to participate in the program. There is little doubt that the GSL program has helped millions of needy students, particularly students attending the higher-cost colleges. But the sheer size and scope of this program has thrown a publicity spotlight on it along with criticism that the program lacks accountability. This criticism has been triggered by a high loan default rate by some students. Basically, subsidy costs of the GSL are "back-loaded" in that the loan costs occur primarily after a GSL loan has been made to a student and not at the time of loan origination. Most of the subsidies "pile up" and come due years later. The compounding effect of the subsidy program has made the GSL program come under fire as the subsidy costs rise virtually unabated into the 1990s.

Obscured in the loan default aspect of the GSL program is the fact that colleges and universities are but one player on the student loan stage. In fact, many college leaders feel they are being unfairly criticized for lax agency and private-lending-institution loan collection policies. The loans are made by the lending agencies and not the colleges. Colleges have little or no input in deciding which students should receive loans. Bluntly put, there is little accountability in the current GSL program, and colleges and schools, particularly those serving low-income students, are being blamed for student defaults.

There can be little doubt that the 1990s will see the federal loan program overhauled and significantly modified. Editorial writers who have been long-term supporters of the federal student financial aid are now urging that changes be made.

> Both House and Senate appropriations committees also charge in their report that the aid programs have been allowed to drift away from their original purpose of producing college graduates, that too much money is now taken up by suspect proprietary schools and that too much— nearly $2 billion a year—is required to cover loan defaults on student loans. The government needs to maintain support for higher education. No federal investment is more important; none has greater equalizing effect. At the same time there is a need, neglected in the past, to make sure that this large amount of money is being usefully spent.[10]

281

Even Frank Mensel, vice president for federal relations of the American Association of Community and Junior Colleges, and one of the longtime advocates for increasing federal student financial aid, is now advocating that public community, technical, and junior colleges move out of the GSL program and leave the program for private sector schools and colleges.

However, the good news is that as students begin to repay their college loans of the 1980s, as the loan default collection procedures are improved, and as school and colleges learn how to better counsel prospective students on the payment accountability for the loan, the GSL program will improve and remain a stable source of funding for needy students. Add to this good news the efforts that states and private organizations are making to provide other avenues for student financial aid.

The state of Michigan became the leader in establishing the first state government-run tuition-guarantee program. Today twenty-eight states have plans in the works to promote "savings for college" programs. The Michigan model of the college savings program allows parents and benefactors to pay for tuition years before the student goes to college, and they are guaranteed that their contract will cover college tuition costs no matter how much they rise. Payments are made based upon the age of the prospective student and an estimate of interest to be earned on the payments. However, the more common pattern that seems to be emerging in other states is the tax-exempt savings bond approach.

The large and unresolved worry for the 1990s is how middle-income families and individuals will finance a college education. The relatively well-off and the most needy students will usually find ways to pay for college, but that large segment of the population called "middle incomers" will continue to find it difficult to finance college costs. This observation argues for a low-tuition policy, and providing access as well as choice in the college financing debates of the future.

Dateline 2000 Forecast

1.   In the short term, through 1993 or 1994, it will continue to be difficult to raise the necessary public and private funds to support college programs. In the longer term, through the second half of the decade, the financial pressures should ease somewhat. The student loan default issue will fade into the background, cost containment programs will be well in place, the federal deficit problem will likely be solved, or on the way to solution, and the need for better educated and trained individuals to meet workforce needs will be great.

2.   Cost containment will become a major point of discussion and action among college and university leaders during the decade ahead.

3.   The media, as well as finance institutions, will begin reporting on college costs across the diversity of institutions, including the lower-cost colleges, and thereby giving more individuals hope that they can afford to go to college.

4.   Tuition and fee costs will rise during the 1990s, but about even with the cost of inflation.

5.   The tax-exempt college savings bond will become as common-place in the 1990s as war bonds were during World War II, with grandpas and grandmas investing heavily for the college education of the grandchildren.

6.   The larger public and private universities will downsize by placing ceilings upon enrollment. This will result in more students enrolling in public community colleges and four-year public regional state colleges.

7.   Faculty shortages will drive up faculty salaries, particularly in certain fields.

8.   The entire federal student financial aid program will be dramatically reshaped in the 1990s, perhaps developing different pro-

grams for different segments of the postsecondary education community.

9. A set of common college financial indicators will be developed and linked to accountability indicators whereby colleges and universities within various categories will be called upon to report upon the health of the college utilizing these indicators.

10. Students will become increasingly active in debating and influencing college cost-versus-quality issues.

Executive Summary

The cost of higher education has been considerably overstated. College students attend institutions where the annual tuition-fee costs vary as much as from $100 per year to $16,500 per year. Yet, three out of four college students attend institutions where the annual tuition and fee costs are under $2,000.

College and university leaders are faced with a rising public sentiment that even though a college education is worth the investment, the costs are too high. Federal officials, governors, and other leaders are beginning to wonder out loud about matching state funding for colleges and universities with accountability for results. This will mean that college leaders must clearly communicate the mission of the institution. It will be inappropriate to compare institutions with different goals, purposes, and student bodies.

There are many valid reasons as to why college costs continue to rise. But cost containment will be a motivational force in the decade ahead for colleges and universities of all kinds. Cost containment discussions will not be limited to college presidents, but will involve the entire college community.

Student financial aid for needy students will continue to be up at the front of the college finance agenda during the 1990s. There will be a greater push for financial aid help from middle-income individuals. As a result, the tax-exempt college savings bond program will take off and be fully airborne by Dateline 2000.

Notes

1.   Robert Atwell, *President's Letter*, American Council on Education (September 1989).

2.   *Money Talk*, Dean Witter Reynolds, Inc. (Autumn 1989).

3.   *Higher Education and National Affairs* (October 1986).

4.   *Chronicle of Higher Education* (4 October 1989).

5.   *Chronicle of Higher Education* (4 October 1989).

6.   *Chronicle of Higher Education* (1 November 1989).

7.   *Chronicle of Higher Education* (11 October 1989).

8.   Council for Advancement and Support of Education, *Attitudes About American Colleges* (Washington, D. C.: Council for Advancement and Support of Education, 1989).

9.   *Washington Post*, 25 August 1989.

10. *Washington Post*, 15 October 1989.

References

Adelman, Clifford. "A Basic Statistical Portrait of American Higher Education." Unpublished paper, 1987.

American Association of Community and Junior Colleges. *Keeping America Working Project Report.* Washington, D. C.: American Association of Community and Junior Colleges, 1988.

——. *Policy Statement on Access.* Washington, D. C.: American Association of Community and Junior Colleges, 1987.

——. *Statistical Yearbook of Community, Technical, and Junior Colleges 1987/88.* Washington, D.C.: American Association of Community and Junior Colleges, 1987.

American Association of Community and Junior Colleges, Commission on the Future of Community Colleges. *Building Communities: A Vision for a New Century.* Washington, D. C.: American Association of Community and Junior Colleges, 1988.

American Association of State Colleges and Universities. *To Secure the Blessings of Liberty: Report of the National Commission on the Role and Future of State Colleges and Universities.* Washington, D. C.: American Association of State Colleges and Universities, 1986.

American Council on Education. *1989-90 Fact Book on Higher Education.* New York: American Council on Education and Macmillan Publishing Co., 1989.

Andrist, Ralph K. *American Century: One Hundred Years of Changing Life Styles in America.* New York: American Heritage Press, 1972.

Angel, Dan. "The Academic Skills Program." Unpublished paper, 1989.

Applebee, Arthur N., et al. *Learning to Be Literate in America: Reading, Writing, and Reasoning. The Nation's Report Card.* Princeton: National Assessment of Educational Progress, Educational Testing Service, 1987.

Arbeiter, Solomon. *Enrollment of Blacks in College: Is the Supply of Black High School Graduates Adequate? Is the Demand for College by Blacks Weakening?* Research and Development Update. New York: College Entrance Examination Board, 1987.

287

Astin, Alexander W. *Minorities in American Higher Education*. San Francisco: Jossey-Bass, 1982.

Atwell, Robert. *President's Letter*, American Council on Education (September 1989).

Becker, Betsy Jane. Review of *The Case Against the SAT*, by James Crouse and Dale Trusheim. *Thought & Action* (Spring 1989).

Bell, Terrel H. *The Thirteenth Man: A Reagan Cabinet Memoir*. New York: Free Press, 1988.

Bowen, Howard, and Jack Schuster. *American Professors: A National Resource Imperiled*. New York: Oxford University Press, 1986.

Boyer, Carol M., et al. *Assessment and Outcomes Measurement. A View from the States*. Denver: Education Commission of the States, 1987.

Boyer, Ernest. *College: The Undergraduate Experience in America*. New York: Harper & Row, 1987.

Boyer, Ernest, and Fred Hechinger. *Higher Learning in the Nation's Service*. Princeton: Carnegie Foundation for the Advancement of Teaching, 1981.

Breneman, David W., and Susan C. Nelson. *Financing Community Colleges: An Economic Perspective*. Washington, D. C.: Brookings Institution, 1981.

Brock, Michael. "Who Gets to the University." Unpublished paper, 1986.

Cetron, Marvin, and Owen Davies. *American Renaissance*. New York: St. Martin Press, 1989.

Chronicle of Higher Education (3 July 1989, 4 October 1989, 11 October 1989, 1 November 1989).

Clarke, Marianne K. *Revitalizing State Economies*. Washington, D. C.: National Governors' Association, 1986.

College Entrance Examination Board. *The College Cost Book, 1987-88*. New York: College Entrance Examination Board, 1987.

———. *Today's Urban University Students: Part 2. A Cast Study of Hunter College*. New York: College Entrance Examination Board, 1985.

———. *Trends in Student Aid: 1980-89*. Washington D. C.: College Entrance Examination Board, 1989.

College Entrance Examination Board, Advisory Panel on the Scholastic Aptitude Test Score Decline. *On Further Examination*. New York: College Entrance Examination Board, 1977.

Congressional Record. 98th Cong., 2d sess., 14 June 1984.

Corporate Video Decisions (April 1989).

Council for Advancement and Support of Education. *Attitudes About American Colleges.* Washington, D. C.: Council for Advancement and Support of Education, 1989.

Council for International Exchange of Scholars. Fulbright Scholar Program, 1986 Annual Report.

Council on Postsecondary Accreditation. *Educational Quality and Accreditation: A Call for Diversity, Continuity and Innovation.* Washington, D. C.: Council on Postsecondary Accreditation, 1986.

Cyert, Richard M., and David M. Mowery. *Technology and Employment: Innovation and Growth in the U. S. Economy.* Washington, D. C.: National Academy Press, 1987.

Drucker, Peter. "How Schools Must Change." *Psychology Today* (May 1989).

Eaton, Judith. "A Message Sent to Students." *Philadelphia Inquirer,* 29 May 1987.

Edelman, Marian Wright. "The Future at Risk." *Liberal Education* (May/June 1987).

Elam, Stanley M., and Alec M. Gallup. "The 21st Annual Gallup Poll of the Public's Attitudes Toward the Public Schools." *Phi Delta Kappan* (September 1989).

El-Khawas, Elaine. *Campus Trends, 1986.* Washington, D. C.: American Council on Education, 1986.

——. *Campus Trends, 1988.* Washington, D. C.: American Council on Education, 1988.

Francis, Carol. "Where Income Is Keeping Up." Unpublished paper, 1987.

Gordon, Mary, and Meredith Ludwig. "Addressing the Problems of Youth: Public Four-Year Colleges Respond." *Memo to the President,* American Association of State Colleges and Universities (4 August 1989).

Harris, Louis. *Inside America.* New York: Vintage Books, 1987.

Harvard Institute for the Management of Lifelong Education. Annual Report, 1989.

Hesburgh, Theodore M. *The Hesburgh Papers: Higher Values in Higher Education.* Kansas City, Kan.: Universal Press, 1979.

Higher Education and National Affairs (20 October 1986).

Honig, Bill. "The Educational Excellence Movement: Now Comes the Hard Part." *Phi Delta Kappan* (June 1985).

Hudson Institute. *Workforce 2000: Work and Workers for the Twenty-first Century.* Indianapolis: Hudson Institute, 1987.

Institute of International Education. *Open Doors: 1985-86 Report on International Educational Exchange.* New York: Institute of International Education, 1985.

Kaplan, Robert B. "Foreign Students: Developing Institutional Policy. *College Board Review* (Spring 1987).

Kiplinger Washington Letter Staff. *The New American Boom: Exciting Changes in American Life and Business Between Now and the Year 2000.* Washington, D. C.: Kiplinger Washington Editors, 1986.

Kosnett, Jeff. "Telecommuting Is Finally Coming." *Changing Times* (November 1989).

Lakoff, George, and Mark Johnson. *Metaphors We Live By.* Chicago: University of Chicago Press, 1980.

Lindgren, Richard. "Gut-Wrenching Changes Loom Ahead." *Michigan Business* (July 1989).

Lippmann, Walter. *Public Opinion.* New York: Harcourt-Brace, 1922.

Lynton, Ernest A., and Sandra E. Elman. *New Priorities for the University.* San Francisco: Jossey-Bass, 1986.

Main, Jeremy. "Business Goes to College for a Brain Gain." *Fortune* (16 March 1987).

McClain, Charles J. *In Pursuit of Degrees with Integrity: A Value-Added Approach to Undergraduate Assessment.* Washington, D. C.: American Association of State Colleges and Universities, 1984.

Money Talk, Dean Witter Reynolds, Inc. (Autumn 1989).

Naisbitt, John. *Megatrends.* New York: Warner Books, 1984.

National Science Teachers Association. *Essential Changes in Secondary School Science: Scope, Sequence, and Coordination.* Washington, D. C.: National Science Teachers Association, 1989.

Nettles, Michael T., et al. "Comparative and Predictive Analysis of Black and White Students' College Achievement and Experiences." *Journal of Higher Education* (May/June 1986).

Newman, Frank. *Higher Education and the American Resurgence.* Princeton: Carnegie Foundation for the Advancement of Teaching, 1985.

New York Times, 9 May 1983, 23 March 1989, 6 September 1989.

Oliver, Leonard P. "Teaching Civic Value and Political Judgment in the Community College." In *Colleges of Choice: The Enabling Impact of the Community College,* ed. Judith Eaton. New York: Macmillan, 1988.

Parade (4 June 1989).

Parnell, Dale. *The Neglected Majority.* Washington, D. C.: Community College Press, 1985.

Paul, Faith. *Declining Minority Access to College in Metropolitan Chicago.* Working Paper No. 2, Metropolitan Opportunity Project. Chicago: University of Chicago, 1987.

People For the American Way. *Democracy's Next Generation.* Washington, D. C.: People For the American Way, 1989.

Pickens, William. "California Response to Faculty Supply and Demand." Paper presented at the Annual Meeting of the Western College Association, Los Angeles, California, 1988.

Pyle, Cassandra. "Our Shortfall in International Competence." *AGB Reports* (March/April 1984).

Ravitch, Diane, and Chester E. Finn, Jr. *What Do Seventeen-Year-Olds Know? A Report on the First National Assessment of History and Literature.* New York: Harper & Row, 1987.

Reader's Digest Editors. *Reader's Digest Almanac & Yearbook, 1986.* New York: Reader's Digest Association, 1986.

Rentschler, William H. "The Logics of Low Tech." *American Way* (May 1987).

Roueche, John E., and George A. Baker. *Access and Excellence: The Open-Door College.* Washington, D. C.: Community College Press, 1987.

Simon, Paul. *Tongue Tied American: Confronting the Foreign Language Crisis.* New York: Continuum, 1980.

Smith, Bruce. "The Personal Development of the Commuter Student." *Community College Review* (Summer 1989).

Southern Association of Colleges and Schools. *Resource Manual on Institutional Effectiveness.* Decatur, Ga.: Southern Association of Colleges and Schools, 1989.

Southern Growth Policies Board, Commission on the Future of the South. *Halfway Home and a Long Way to Go.* Atlanta: Southern Growth Policies Board, 1986.

State Higher Education Executive Officers Association. *A Difference of Degrees: State Initiatives to Improve Minority Student Achievement.* Denver: State Higher Education Executive Officers Association, 1987.

Stokes, Bruce. "Moral Leadership." *National Journal* (24 January 1987).

Trends and Learning Newsletter (Summer 1989).

U. S. Department of Commerce, Bureau of the Census. Current Population Reports. Washington, D. C.: GPO, 1973, 1978, 1984, 1986, 1987.

——. *Statistical Abstract of the United States, 1989.* Washington, D. C.: GPO, 1989.

U. S. Department of Education. *Schools That Work: Educating Disadvantaged Children.* Washington, D. C.: GPO, 1987.

U. S. Department of Education, National Center for Education Statistics. *The Condition of Education, 1989.* Washington, D. C.: GPO, 1989.

——. *Digest of Education Statistics, 1987.* Washington D. C.: GPO, 1987.

——. *State Higher Education Profiles, 1988.* Washington, D. C.: GPO, 1988.

U. S. Department of Education, National Commission on Excellence in Education. *A Nation at Risk: The Imperative for Educational Reform.* Washington, D. C.: GPO, 1984.

U. S. Department of Health and Human Services, National Center for Health Statistics. Vital Statistics of the United States. Washington, D. C.: GPO, 1986.

U. S. Department of Labor, Bureau of Labor Statistics. Employment and Earnings. Washington, D. C.: GPO, 1986.

USA Today, 18 June 1987, 5 August 1989, 29 August 1989.

Wall Street Journal, 7 June 1989.

Washington Post, 5 May 1985, November 1986, 25 August 1989, 15 October 1989, 23 October 1989.

Washington Times, 8 September 1987.

West, Joel. "Changing Patterns of Finance in Higher Education." Unpublished paper, 1988.

Whitlock, Baird. *Don't Hold Them Back: A Critique and Guide to New High School–College Articulation Models.* New York: College Entrance Examination Board, 1978.

Index of Proper Names

Johnson County Community
College, 56
Jordan, King, 16
Journal of Teacher Education, 179
Judah, Oma Ruth, 122-23

Kalamazoo College, 84
Kaplan, Robert, 75
Kassebaum, Nancy, 10
Kean, Thomas, 259
Keith, Leroy, 16
Kennedy, Donald, 181
Kennedy, Edward, 184
King, Martin Luther, Jr., 208
Kingsborough Community
College, 84
Kingsford Charcoal Company,
57
Kiplinger, Austin, 4
Kropp, Arthur, 173
Kozol, Jonathan, 115

LaGuardia Community
College, 124
Lakoff, George, 27-28
Lane Community College, 273
Lang, Eugene, 128
Lansing Community College,
84
Lawrence University, 182
Learning Channel, The, 243
*Learning to Be Literate in
America*, 115
Lears, 199
Lewis and Clark College, 84
Lindgren, Richard, 226-27
Lingua, 91
Lippmann, Walter, 185-86

*Looking Backward—
2000–1887*, 6
Los Angeles City College,
204-5
Luskin, Bernard, 228
Lynton, Ernest, 60

Manufacturers Hanover Trust
Company, 20, 246-47
Maricopa County Community
College District, 183
Mark Twain Public Library
(Detroit), 123
Marshall Plan, 126, 129
Massachusetts Institute of
Technology, 48
McCabe, Robert, 147
McClain, Charles, 149-50
McDonnell Douglas, 240
MDC, Inc., 208-9
Meese, Edward, 142
Mensel, Frank, 282
Meredith, James, 141
Merrifield, Bruce, 45
Metropolitan Opportunity
Project, 118
Metropolitan Re-employment
Project, 122
Mexican American Legal
Defense Fund, 152
Miami-Dade Community
College, 90, 147-49
Mirabella, 199
Missouri Department of
Vocational Education, 122
Missouri Job Service, 122
Monsanto Company, 48
Moran, James, 210

Office of Naval Research, 46
Ohio Board of Regents, 50
Ohio Department of
  Development, 50
Ohio Technology Transfer
  Organization, 50-51
O'Leary, Michael, 259
Oliver, Leonard, 186
Oregon State System of Higher
  Education, 82

Pan Am, 234
Panel on Technology and
  Employment, 49-50
Parade, 136
Passaic County College, 125
Paul, Faith, 118-19
Peace Corps, 85, 184
Pell, Claiborne, 269
Pennsylvania Higher
  Education Assistance
  Authority, 13
People For the American Way,
  173
Peter D. Hart Research
  Associates, 173
Pickens, William, 21
Pierce, David, 22
Points of Light Foundation, 185
Principles of Alphabet Literacy
  System, 122
Professional Student Assistant
  Program, 272
*Profscam: Professors and the
  Demise of Higher Education*,
  259
Project 87, 187
Psychology Today, 15

Public Broadcasting Service,
  115; Adult Learning Service,
  234
Pyle, Cassandra, 75

Reagan, Ronald, 74-75, 142
Regional Commerce and
  Growth Association, 122
Rentschler, William, 46-47
Republic Airlines, 234
Richmond Community
  College, 245
Richmond County Public
  Schools, 245
Rio Salado College, 183
Roosevelt, Theodore, 6
Roper Confidence/Efficacy
  Poll, 189
Rosser, Richard, 279
Rural Extension Act, 127
Ryder System, 275

St. Louis Community College,
  122; at Meramec, 274
St. Louis Labor Council, 122
San Diego Community College
  District, 123-24
San Diego Educational
  Cultural Complex, 124
San Joaquin Delta College, 203
*Schools That Work: Educating
  Disadvantaged Children*, 107
Schulhof, Michael, 230-31
Schuster, Jack, 22
Senior Service Agency, 203
Servicemembers Opportunity
  College, 217
Service to America Act, 185

301

If we are resourceful enough, there will be many ways for us to adapt and many unanticipated events that may change the picture. In the end, perhaps our greatest protection lies in our growing importance to the society that sustains us.

Derek Bok
President
Harvard University